MAN AND NATURE

Selected Essays
by Giorgio Del Vecchio

Giorgio Del Vecchio

MAN AND NATURE

Selected Essays by

GIORGIO
DEL VECCHIO

Ralph A. Newman, *Editor*

Translated by

A. H. CAMPBELL

UNIVERSITY OF NOTRE DAME PRESS
Notre Dame London

Library of Congress Catalog Card Number: 72-75156
Manufactured in the United States of America

CONTENTS

PREFACE:
DOCTOR VENERABILIS

SINCE THE CHILDHOOD OF THE RACE WHEN MEN FIRST CULTIvated grain in the river valleys of the Tigris and the Euphrates and settled down to a sedentary life, human history has consisted largely of the record of man's struggle to pit his feebleness against the overwhelming forces of nature. At first his chief reliance was on the gods, to be won to his side by appeasement and flattery. As time went on, the key to man's control of his environment was seen to be his ability to cooperate with his neighbors; as Bronowski has put it, his ability to find a compromise between man and men.[1]

Our first glimpse of a society ruled by moral law is on the borders of a desert of the Middle East, where men first conceived of a god of benevolence, concerned not with his own aggrandizement but with the well-being of his people. From the concept of the fatherhood of God flowed the concept of the brotherhood of men. From this concept there followed the concept of justice in men's relations with one another. Men found in the Divine Law the sanction for the employment of their concerted strength in the struggle against the impersonal forces of nature and against the selfish forces of men. In this theology natural law had no place.

In neighboring Greece, under a theology staffed by more earthy gods, nature was personified in the gods themselves. It is no coincidence that the pagan gods of Greece dwelt in the forests and streams and on the mountains. In the philosophy of the Greek Stoics the law of nature was not attributed to divine origin. The Greeks, because they found it unpleasant to contemplate the infinite, never attempted to define the eternal. Plato said that "to find the Father and Maker of all is hard, and having found him it is impossible to utter him."[2]

Nature was both ruthless and benign, but in nature alone was help to be found, since the gods who personified nature were created not only in man's image but possessed of all his frailties.

How could the forces of nature be enlisted in the struggle to set men free from its evil forces? From Homer on, men thought they detected in the orderly processes of nature a prototype, to be determined by reason, as a guide for their own conduct. As men trusted themselves to the benevolence of a god who was not always merciful, so men relied on nature to set them free from nature itself. This solution, involving the cooperation of puny individuals in a mighty community, was too simple to be easily recognized; to the philosopher, as Schopenhauer said, the simple things are the most mysterious. Men turned to nature as a guide to a better life by availing themselves of its benign aspect, and found in the ecology and self-regeneration of nature the prototype of a community of human brotherhood.

No man, nor any god, said "let there be law"; but justice, in the words of a philosopher who was a poet, "emerged from social life and soared above it, categorical and transcendent,"[3] and there was law, decreed by nature itself. The orderly control of men's relations with one another, according to rules of law modelled on the laws of nature as they were interpreted by reason, became the key to the attainment of all their aspirations, never fully understood, but glimmering faintly just beyond the horizon of their dreams.

Embodied in Cicero's concept of a *lex naturalis et immutabilis*,[4] natural law became the central core of the *ius gentium* that was administered in the praetorial courts of Rome, and of the doctrine of *aequitas*, the progenitor of equity in both the civil law and the common law. During the Dark Ages natural law lay buried and forgotten. In the thirteenth century St. Thomas, building on the foundation of the Judaic-Christian ethos of human brotherhood—expressed in Christian doctrine as charity—and on a revived natural law, erected the first complete system of law since the *corpus iuris* of Justinian.

Until the Age of Reason, religion maintained its control of men's minds and lives and determined the moral shape of their laws. Men sought to save their souls, and resigned themselves to a desolate existence in what they persuaded themselves was the vestibule to eternity. In the seventeenth century a group of courageous thinkers, Kant, Bacon, Descartes and Grotius, later fortified by the French *philosophes* from Bayle to Condorcet, struggled to wrest from the Universal Church its monopoly of moral authority, and to restore the moral autonomy of law.[5] Their success left men groping for a new light to replace the old. For three centuries, from the beginning of the sixteenth to the end of the eighteenth, the flame of natural law flickered faintly and almost disappeared.

In the eighteenth century an Italian philosopher, Giambattista Vico, conceived, on the lines of Kant's later concept of a *Weltbürgerrecht*, the ideal of what Vico called a *civitas humani generis*. This was an ideal world community, guided by a universal law based on the essentially similar moral and ethical ideals of all civilized societies, and drawn from politics, law, commerce (which to Vico meant economics) and philosophy.[6] There is a close similarity between Vico's conception of a small body of universal truths and the thought of legal philosophers of other cultures who followed him in time; of Würzel, an Austrian, who speaks of "the concepts, relatively few in number, which embody the phenomena of social life as they would appear if there were no laws";[7] of Ripert, a Frenchman, who speaks of "the essential rules upon which are scrawled secondary rules of application,"[8] and of a distinguished contemporary American philosopher who has recently spoken of "certain values common to all mankind and conducive to self-fulfillment and civilized living."[9]

Early in the twentieth century another Italian philosopher, Giorgio Del Vecchio, kindled into flame the flickering embers of natural law, and provided an explanation of the nearly world-wide similarity of the moral principles of law. "Every man," Del Vecchio has said, "carries within him the principles of law; every conscience has within it the elements to rise above its empirical personality and to coordinate ethically with that of another."[10] Piercing through the distinction between human and inanimate nature, he tore law free from a materialistic ontology. Del Vecchio reminds us that man himself is a part of nature, and that the laws of nature embodied in humanity constitute what he describes in one of his most magnificent phrases as the eternal postulates of reason.[11] Law and morals, both emanating from the human spirit,[12] transcend, in his philosophy, the laws of the world of nature,[13] and create a natural law immutable in its essential content,[14] but susceptible of varying applications in place and time.[15]

Thenceforth nothing in legal philosophy would ever be quite the same. Man could now find in his own moral virtue the strength to live in harmony with his fellowmen, and to grow materially and spiritually; that is to say, he could follow the path toward his Unknown Goal. The similarity of moral principles of almost all legal systems stems from their origin in deeply rooted emotions of the human spirit. Del Vecchio has found the source of virtue to be immanent in man himself.[16] From this starting point he turns from the traditional scholastic approach to natural law and attaches primary emphasis to the moral aspect of conduct, not exclusively with reference to subjective morality but also with reference to social utility, that is, the effect of the actor's conduct on the objectives of society as a whole. In thinking of man as a moral and social being he has provided a moral base for the evolving law of today and tomorrow.

Del Vecchio's theory of the origin of the sense of justice in human nature is strongly corroborated by the presence in widely scattered parts of the world, under different conceptual formulations, of what prove to be substantially similar moral concepts: the concept of righteousness found in biblical[17] and Hindu[18] law; the concept of the brotherhood of man in the Old Testament[19], which found expression in Christianity as the doctrine of charity;[20] the concept of conscience in canon law and English equity[21]; the moral principles of Zoroastrian[22] and Chinese[23] philosophy, and the concepts of reason, equity and natural justice in many civil codes.[24] Transplanted from Roman law in the thirteenth century to England by the Franciscan and Dominican canonists, natural law became the basis for the doctrine of conscience in English equity. Between the twelfth and eighteenth centuries the civil law fell heir to a system of Roman law in which, by the time of Hadrian, moral doctrine had become woven firmly, like a golden thread, into the fabric of the law.

In our own legal system we have been less successful in absorbing the moral principles of natural law into our general law. Partly, perhaps, this has been due to our failure to see that the source of justice is in human nature. On the tide of an awakening social conscience many of the doctrines of natural law have penetrated into the mainstream of our law, but the absorption has been sporadic and imperfect. The principles of natural law embodied in the *Digest*, particularly in the last title, *De regulis iuris antiqui*, and which, in Lord Mansfield's magnificent phrase, have worked themselves pure in Anglo-American equity, form a system of moral principles which constitutes the supreme contribution of a long line of illustrious chancellors. We have tasted only lightly of this source. When we realize that human nature, like physical nature, is not wholly evil, as Hobbes conceived it, but in part benign, and when we translate its benign impulses, as they have been translated in all systems of ethics and morals, into law, we will have mastered the most difficult of all the arts, the art of living together as neighbors.[25]

From *Il sentimento giuridico*, written in 1902, to *Lezioni di filosofia del diritto*, written in 1930 and published in its thirteenth edition in 1965, Del Vecchio has had much to do with stimulating the revival of natural law. This revival has manifested itself, during what Pound has called the period of equity and natural law, in correcting the undue scope of discretion involved in the identification of law with morals,[26] and in helping to create a body of law which is both sufficiently stable and sufficiently liberalized by the introduction of the principles of equity. Del Vecchio's variety of Neo-Kantianism, encompassing a body of unchanging basic principles susceptible of changing application to meet expanding concepts of social needs,[27] has provided a counter-balance to the parallel growth of the influence of Neo-Scholastic natural law, consisting solely of absolutes.[28]

His influence on contemporary scholars is sometimes specifically acknowledged, but is often unrecognized. Lord Denning, in 1953, pointed out that equity "involves the principles of natural justice";[29] and Tillich, writing in 1960, felt that "the roots of the moral imperative . . . can be elaborated only in terms of an analysis of man's being and universal being."[30] Early in the present century, the idea of natural law possessing a changing content provided for Stammler the solution to the perennial problem of establishing a balance between certainty of law and discretion in the application of its principles.[31] Aldous Huxley's evolutionary humanism shows close similarities to natural law.[32]

Del Vecchio's writings have been translated into eighteen languages. A bibliography of his writings published at Bologna in 1949, *Bibliografia di Giorgio Del Vecchio*, second edition, comprises 121 pages. His writings since then have been collected in a massive compilation of ten volumes. His essays, many of them written within the past twenty years, constitute the culmination of the magnificent structure of the philosophy of law which, with the aid of a stupendous knowledge of classic, medieval and modern philosophic thought, he has erected over the past sixty years. More than fifty of his essays have been published in English translation. When under the editorship of Dean Wigmore the Association of American Law Schools undertook, some fifty years ago, the compilation of a series of volumes on Modern Philosophic Thought, it was Del Vecchio who was selected to write the volume on Natural Law. In 1921 he founded the *Rivista internazionale di filosofia del diritto* and resigned from its board of editors in 1967. In 1947, on resuming the direction of the *Rivista*, a post from which he had been deposed by the Fascists in 1938, Del Vecchio appealed for a return to "the eternal idea of a natural law, to that pure principle of justice which rises above the contingent vicissitudes of positive legislation as a permanent criterion and which alone, if it is respected, can lead men to a true and lasting peace."[33] At a ceremony honoring Goethe, Shakespeare and Dante held in the Capitol at Rome, near the Forum where Cicero and Marcus Aurelius had addressed the Roman people, Del Vecchio emphasized the vital element in Dante's political thought: the goal of a society of the human race, an alliance of nations built on the concepts of freedom and justice. Del Vecchio's latest book, *Lo Stato Moderno e i Suoi Problemi*, was published at Turin in 1967. He was formerly Rector of the University of Rome, and for many years the Dean of its Faculty of Law. He retired as Professor Emeritus Ordinarius at the age of seventy-five. On August 26, 1968, he celebrated his ninetieth birthday.

It has been my good fortune to know Del Vecchio. His greatness extends beyond his vast learning and the profundity of his philosophic thought, to his character. As Pollock said of Holmes, the dignity of his bearing is wholly free from arrogance, the brilliance of his intellect from vanity. He has the humility of greatness. His reflections come to us, to borrow from a phrase of Tagore, with the ceremony of a king. The old saying that "words that come out of the heart, enter all hearts,"[34] is in part the explanation of his influence. The preface of his book on Justice reads ". . . the discovery of the truth. Who labors with purity of heart to that end will find therein a sufficient reward for his toil, however great."[35] The statement is particularly applicable to Del Vecchio himself. "Nec fas est propior mortali attingere divos"; it is not allowed to any mortal to come closer to the gods.

Ralph A. Newman

San Francisco, California
August 30, 1968

NOTES

1. Bronowski, *Science and Human Values*, 87 (1956; ed. 1959).
2. Plato, *Tim.*, IX. In the philosophy of the Greek Stoics the law of nature was not attributed to divine origin. Reference to a divine origin of natural law is to be found in Cicero, *De Republica*, Bk. 3, c. 22. St. Augustine added the divine law, *lex aeterna*, to Aristotle's *lex naturalis*. St. Thomas, who integrated the principles of natural law into his massive theological system, felt that such concepts as justice, dignity and tolerance have "an inwardness which is inaccessible to experience," according to Bronowski; see *op. cit.*, pp. 48-51.
3. Bergson, *The Two Sources of Morality and Religion*, 76 (17th ed., Aufra and Brereton transl. 1956).
4. Cicero, *De Republica*, Bk. 3, c. 11, p. 355 (Bohn's Classical Library ed. 1853). The cleavage in the philosophy of natural law between the concept of natural law as divinely inspired, and as

based on altruistic elements of human nature, does not concern Del Vecchio, who feels that the general principles of law can be philosophically discovered and demonstrated without reference to theological premises, although theology leads, generally, he feels, to the affirmance of the same principles. It is to the cleavage between natural law and positivism that Del Vecchio directs his primary attention.

5. The characteristic of the Renaissance, as Del Vecchio points out in his essay, "Grotius and the Foundation of Natural Law," in *Humanité et Unité du Droit*; *Essais de Philosophie Juridique*, 190 (1963) was to liberate scientific and philosophical speculation from theological premises. Subsequent references to essays of Del Vecchio will be, unless otherwise designated, to this collection of his essays, as *Essays*.

6. Vico, *Principi di una scienza nuova d'intorno alla commune natura della nazioni* (2nd) (1725).

7. Würzel, *Das Juristische Denken* (sec. 26) (1904).

8. Ripert, *2 Recueil des cours d'Académie du droit international*, No. 6, p. 575 (1933).

9. Bodenheimer, *Reflections on the Rule of Law*, 8 Utah L. Rev. 1 (1962).

10. Del Vecchio, *La Communicabilità del Diritto*, 15 (1911).

11. Del Vecchio, "The Word of Pius XII and the Jurists," *Essays*, 133.

12. Del Vecchio, "Concerning the Asserted Political Character of Law," *Essays*, 97.

13. Del Vecchio, "*Homo Juridicus* and the Inadequacy of Law as a Norm of Life," 11 Tul. L. Rev. 503, 526 (1937).

14. Del Vecchio, "Mutability and Eternity of Law," *Essays*, 31.

15. Del Vecchio, "Mutability and Eternity of Law," *Essays*, 31.

16. Del Vecchio, "Mutability and Eternity of Law," *Essays*, 26, 38.

17. *Is.* 59.14; *Isaiah*, Soncino Books of the Bible, 290 (1949).

18. Venkateswara, 1517, cited in Monier-Williams, *Indian Wisdom*, 448 (1893); "Do naught to others which if done to thee would cause thee pain."

19. *Lev.* 19.18, 34.

20. *Paul,* 1 Cor. 13.13; *Luke* 17.33 (King James); see especially Crampton edition of the Bible (French), *John* 12.25.

21. Baildon, *Sel. Cas. Ch.* (Selden Soc. 1896), introduction, p. xxix.

22. Dawson, *The Ethical Religion of Zoroaster*, 125 (1931);

"The golden rule; that nature alone is good which shall not do unto another whatever is not good unto its own self."

23. Confucius, *Analects* xii, ii; "Not to do unto others as you would not wish done to yourself."

24. Swiss Civil Code (art. 4): "equity." Egyptian Civil Code (art. 4): "equity and justice." Civil codes of Colombia (art. 32), Ecuador (art. 17, 18), and Honduras (art. 20): "natural equity." Chinese Civil Code (art. 1), Italian Civil Code (art. 12), Portuguese Civil Code (art. 16) and Spanish Civil Code (art. 6): "the general principles of law" (in the Italian Civil Code the reference is to "the general principles of law of the legal system of the State."). The provision in the Spanish Civil Code is derived from the *Siete Partidas*. The Argentine Civil Code (art. 16), the Austrian Civil Code (sec. 7), the *Avant-Projet* for the French Civil Code (art. 21) and the Constituent Assembly Law of Ghana (art. 4) refer to "natural law." See also Montenegro Civil Code (art. 3); Panama Civil Code (art. 7); Proposed General Law Pertaining to the Application of Judicial Norms, Brazil, art. 9.

25. Wyzanski, speech at the dedication of the new Illinois College of Law building (1956): "Of all the wonders of the world the greatest wonder is Man, who . . . has mastered . . . the art of living together in neighborliness."

26. Pound, Introduction to Del Vecchio, *General Principles of Law* (ed. 1956).

27. "There is an unchanging, eternal idea of what is just" (Del Vecchio, "The Bases of Comparative Law and the General Principles of Law," *Essays*, 31) "but this is not to deny the possibility of change in its application, which must correspond to the circumstances of time and place" (*ibid.*, 31).

28. Ideas of justice ceased to be absolute in the Age of Pericles, when the rights of the individual first became recognized; Hamilton, *The Greek Way to Western Civilization*, 64 (1930).

29. Denning, *The Changing Law*, 73 (1953).

30. Tillich, *Love, Power and Justice*, 72 (1960).

31. Stammler, *The Theory of Justice*, 247-48 (1925).

32. Aldous Huxley, *Knowledge, Morality and Destiny*, c. 2, p. 252 (1960).

33. "Premessa alla Terza Serie," 24 *Riv. int. di fil. del dir.*, 3 (1947).

34. Haim Cohn, Justice of the Supreme Court of Israel, at International Lawyers Convention in Israel, 325 (1958).

35. Del Vecchio, *Justice* (ed. 1952).

INTRODUCTION

GIORGIO DEL VECCHIO, SON OF THE ECONOMIST GIULIO DEL Vecchio, born at Bologna in 1878, university teacher for fifty years, Professor (from 1920) and Rector (1925-27) of the University of Rome and Dean of the Faculty of Law (1930-38), founder (1931) and editor of the *Rivista internazionale di filosofia del diritto*, founder (1933) of the Società Italiana di filosofia del diritto, and prolific writer, has been one of the most important influences on twentieth-century legal philosophy in Italy and in many other countries.

Before attempting to summarize his doctrine, let us clear away a misunderstanding and correct an injustice. Del Vecchio, having served with distinction as a volunteer in the first world war and having seen in his native city the postwar collapse of government before communism and anarchy, joined, like other veterans, the nascent Fascist movement at a time when its professed ideals were patriotic, democratic, and anti-imperialist. He remained nominally a Fascist, although never holding office in the Party, until 1938, when because of his Jewish blood he was expelled and was dismissed from his University posts. In 1944 he resumed teaching, but was again suspended, this time because of his past Fascist connection. From 1947-1953 he taught again and in 1955 received the title of Professor Emeritus.

Superficial critics have been misled into labeling him as a "Fascist philosopher." The utmost that can be laid to this charge is that for a time he did hope that the Fascist plan for the "Corporate State" (a fair-enough seeming plan on paper) might provide the framework in which could be realized his vision of the ethical State, which by harmonising individual freedom and corporate interests should enhance the value of individual personality. (See certain passages in the original version of his "Individual, State and Corporation," translated in *Political Science Quarterly*, 1935.) But he yielded no part of his fundamental beliefs, and throughout the Fascist period he continued in writing and teaching to assert the validity of natural law and human rights, and to defend academic freedom against the statolatry of the Fascist doctrine as preached by Gentile. (See especially his "Ethics, Law and the State," an address delivered in Italy in 1934, English translation in *International Journal of Law and Ethics*, XLVI, Chicago, 1935, and "Individual, State and Corporation," especially pp. 537-538 of the English translation.)

I should like to modify some words which I wrote seventeen years ago in my Introduction to his book on *Justice* (Edinburgh, 1952). Although in the course of his long life of reading, reflection, and practical experience his views on the practical application of his doctrines may (as I suggested) have altered on some points, their philosophical foundation has remained unshaken.

In Descartes, as Del Vecchio observed in the lecture on "Right and Human Personality" which he delivered in 1904, we find the primacy of thought, the conception of the spirit as *res cogitans* and the recognition of the absolute value of the human person in its theoretical aspect, of man as an absolute *prius*. When we transfer this conception from the realm of epistemology to the realm of morality and law, it means that the foundation of social order must be not in external authority but in reason and the nature of man. The self, to conceive itself, must posit the other, and it must conceive the other as not merely an object of its own thought and action but as a subject. The subject cannot conceive himself as having claims on others without conceiving them as having, potentially, claims on him, that is, as being themselves subjects. This *alteritas* is the foundation of Del Vecchio's theory of law. In his terminology, Practical Philosophy (Ethic in the wide sense) is divided into (i) Morality, which is concerned with myself and my duties as an individual, and (ii) Law, which is concerned with what others may rightly claim of me, and thus (but only in a secondary sense) with my duties to others. Charity, for instance, falls within the moral sphere; the repayment of debts falls within the juridical sphere. (We might compare Petrazhitsky's observation that the distinguishing mark of law lies in its imperative-attributive character.) For Del Vecchio, morality and law, thus defined, are necessary *a priori* forms of consciousness, and also necessary conditions of social life. "No common life nor even any collaboration among individuals is possible without a determination . . . of the sphere of activity belonging to each, and, consequently, of their respective obligations and powers" (*infra*, p. 142).

This is the formal meaning of juridicity. But there is an infinite number of possible juridical systems, that is, of systems of rules defining mutual claims and obligations. These may have a greater or less degree of positivity, that is, they may be more or less effective; they may be imposed by authority or they may rest upon definite usage or merely on a vague common consciousness shared by the persons concerned. (See especially, in this volume, "The *Homo Juridicus*" and "On the State-Character of Law.") Moreover, several such systems may coexist at the same time, claiming authority over the same people.

Any type of society may produce its own (more or less) positive law. The name of "law" should not be denied to the rules of the Church, of the international society, of groups which existed before the State or which arise within the State, even of groups which seek to subvert the State or which, in the eyes of the State, are simply criminal associations. Del Vecchio's essay "On the State-Character of Law" and, more fully, his essay on "Individual, State and Corporation" discuss the various possible forms of relationship (opposition, tolerant coexistence, mutual acknowledgment, subordination and incorporation) between the law of such groups and that of the State. The State is "that one among several possible juridical systems which corresponds to the predominant will and which has therefore reached, as compared to the others, the highest degree of positivity" (*infra* p. 149).

But the mere fact that the State corresponds to the predominant will does not ethically justify its authority. Here Del Vecchio parts company with the statolatrists. Rules may be juridical in character and they may form part of a positive system, yet they may be unjust. The second and more important part of Del Vecchio's teaching concerns the notion of justice as the ideal of law, from which we can deduce the proper substance of legal rules. The concept of *alteritas* involves the recognition of the other as a being with equal value to oneself and equal claim to recognition. This for Del Vecchio is not merely a formal requisite but is a deeply rooted, irrepressible, and ineradicable *attitudine* (an Italian word whose translation may vary between "attitude" and "aptitude" or "potentiality") of man's *coscienza* (which may be translated "consciousness" or "conscience"). Even those who act unjustly act in accordance with their own misguided conception of justice; they claim what in their selfishness they believe to be their due. Properly regarded, however, the concept of *alteritas* should yield certain fundamental notions of what is objectively just between man and man, and Del Vecchio deduces from it a number of conclusions which in substance correspond with traditional notions of fundamental human rights. These rights (and this is a novel and interesting suggestion of Del Vecchio's) may all be deduced from an original *diritto alla solitudine* ("right to solitude"), namely, the inborn freedom of every individual to find *in interiore homine* the motives and determining conditions of all his social relationships, and his claim that others shall respect this his autonomy. Thus Del Vecchio upholds the idea of Natural Law as a law based on human nature and on reason.

The notion of the *Rechts-staat* (or "State acting according to law") is adapted by Del Vecchio to give the idea of the *Stato di giustizia* (or "State acting according to justice"), whose law is in accordance with natural law and protects the essential rights of the individual. It is impossible for either the international lawyer or the municipal lawyer to justify law as being simply "the will of the State," if by this is meant an arbitrary will, not subject to reason. Commands of a State not based on justice are in substance not truly law; there is (as Aquinas observed) a certain obligation to obey them *propter vitandum scandalum vel turbationem*, but, if they go beyond measure, there remains the ultimate, terrible right of revolution (*infra* p. 184).

The idea of the Justice-State is developed by Del Vecchio in various applications. The rules for admission to the United

Nations Organization and the terms of its membership are, he suggests, too wide. Full membership (voting membership) should have been confined to States whose internal constitutions give adequate guarantee that they will observe the requirements of justice. (We remember Kant's proposals in *Zum ewigen Frieden*, and we may recall as a historical fact that occasionally the international recognition of a new State has been made conditional on the holding of democratic elections.) Voting in international assemblies should take account not only of the formal equality of States but also of the number of human beings who compose their populations. ("It does not seem reasonable that a vote which represents a population of a few thousands should receive the same weight as a vote representing many millions. These requirements might be reconciled by a system which required a majority by both counts for decision." See *infra* p. 165).

In internal constitutional matters, too, Del Vecchio is an advocate of weighted voting, the object here being to take proper account of the differing capacity of voters according to age and education (*infra* p. 163).

The fundamental principles of natural law should (perhaps someday will) serve as the basis of a uniform law for the whole world. (On the "progressive unification of the positive law of the various countries" see *infra* p. 36). In the meantime, the unification of humanity could be helped by a uniform programme of education (from the elementary school upward) based on incontestable elements of fact and on generally recognized moral ideas (see "A Unitary Programme of Education").

To many readers Del Vecchio may seem most startlingly heterodox in his teaching on "penal justice" (*infra.* pp. 165-7 and more fully developed in the Appendixes to his book on *Justice*). The notion of "punishment" should be abandoned. Apart from necessary "measures of defence" (which may have to be taken against certain criminals in the same spirit as they have to be taken against the violent insane or against those who suffer from contagious diseases), what justice requires, and all that justice allows, is that the offender should make what reparation he can for the harm he has done to his victim and to society; this, if not made voluntarily, should be secured by a system of "attachment" of his earnings and, if necessary, compulsory labor under supervision.

The impatient reader may be inclined to dismiss these teachings as those of an optimistic, unpractical theorist. Yet, to take only the last-mentioned, we should note certain developments in the actual penal law and administration of some countries which are in accord with Del Vecchio's ideas: in Britain, for instance, the "corrective training" of offenders and the introduction of payment for prison labor and of State compensation for the victims of violent crime. Del Vecchio is taking a long view, and the philosopher in his study sometimes sees farther than can the practical man whose eyes are focused on immediate problems and immediate difficulties.

Del Vecchio is certainly an optimist, but not of the foolish kind who think they possess a magic formula which will dispel all practical difficulties, nor is he one of those who imagine that man's progress is continuously onward and upward to ever better things. The history of man—in particular, the history of law—shows changes of direction, regressions, decadence, the decay and disappearance of particular institutions and of entire systems, phenomena which have been analyzed by Del Vecchio with subtlety and erudition in his "Evolution and Involution in Law." Yet, as he there writes (*infra*, pp. 53-4): "All decadence and regression has in itself the promise of a revival and a resurrection . . . it is not in us to conceive the total disappearance of being, the complete death of the spirit."

A. H. C.

THE ESSAYS INCLUDED IN THIS VOLUME HAVE ALREADY APpeared in various English translations. Many of these translations are now difficult of access; some are far from complete; some, regrettably, contain serious errors of translation or, even if accurate, make for difficult reading by too close adherence to the style of the original Italian. For the present volume these translations, where available, have been used as a foundation but they have been revised throughout and almost completely rewritten with reference to the authentic Italian text in the excellent reprinted collections of Del Vecchio's work published by Giuffrè of Milan: *Studi sul Diritto*, 2 vols. (1958); *Studi sullo Stato* (1958); *Contributi alla Storia del Pensiero giuridico e filosofico* (1963); and *Parerga*, 3 vols. (1961, 1963, 1966), and other volumes of miscellaneous writings, many of which remain unknown to the English reader.

The essays in the present volume have been selected to display as many as possible of the aspects of Del Vecchio's thought, illustrating the application of his fundamental principles to particular questions. They touch occasionally on points of practical contemporary import; but nothing is here included of his extensive miscellaneous writing on politics or on Dante, or of his poems.

The present translator has aimed, above all, at a clear presentation of Del Vecchio's thought. Considerations of space have compelled some abbreviation, but care has been taken to omit only passages which seemed to be mere amplification or illustration of a thesis already stated, or which restated a position already set out in another essay.

The notes have been translated directly from the Italian editions. Here, too, some compression has been necessary; for instance, lists of works in Italian on points of Italian law have been omitted as of little use to readers of the present volume. Where Del Vecchio has used an Italian translation of a work originally written in some other language, an attempt has been made to replace his reference by a reference to the original or to an English translation thereof, but in one or two instances this has not been possible.

A. H. C.

ACKNOWLEDGMENTS

Grateful acknowledgment herewith is made to the following for permission to translate or retranslate and publish the material listed below:

Casa Editrice Dott A. Giuffrè of Milan, Italy, for permission to utilize the writings of Del Vecchio selected from *Studi sul diritto*, 2 vols. (1958), *Contributi alla Storia del Pensiero giuridico e filosofico* (1963), and *Parerga*, 3 vols. (1961, 1963, 1966).

"Man and Nature: Transcendental Parellelism" from *Parerga*, II (1963), originally written 1958, published in English in *The Philosopher* (1965) and in *International Philosophical Quarterly*, IX, 1 (March, 1969), pp. 3-10.

"Historical Materialism and Psychologism" from *Studi sul diritto*, II (1958), pp. 61ff., originally written 1947, published in English in *Seminar* (*The Jurist*), XIII (1955-1956), pp. 17-32, and in *Scienza Nuova*, I, 2 (1955), pp. 5-14.

"Natural Law as the Foundation of a Society of Mankind" from *Parerga*, II (1963), pp. 3ff., originally written 1962, published in English in *Loyola Digest* (1963) and, as "Natural Law as the Foundation of a Society of the Human Race," in *World Justice*, IV, 3 (March, 1963), pp. 307-314.

"The Unity of the Human Mind as a Basis for Comparative Legal Study" from *Studi sul diritto*, II (1958), pp. 51ff., originally written 1950, published in English as "The Unity of the Human Mind as a Basis for Juridical Comparison" in the *Notre Dame Law Review*, XXVI (1951), pp. 268-276.

"Evolution and Involution in Law" from *Studi sul diritto*, II (1958), pp. 79ff., originally written 1938, published in English in *The Georgetown Law Journal*, XXVII, 6 (1939), pp. 732-750, and in *Acta Juridica* (1958).

"The *Homo Juridicus* and the Inadequacy of Law as a Norm of Life" from *Studi sul diritto,* I (1958), pp. 279ff., originally written 1935, published in English in the *Tulane Law Review,* XI (1937), pp. 503-526.

"Truth in Morality and Law" from *Studi sul diritto,* I (1958), pp. 177ff., originally written 1947, published in English in *Interpretations of Modern Legal Philosophies* (Oxford University Press, 1947) and *Iowa Law Review,* XXXIX (1953), pp. 16ff.

"A Unitary Program of Education" from *Parerga,* II (1963), p. 79, originally written 1962, published in English in *The Scottish Schoolmaster* (1963).

"On the State-Character of Law," from *Studi sul diritto,* I (1958), pp. 89ff., originally written 1928, published in English, as "On the Statuality of Law," in *Journal of Comparative Legislation and International Law 1*, 3rd series, nos. I-IV, part I, XIX, 1 (1937).

"Equality and Inequality in Relation to Justice" from *Parerga,* III (1966), pp. 29ff., originally written 1965, published in English in the *Natural Law Forum*, XI (1966), pp. 36-46.

"The Crisis of the Science of Law" from *Studi sul diritto,* I (1958), pp. 165ff., originally written 1933, published in English in *Tulane Law Review,* VIII (1934), pp. 321-336.

"The Posthumous Fate of Alberico Gentili" from *Contributi* (1936), pp. 59ff., originally published in English in *The American Journal of International Law,* L (July, 1956), pp. 664-667.

MAN AND NATURE: TRANSCENDENTAL PARALLELISM

THE PROBLEM OF THE RELATIONS BETWEEN MAN AND NATURE is bound to present itself to the mind of every philosopher. Many years ago I ventured to express some thoughts on this problem, briefly indicating the lines along which it seemed to me that a solution might be found. These thoughts I hoped to develop into a system, but for various reasons this hope (like so many of the dreams of youth) has remained unfulfilled. In the study of legal philosophy to which I subsequently devoted myself I still held to the general principles which I had thus briefly indicated, and I occasionally referred to them, but seldom explicitly, so that they attracted little critical attention. Now I have the opportunity to restate and clarify my profession of philosophical faith, which may be summarized in the phrase: transcendental parallelism.

Man is a part of nature and is therefore comprehended in nature. But man also comprehends nature, which in this way becomes a human idea or representation. We thus have two opposite points of view which are both in certain respects correct, so that neither can be rejected, while they open up another problem, namely, whether and how they can be unified.

This antithesis substantially corresponds to that between subject and object, and it is, broadly speaking, analogous to such others as those between ego and non-ego or spirit and matter, which are found in all philosophical systems but differently conceived in each. On the differences we need not dwell. What we should bring into light is the sort of equilibrium or equipollence which, I believe, must from the theoretical aspect be established between these two points of view; from the practical aspect things are somewhat different.

From an objective point of view (that is, one which starts from an object) all things are considered in the order of their external genesis. There is a reality which has its origin outside of us, which is prior to us and infinitely greater than us, moving by its own energy and its own laws, to which all our life —which is but a minute particle of reality—is subordinated. From a subjective point of view, on the contrary, the *prius* of all cognoscible reality is in the subject himself; the world is a reflection of ideas whose center is in the subjective consciousness, and the laws of reality are nothing but the laws of this consciousness.

Object and subject are not "things" or matter but transcendental criteria, that is to say, *a priori* necessary regulative principles. Reality is disposed and apprehended in both senses; it has, so to speak, a bipolar aspect. This duality cannot be abolished, because our intellect is equally disposed by its native structure to either the one or the other orientation. Neither of the two fundamental antithetical terms can eliminate the other, since each in a way embraces and dominates the other and (inverting the angle of vision) is itself embraced and comprehended by the other.

Nature, according to the first conception, is the complex of phenomena or physical facts which extend indefinitely in space and time and are linked to each other by the relation of cause and effect (without which we could not speak of nature but only of chaos). Into this conception there enter human acts and so-called social facts, for these too, whatever may be their significance and their value from other aspects, undeniably have a physical substratum and belong to nature generically considered, so that one can with reason apply to them, as to all other phenomena, the criterion of causality. By this standard everything appears as necessarily determined in the world, and if no other conception than this were possible, we should have to regard the idea of freedom as a mere illusion and to deny the scientific legitimacy of all value-judgments.

Even if we add to the causal the final or teleological consideration, which is especially applicable to the organic world and to human facts, we should still remain within the bounds of an "objective" conception of nature, which, in the words of Aristotle, "does nothing by chance" and "does nothing in vain." We can, of course, make a distinction between the normal and exceptional cases, between the physiological and the pathological, and we can say, for instance, that abortions and monstrous births are "unsuccessful attempts" by nature; but, even so, our judgments are made with reference to nature. Disturbances and anomalies—that is, phenomena which do not conform to the ordinary course of things—can sometimes be described as "against nature" (for instance, according to the jurist Julian, fever was *contra naturam*), yet, inasmuch as these phenomena too are determined by sufficient causes, they must be deemed to be natural in the strict sense of the term. As Goethe wrote, "He who does not see nature everywhere does not see nature rightly anywhere."

Reflection, however, shows us that both the criterion of causality and the criterion of finality are inborn in our intellect as categories proper to it, that is, as functional modes of apprehending the external world. They thus have a subjective validity, which does not mean that they do not also have an objective validity. Investigating nature, we find, as it were, a translation therein of the laws of our spirit, as if nature were a mirror to our spirit or our spirit a mirror to nature. We find in the order of the universe the same ideal imprints which we find given *a priori* in our consciousness. This leads us to think that subject and object may be like the refraction of the one same absolute unity.

When reality is regarded *sub specie subjecti*, its determinations show themselves as forms of thought, but of a thought which, as the subject himself realizes, is not peculiar to his own individuality but belongs to a transcendental order of universal character. It is in this sense, and not in any empiric sense, that we understand the "primacy of the ego" or the primacy of consciousness in the subjectively orientated conception of the world. Inasmuch as the subject belongs, at least potentially and by inclination or vocation, to an order of universal ideas, he feels himself to be free and responsible in his actions and not bound to the strict and infrangible chain of cause and effect. Insofar as, according to the objective orientation, man is part of nature, it may be that he is bound by physical laws and that his actions are always necessarily in coherence with all other phenomena, so that it can be said that he does not himself act but nature acts in him; yet in his quality of a principle or origin, as an intelligible being, man has in himself the possibility of determining himself, and nature is only the means or the field in which his determinations unfold and take sensible form. In this view man's actions are considered no longer in the empiric nexus which binds them to the phenomena that precede and follow them but in their transcendental dependence on the noumenal being of the subject and the ideas of which he is in possession.

The faculty of abstracting and recognizing oneself outside of physical nature, the faculty of referring to the ego, by way of ideas, all the reality which converges in it, constitutes for the subject his proper and specific being, that which is preeminently his *nature*. And this faculty or vocation reveals itself to every man in his never-failing consciousness of his power of free choice and of the responsibility which attends thereon. Here lies the transition from theoretical philosophy to ethics, or, rather, here is the meeting point between these two branches of the knowable.

To act as a subject and not as an object is for man not merely a psychological possibility. It is also an ethical requirement which imposes itself on his conscience and does so all the more clearly and strongly the more sensitive and alert his conscience has become. If man were simply a phenomenon, he would not be confronted by the problem of ethics and the notion of an imperative would have no meaning for him, because human actions as phenomena, being always and necessarily in conformity with nature in the objective sense, would not be susceptible of any further critical examination or evaluation. Fact would be, as in the physical sciences, the criterion of truth. But since man, while belonging to the phenomenal order, is, and feels intimately that he is, something more than a phenomenon, the fulfillment of his own essence and realization of his nature is for him not a mere fact but a problem and a task which is continuously set before him so long as he lives—that is, so long as he exists as a subject. Indeed, the notion of an imperative depends precisely upon this peculiar condition of man by which he participates in two natures or, to put it better, belongs to a double order of reality, the physical and the metaphysical. From the latter aspect, each of his actions has its origin in man himself and thus bears the mark of an absolute beginning.

The fundamental norm of action is derived from man's essence insofar as it surpasses physical nature, in other words, from his spiritual nature. The validity of the norm, therefore, does not depend on experience but is absolutely *a priori*. This does not mean that every individual is at all times fully conscious of the norm which is implicit in his spirit, nor does it mean that the norm cannot be physically transgressed or violated. Logical and deontological validity must not be confused with psychological actuality or with the accidental fact of observance. Only by making these distinctions can we rightly grasp the meaning of the necessary and universal ideas against the fallacious arguments of sensism and empiricism. As Leibniz said, we have to *learn* even our innate ideas.

Logical forms, and ideas in general, have a specific *raison d'être*, by virtue of which they do not depend on the historical condition of becoming and are free from the factual repercussions of causality. No fact can act upon or modify an idea; it is only the presentation of the idea in the empirical world (that is, its conception and translation into act by someone) that is subordinate to the natural laws of actual happening. Considered in itself, the idea is not subject to the flux of time; in its essence it lies outside thereof. We cannot speak, strictly, of an idea having an origin in the historic sense. What we see appearing is the assertion of ideas, not ideas themselves. We must see ideas in their essence as placed in an order in which the connections between them are established, not according to priority of appearance but according to their own intrinsic tenor, that is to say, in a purely logical systematic order. Even if the presence of physical objects and factors may offer the occasion or the means for the conception of certain ideas and so help to explain their psychological genesis, it can never be the cause of the logical significance of an idea or a concept; this significance always transcends the limits of its psychical origin. As the concept gradually takes form in our consciousness, it retrospectively demonstrates its validity, until it eventually reveals itself as an extratemporal condition of every possible object of the kind under consideration.

All this is valid, *a fortiori*, when we come to deal with necessary ideas, that is, those which originate directly from the spirit without any reference to empirical elements. Such is that fundamental norm which imposes on the subject the duty of acting not as a means or as a vehicle of the forces of nature but as an autonomous being which is in itself a beginning and an end; not impelled by or drawn in the train of passions and physical affections but dominating them; not as belonging to the world of perception but as partaking in the intelligible world where its contingent individuality is lifted up and, as it were, transfigured in the form of universality, as it acquires consciousness of its own identity of substance with the being of every other subject.

The ambiguity of language and particularly of the word "nature" should not mislead us, since it is clear that when we speak of human nature in the proper and specific sense, we distinguish it from nature generically considered. Confusion between the two concepts has arisen either from imperfect notions of nature in general and of human nature, or, sometimes, from the declared intention of denying all difference between physical and spiritual phenomena, thus refusing to recognize essential truths and, incidentally, rendering impossible the foundation of a true and proper ethic.

In the human spirit there are many motives or impulses, more or less deeply implanted, which make themselves apparent in differing measure in different persons. To analyze these is the task of psychology as an empirical or positive science. Inasmuch as they all exist, they are undoubtedly all "natural" in the objective sense of the term—that is, they are determined by sufficient causes. We must reject as erroneous all theories which presume to reserve for only one of them (for instance, egoism or sociality or compassion and so on) the title of "natural," and the error is redoubled when an attempt is then made to deduce an ethical law directly from a simple psychological fact.

No such impulse can by itself suffice to give a rule for human life. The essence of the subject and his supreme law do not consist in this or that empirically observable tendency; it might rather be said that the whole gist of this law is that it requires him to overcome the impulses and tendencies by which subjective being appears bound to the world of experience as a determinate part thereof.

It is another common error to treat as "natural" only what first appears in the temporal phenomenal order, as if naturalness in the objective sense was not to be found indifferently in all phenomena. Even the famous words of Vico, "The nature of things is nothing else than their birth in certain times and certain modes," are not free from this error (although to Vico himself they probably had a deeper meaning), and they have perhaps helped to spread it. No one denies that etymologically the word *natura* implies the notion of birth (*nascita*). St. Thomas observed: "Sciendum est quod nomen naturae a nascendo est dictum vel sumptum. . . . natura quasi nascitura," but he did not stop at the etymological meaning, for he well knew that this is seldom if ever sufficient for the exact definition of a concept. This prejudice has led many earlier writers to speak of the conditions of primitive ages as man's "natural state" and the law appropriate to such conditions as "natural law." They have even sought to contrast the "state of nature" with the "state of society," as if the latter followed on the former, although the slightest critical reflection would have shown that, on the contrary, the natural state for man is the state of society.

Nor is the problem philosophically solved by holding that by "nature" must be meant only that which is independent of the act of man. The activity of man can enter into phenomena of any kind; even physical phenomena in which man participates are "natural," and "natural" too is the fact of man's intervention and participation. From the point of view which we have called "objective orientation," the actual modes of behavior of individuals and of people, their customs, inasmuch as they have determinate causes which are in relation with all other phenomena, belong to the science of nature. In this sense we can say that all positive law—that is, all law existing in fact—is "natural"; by examining its determining factors and conditions we may come to understand its relative necessity and, as we say, explain it historically, but this does not imply any judgment concerning its intrinsic value as measured by the ideal standard of justice. This ideal is defined by the supreme law which corresponds to the spiritual essence of man, that is, to his hyperphenomenal nature. It is only in this latter sense that we can properly speak of natural law, as a paradigm and a rational criterion standing above positive law and enabling us to judge its value.

The supreme rule of action is expressed in two orders of precepts, equally imperative and logically coherent with one another according as the rule is applied to each subject in himself or to the relations between one subject and another. These two orders are the forms of morality and of law. In morality, the fundamental rule requires each man to overcome, through an absolutely pure determination of his own being, all external motives and all particular and sensible impulses, so as to give to his own acts the universal character of reason and make himself one with the being of every other subject. He who acts morally or "according to conscience" (this popular phrase can have a precise philosophical meaning) acts as if his decision embraced, and in him there acted, the whole of humanity. In this is affirmed the truth of the precepts of the Gospel: "Love thy neighbor as thyself" and "Whatsoever ye would that men should do to you, do ye even so to them."

In the form of law, the supreme ethical rule requires the reciprocal recognition of the absolute character of personality. Hence is derived a series of correlative claims and duties equally founded on that same presupposition and therefore universally valid. Every man, solely in virtue of his nature, can claim that no other shall treat him as if he were nothing but a means or an element of the sensible world, but rather shall behave toward him with respect for that ideal principle of autonomy which is implanted in his very nature. Under this aspect there is among all men a fundamental equality, whence it follows that the liberty of each should be harmonized and raised to the universal according to the idea of a possible coexistence. On this basis is developed the system of the natural rights of man.

We need not linger on this point, which has been sufficiently developed elsewhere, but one last word should be added.

Both ways of regarding nature imply reference to an absolute. If the limitations of our intellect do not allow us fully to apprehend it, they yet allow us to assert it as an inevitable premise and integration of all our concepts. It need hardly be said that the absolute, even though reached from two different points of view, can only be one. An absolute which was limited by another absolute would no longer be absolute. The law of causality, which guides us in the study of physical phenomena, throws no light on the origin of nature, and that which is for us the supreme law of conduct (the ethical imperative) does not *per se* reveal the source of the transcendental order to which it bears witness.

All this leads to the conclusion that we must bow before the immense mystery which surrounds us and which it would be vain to seek to penetrate by the methods of scientific research alone. An inward and indestructible sentiment draws us to respect this mystery and the absolute which it encloses; not only to respect but to invoke it and seek refuge in it, especially when our soul is shaken by the tremendous contrast between ephemeral physical life and the eternity of ideas. The more this contrast is felt, the more widely is the door opened to the legitimate appeal of faith arising from the postulates of our moral consciousness, to those aspirations and hopes of an order not of this world, which find no satisfaction in our earthly life and which experimental science can neither explain nor disprove.

(1958)

HISTORICAL MATERIALISM AND PSYCHOLOGISM

THE TERM "HISTORICAL MATERIALISM," INTRODUCED BY ENgels to describe the doctrine which, in the study of social phenomenology, attributes a preponderant value to economic relations, has been pronounced inexact by some of its most authoritative exponents (Croce and Mondolfo, for instance). This doctrine should not be confused with doctrines which are typical expressions of true and genuine materialism.[1] It has also been observed that the same term could just as well be applied to other currents of thought—the sociology of Spencer, for instance, which is derived from biological principles.

However, it must be admitted that the prominence which the doctrine's principal exponents, Marx and Engels, assigned to "material productive forces" in determining the structure of human society, and thus of the life and the modes of thought, resemble the doctrines of the materialist philosophers who denied the priority of ideas, declaring them to be mere derivations of matter or even "secretions of the brain." Therefore we need not reject the name given by Engels; besides, the name has entered common usage to such a degree that it would be difficult to replace it.

A more fitting name, certainly, is "economic determinism," although this too has been attacked by some authors. It is true that Marx often talks of "what men do," and admits explicitly that society is "made by men." This offers an obvious comparison with Vico's famous doctrine, but the agreement is only apparent, for it is a question of seeing *how* men act: whether they are dominated and constrained by the material necessities of existence, or guided by the immanent final cause inside them, which in its transcendent principle can be identified with Providence. The two conceptions are really so radically different that it would be difficult to imagine a greater contrast.

We do not here seek to analyze Marx's thought in all its particulars or to trace its fluctuations in its varying expressions. In the works of all thinkers, not excluding the greatest and the most representative, it is always possible to assemble sayings which, considered separately, apparently point to theories that differ from and even contradict the mainstream of their author's teachings. Thus some writers have been pleased to uphold the moralism of Machiavelli, the scepticism of Kant, or the optimism of Leopardi, in essays which are ingenious but have not as a rule contributed to the cause of truth.

The substantial nucleus of Marx's teaching is formed by his preliminary remarks to the *Kritik der politischen Oekonomie:* "In the social production of their life, men enter into relations that are determinate, necessary and independent of their will; these relations of production correspond to a determinate stage of development of their material productive powers. The totality of these relations of production constitutes the economic structure of society—the real foundation, on which arises a legal and political superstructure and to which correspond determinate social forms of consciousness. The mode of production of material life determines the social, political and spiritual process of life in general. It is not the consciousness of men that determines their being but their social being that determines their consciousness."[2]

The interpretation of this passage seems to leave no room for ambiguity. It is a case for applying the maxim: "Where the letter is clear, do not make an obscure gloss." These statements, moreover, are in agreement with others, no less explicit, in Engels' writings and, if we wish for still clearer proof, we have only to turn to the many writers who defend and disseminate this same teaching. Loria (to give a single example) expresses himself thus: "The economic fact is endowed with characteristics that attribute to it an evident preeminence in the ordering of human society." "The economic fact is simpler than all other social phenomena," and it "precedes them chronologically." It is, in a word, "the basis of social order." Thus "the secret of the juridical relationships which prevail in any age should be sought not in the supra-sensible principles on which the old philosophy of law feeds but in the prosaic and material structure of economic relationships. In other words, the philosophy of law is political economy."[3] These are clear-cut, unambiguous declarations which render further quotation superfluous.

Let it be said at once that this conception is, to our way of thinking, fundamentally mistaken, but, like all errors, it may contain particles of truth—as will appear.

Material things enter into economic relationships insofar as they correspond to the needs, inclinations or aspirations of human beings, thus constituting a way or a means for their possible satisfaction. They are not, however, the cause of these same needs or aspirations. They do not determine their beginning, but only the manner in which they are satisfied, which is always a *consecutivum* in regard to the primordial psychological datum. Agriculture could certainly not exist where the soil is absolutely sterile, nor industry develop where coal mines or sources of electric energy are lacking, just as there can be no hunting where game is lacking. But the presence of physical elements is not enough of itself to explain the commencement of any activity, the roots of which must always rest in the subject's state of mind, even if this means the obscure and prerational form of instinct or of the subconscious. The need for food can be satisfied in various ways, depending on what the surroundings have to offer. The kinds of activity aimed at satisfying such a need will vary according to varying external conditions; but only in a partial and improper sense can such activities be said to be determined by these conditions and to have their cause in them. The most that can be admitted is that such conditions are secondary causes; but the prime and truly determining causes are inherent in the very being of the subject, that is to say, they are the motives of his action.

The logical error committed by exponents of historical materialism or economic determinism consists in confusing the condition with the cause; or, if you prefer to say, in confusing the necessary with the sufficient conditions for a certain relationship to life to arise and assume a specific concrete form. If proof were needed, it would be enough to observe that the same factual elements (for instance, the existence of sea coasts, of mineral deposits, etc.) do not produce the same effects among different people or at various times. Many factors of quite another order also play a part in determining the direction and the kinds of activity undertaken by individuals and by peoples.

These considerations seem obvious enough; but it is precisely the elementary truths which are denied or obscured by those who construct artificial and one-sided theories, which sometimes appear attractive and are followed just because of their one-sidedness.

The activity that is directed toward the acquisition, production and exchange of material goods—in a word, economic activity—is but one part of the vast and complex field of human activity, which sets itself many other aims besides these. The phenomena of practical activity are all so linked together that it is impossible either to reduce all human actions to a single economic category or to make a clear separation between various kinds of action. "History and facts," wrote Igino Petrone in his penetrating criticism of Antonio Labriola's well-known essay, "show us the reciprocity, the correspondence and the interdependence of economic phenomena and of other historical phenomena: they do not show the dialectical causality of the one in the other, or the dependence and derivation of the latter from the former."[4] We may even go further and assert that an economic phenomenon is never *only* an economic phenomenon; it is at the same time, insofar as it proceeds from human will, a moral and juridical act, in the sense that it can be evaluated, and is evaluated, by the standard of morality and of law.[5] We do not deny that by a process of abstraction scientific analysis can isolate, or attempt to isolate, the economic criterion of pure material utility from the other criteria that actually control the course of human actions in their historical-social reality. But we do deny that all actions obey this one criterion alone and that even one action exists which does not cross over into several other categories. Many of the most intelligent exponents of historical materialism—or of economic determinism—make the significant admission that, in one and the same phenomenon, economics would represent the content, and law the form. It is true that certain facts (exchange, ownership, etc.) are studied, under different aspects, by lawyers and economists alike. But this admission does not suffice. In the first place, the form they speak of is not (as these authors seem to think) an extrinsic element, a mere chance accessory happening, but an intrinsic factor that is an essential part of historico-social reality. Moreover, it must be recognized that law in its various forms does not always include an economic content, and that many of its most important institutions (such as the essential rights of the person, the right of religious liberty, of suffrage etc.) have no such content at all.

Within the very restricted limits seen from the foregoing considerations, the so-called materialistic conception of history may offer some contribution to the investigation of the elements that form reality. However, we need have no doubt about rejecting its principal thesis, which attributes a chronological precedence and a causal value to the economic phenomenon in its relation to other phenomena. For instance, Loria, faithfully following Marx's footsteps, maintained: "Man must first of all procure for himself the necessary means of livelihood, and only when these have enabled him to stand on his own feet, can he think of promulgating laws, creating moral sanctions, etc. That is, the economic fact takes precedence over all other phenomena of human society."[6] Statements of this kind, often encountered among those who have no legal training, are founded on the mistaken belief that law consists essentially in a system of written rules that have been formally promulgated, or indeed solely in rules that have a penal content. It is strange that, more than two centuries after Vico, after the historical school of jurisprudence, and after innumerable other proofs furnished by ethnologists, lawyers and philosophers, we must still insist upon such elementary notions, which should by now be the common patrimony of educated people, as that law is born, not in enacted form, but as custom; and such custom is, like language, a primary and spontaneous product of the human spirit, preceding all reflection and elaboration, which only much later contrive to formulate in abstract rules what is already alive in fact and at work in the public conscience. Only a person who denies or ignores this can write fables about a primitive "economic arrangement" of society which is not accompanied and determined by a corresponding legal arrangement.

Nor should we argûe differently about morality, which, like law, has its own natural and spontaneous roots in individual consciousness, whence it is reflected and expands into social consciousness. It too expresses itself in custom, in which the two determinants of action, law and morality, appear in the beginning almost entirely fused together, and remain thus connected and correlative to each other even after philosophic analysis and technical elaboration have managed to distinguish them.

Man cannot affirm his own personality without acknowledging that of other persons; hence a limitation is imposed on his arbitrary freedom, and this is the essence of law. Man cannot act without making some kind of choice among the actions that are possible for him, a choice that presupposes a criterion, and thus a distinction between good and evil; and in this there consists the schema of morality. The recognition and love of other human beings, starting with those who are nearest to us, those who have the same blood in their veins, enters as a fundamental motive, alongside the love of self.

However slow and difficult may be the demonstration of these concepts through the *raison raisonnante*, all the more certain, alive and immediate is their presence in even the most primitive human spirit, where they form true and genuine categories, of necessity already operating even in the phases of subconscious and instinctual behavior. And it should be noted that similar manifestations, although inferior in degree, which can be called pre-juridical and pre-moral, are found in animals or at least in some species of animals. These manifestations are, as it were, an embryonic symptom, a tenuous glimmer of that same spirituality which emerges to shine in human nature as its unfailing immanent characteristic.

* * *

The problem which historical materialism—or economic determinism—imagines it is solving with its oversimplified formula is, then, really very complex.

Just as knowledge is not only an objective datum but a relation between a subject and an object, so activity is never determined *sic et simpliciter* by the conditions of the external world, although it necessarily unfolds in relation to it.

The *primum movens* of activity lies in the nature of the subjective being; from this proceed those decisions and inclinations which find the material for fulfilling and externalizing themselves in the elements of surrounding physical nature. It is neither possible to reduce all the subject's activities to this material nor, even if we look at the primitive phases of human activity, to see this activity as directed exclusively towards the satisfaction of the material needs of life.

Human nature includes infinitely diverse tendencies and aptitudes, which it is difficult to reduce to one scheme. If we wish, nevertheless, to count them and to classify them, we should not imagine them as really separated and disposed in series as if they succeeded each other chronologically as parts of a mechanical process. We should conceive them organically as springing from one identical root, the human spirit, and as being in existence, at least embryonically, ever since the subjective being first came to life.

Since the first crude formulations of the materialistic doctrine of history, there have been attempts to refine it so as to meet the objections raised against it. While always upholding the fundamental thesis that the economic structure of society is the substrate and the cause of every other phenomenon and of all ideologies (including those of morality, law and religion), some writers, for instance, Labriola, have sought to distinguish between a primary series of derivations, which are immediate and direct, and a secondary series, mediate and indirect. The former would be exemplified by the forming and the frictions of the various social classes, and the development of a determinate domination of one class over another; the latter, by the tendencies and manifestations of thought in the productions of art, religion and science. The origin of these secondary products is supposed to have been partly forgotten, which is the reason for the illusion that they are independent and autonomous.

This is an ingenious attempt,[7] but it is hopelessly inadequate and wrong. Not only do our general objections remain intact in face of this more refined form of the doctrine but other more specific objections can be added as regards the very facts it alleges. Experience shows us that all the "ideologies" which are denounced by this doctrine as late superstructures, or epiphenomena, do not follow but accompany or even precede the formation of "economic relations" from primitive times onwards. We can see moral behavior already in action, displaying typical forms of altruism (as in the relation between parents and offspring), at the very beginning of any form of human life; human life would not be possible without it. Law defining the limits of what is permitted in relations between persons makes its appearance *ab initio:* for instance, the institution of lawful self-defense did not wait for any article in a legal code before it was sanctioned by usage and by human conscience (it is not by chance that the Romans invoked *naturalis ratio* to justify the principle: *vim vi repellere licet*). As for religion, it is puerile to believe that it is an invention springing from an advanced phase of culture. No men and no people, however savage, but in their own way fear and adore the invisible forces around them, and seek to propitiate them; no one is insensible to the mystery of death and what happens after death. Nor is it true that aesthetic and artistic activity appear only at a late stage, as an indirect effect of material necessity; for it has been proved—however extraordinary it may sound—that primitive men began to wear clothing through a desire for beauty rather than because they needed protection against the weather.[8]

Science, in the broadest meaning of the word, is inseparable from the spirit, which may indeed err but which cannot but aspire to the knowledge of the truth. Even in the uncivilized savage, some kind of knowledge is to be found. If this were not the case, when and how should science suddenly begin? And how could science be born from previous economic relations, if these very relations already presuppose certain notions, however vague and rudimentary?

If by "philosophy" we mean to designate a systematic treatment of first principles, *more scholastico,* no one will expect to find it among uncivilized peoples; and, even among civilized peoples, it appears as an exceptional phenomenon, reserved for a handful of thinkers. But if, in a broader and truer sense, we mean by "philosophy" an orientation of the soul according to certain directive lines, both in theory and in practice, we can venture to say that every man, simply because he thinks and acts, is in some way a philosopher. That is, he cannot help but have in his mind and his life some sort of logic and some sort of morality. And are not logic and morality essential and constituent parts of philosophy, even in the strict sense of the word? Here, too, we are dealing with questions of degree and with transitions leading from dim and almost instinctive forms to forms that are more conscious and reasoned. Long and arduous is the road that leads from the lowest grades to the higher but we must not refuse to recognize the nature of an evolutionary process, the development of a seed, just because its beginnings are remote from its final stage.[9]

* * *

This summary sketch is designed to point only to the methodological requirement that in the scientific and philosophical study of historical reality we should consider as the fundamental factor, not the material as it is given us by the external world, but the human spirit in its diverse and active unity. In opposition to the thesis of historical materialism—or economic determinism, or dialectical materialism—we offer a thesis which we may entitle "historical psychologism."

This thesis, of course, does not deny the importance of the data provided by physical nature, without which the activity of the spirit would be defective, if it were possible at all. But it must be remembered that the laws of human action can never be derived from these data. Nor can the laws governing the succession of historical events, which are, or appear to be, interconnected in their phenomenalistic aspect. In that they proceed from that autonomous source which is the spirit, they invariably contain a moment of creativity and thus, of indeterminism. In confirmation of this we may note that all the alleged proofs and dogmatic assertions of the exponents of materialism have never led (as they should have done, if the doctrine had any true foundations) to any scientific prevision of future events; and when any such forecast has been attempted, it has usually been flatly contradicted by the actual facts.

But we, on our side, should guard against committing an error analogous to that of the doctrine now disproved. This is the error of falling into a kind of psychological dogmatism; that is, attributing to the human spirit one sole motive, or a few motives, determined arbitrarily without a sufficient examination of reality.

A well-known instance of this is furnished by the efforts made in ancient and modern times to reduce all the phenomena of human life to the single psychological motive of self-love (egoism); these attempts have all failed, in that they have left unexplained many facts which are no less certain than those on which the attempts were based. Along with the individual's instinct of self-preservation (*conatus proprium esse conservandi*) is associated the no less commanding urge to preserve the species. The love of self alternates and intertwines with the love of others; it would be equally possible, and equally one-sided, to base the whole theory of human life on the sole motive of sociability. Each of these motives can lead to actions so diverse and so different in value as to constitute extreme vice in one case, supreme virtue in another.

But these are not the only motives. Joined to them are other aspirations of the soul which spring directly from its spiritual essence, not as a *consecutivum*, but as something simultaneous and concomitant: the tendency towards the universal as it is expressed in the forms of truth, goodness, justice and beauty. The activity directed towards these ideals (activity that may be scientific, philosophic, religious, moral, legal, aesthetic) has no physical limit, nor is it tied to any particular object of the empirical world; it is infinite in its very nature, so its practice in the life of the individual resolves itself into a lasting effort to strive towards a goal which transcends it.

Reality being such, how can we assemble the motive forces of human aspirations within a single framework and mark for them courses and laws such as are formulated, for instance, for mechanics? It is strange that the sovereign genius of Giambattista Vico risked making this desperate attempt, with his all too famous theory of "corsi e ricorsi" (that is, of the recurrence of historical facts); I say "too famous," because this is the least happy and least true part of his system, and yet it is the only part that every cultivated person feels obliged to know (proving that philosophers win public fame not by the truth in their teaching but by the errors). It is all the more strange in Vico's case, because he understood better than all others that it is the human mind that gives birth to the whole of history, namely, to "the world of the nations," and the human mind of its very nature virtually participates in the infinite.

Holding firmly to this principle, we deduce from it the necessity of seeking the best possible light to illumine the succession of human events in a broader and deeper psychological analysis, without any mechanical schematism or any dogmatic preconceptions. The dogmatism to be avoided can consist just as much in that historical systematism of metaphysical origin with which Carlo Cantoni reproached Vico's teaching[10] as in the opposite prejudice, which is represented by the doctrine of historical materialism.

It is difficult to keep to the critical "highway," as far from scepticism as it is from dogmatism. In investigating the motives for action, in individuals as in peoples, we must proceed with the greatest objectivity, though we are dealing with subjective phenomena; it is necessary to *intelligere*, in Spinoza's sense, before undertaking to evaluate. It is not enough to understand the original intention which led individuals or peoples to give a certain course to their actions; for often a slight deviation or exaggeration in putting these intentions into practice is enough to change their whole meaning and effect. Consider the possible consequences that can derive from love of country according to the way in which it is understood and according to the limits within which it may, or may not, be held.

Analysis must work in depth, gathering from the innermost sources of history the psychological elements—even those hidden from sight—which have contributed to the genesis, the deliberation, and the execution of actions. Nor should investigation stop here; for the very nature of this material requires that scientific investigation, that is to say, the analysis of motives, should be followed by (while remaining distinct from) ethical or deontological evaluation of these motives and of the actions that correspond to them. It is because we do not believe that historical events should be considered as necessary and fatal consequences of given circumstances that we believe it to be the great task of the philosophy of history to evaluate men ethically, especially those who have played, or who now play, an important part in fashioning the destiny of their people. Fatalism and determinism are to be particularly opposed here, because they are not merely theoretical errors but are factors in the debasement and moral perversion of men. They induce men to give free rein to their impulses, under the deceitful appearance and facile pretext of historical necessity, thus exonerating them from the absolute obligation of answering for their deeds.

There is, indeed, a world tribunal, which is not the same as world history—as in the famous and equivocal saying—which has been invoked to justify a supine adoration of the *fait accompli* and the idolatrous worship of force. It is the human conscience that is the world tribunal; and it is not content with facts without distinction, merely because they are historically determined or imposed by some preponderant power. The victories gained by such a power, forcing its subjects to obedience, are never of themselves a final verdict, for the human conscience is endowed with the faculty of discerning beyond the fact the idea, and beyond dark force the eternal light of justice. Its judgment prevails even after generations or centuries, thanks to the common spiritual nature which binds all men to one another with a sacred and indissoluble chain (*religio*) that carries them beyond their own life on earth. There is no power on earth that can escape this judgment which, if it is honestly and nobly inspired, bears the imprint of the absolute.

The highest expression of consciousness is philosophy, the various branches of which include, as an explanatory and critical synthesis of human action, the philosophy of history. This branch of philosophy has recently been much neglected and sometimes even opposed and repudiated. For this we must blame the prejudices discussed in this article. May we witness the rise of a true and great philosophy of history, founded on the priority and on the freedom of the spirit!

(1946)

NOTES

1. E.g., according to CROCE, "historical materialism has no intrinsic relation to metaphysical materialism and is simply a 'manner of speaking' " (*Materialismo storico ed Economia marxistica*, Milano, 1900, p. 17). MONDOLFO, who has studied the question at length (see *Il materialismo storico in F. Engels*, Genova, 1912; *Sulle orme di Marx*, 3 ed., Bologna, 1923-24; and the article, "Materialismo storico," in the *Enciclop. Ital.*) says that Marx and Engels not only have not adhered to metaphysical materialism, but have "critically demolished it."

2. MARX, *Zur Kritik der pol. Oekonomie*, Vorwort (2 ed., by Kautsky, Stuttgart, 1903, p. xi).

3. A. LORIA, *La sociologia—Il suo compito, le sue scuole, i suoi recenti progressi* (Verona, 1900), pp. 118, 119 *et seq.*, 128. The conclusion agrees with that which Marx says he reached after his critical review of Hegel's *Philosophy of Right:* "Legal relationships and political forms cannot be explained by themselves or by the so-called general development of the human spirit; they are rooted in the material relations of life" (*op. cit.*, p. x).

4. LABRIOLA, *Del materialismo storico. Dilucidazione preliminare* (Roma, 1896). PETRONE, *Un nuovo saggio sulla concezione materialistica della storia* (1896; repr. in *Filosofia del diritto con l'aggiunta di vari saggi*, Milano, 1953, p. 183).

5. Cf. DEL VECCHIO, "*Law and Economics*," in *1*, *Journal of Social Philosophy*, 1936, New York.

6. LORIA, *La sociologia*, *op. cit.*, pp. 119-120.

7. As is recognized, with perhaps excessive indulgence, by PETRONE, *op cit.*, p. 181 *et seq.*

8. Noted by CATTANEO, *Del pensiero come principio d'economia pubblica* (in *Op.*, vol. V, Firenze, 1888, p. 371) and confirmed by later observers.

9. If the trite saying, *primum vivere, deinde philosophari*, is to have any truth in it, it cannot be taken (as, mistakenly, by LORIA, *op. cit.*, p. 119) as proving that spiritual activity can begin only after the material needs of life have been satisfied, i.e., in a phase historically subsequent to the "economic" phase.

10. CANTONI, *G. B. Vico—Studi critici e comparativi* (Torino, 1867), p. 229 *et seq.* Cf. DEL VECCHIO, *The Formal Bases of Law* (Boston, 1914, and New York, 1921), p. 27 *et seq.*

NATURAL LAW AS THE FOUNDATION OF A SOCIETY OF MANKIND

TO STUDY AND, IF POSSIBLE, TO SOLVE THE PROBLEM OF THE foundation of international law it is well to start from two facts which have never been disputed. There is among all men a certain community of nature (without which one could not speak of "the human race"); but men actually live grouped in various organizations and there does not, in fact, exist any unitary world system.

Among these organizations there are agreements of greater or less scope and certain generally accepted conventions taking the form of customs. This constitutes the so-called international juridical community. But neither the agreements concluded between various States nor the norms accepted by custom are sufficient to bring into being a complete system uniformly regulating the lives of all peoples.

When we look at the facts, we must acknowledge that only within the separate States does there exist a central power from which emanate the norms constituting the body of law in force inside their frontiers, and there still exists no such power for relations between States. What is called international law (and ought more exactly to be called interstate law) has an imperfect degree of positivity precisely because of the lack of a sovereign power to give it real force.

It may be remarked that if such a power were established mankind would form one single State; what is today international or interstate law would become a system of internal law; the States of today would become subordinate parts of this system and, properly speaking, should no longer be called States, if by this name we mean an organization that possesses absolute sovereignty. All this follows if we start from the premises of a rigorous positivism; but the problem assumes a somewhat different appearance if we start from other premises.

The present imperfection and instability of international relations have led some thinkers to deny that international law is really law. Thus, according to Adolf Lasson, treaties between States do not create a real juridical bond but express solely a power relationship, and they cease to be valid when one State has the desire and the capability to disregard them.[1]

The juridical validity of treaties is, however, accepted by almost all authors, the majority of whom consider this principle the sole basis of international law. This doctrine goes back to the idea formulated in the Peace of Westphalia (1648) that States are absolutely independent and free of all bonds with the exception of those which they have voluntarily taken on themselves. Hence the fundamental importance assigned to the maxim: *Pacta sunt servanda.*

We may, however, make a few comments. According to this doctrine, the will of a State is a simple arbitrary choice, which can be exercised unconditionally and illimitably, and which is always valid. This is contrary to the most elementary juridical logic, as can be seen by comparison with the norms of civil law. Such norms subordinate the validity of contracts to certain conditions, such as the capacity of the contracting parties, the absence of defects in consent, and the legality of the object. As an arbitrary act of will can be either right or perverse, it is not in itself a rational principle; it has, therefore, no ethical validity. To accept it as the basis of international law is equivalent to reducing the latter to a string of accidental facts, indefinitely changeable and subject to no universal criterion whatsover; it means denying that there is any bond between men that is based on their common nature.

The maxims *pacta sunt servanda, juris naturae est stare pactis* are acceptable when understood in their proper sense and within their proper limits; they cannot stand on their own but must be deduced from a more general principle, namely, the value of the human person as an entity endowed with reason and liberty. They belong to a system of rational truths, which is not generally accepted by the supporters of the above-mentioned doctrine, who confine themselves to a mere "positivism." Given, on the one hand, the rejection of natural law and, on the other, the absence of a higher organ having effective power over the separate States, international law would be reduced to a simple statement of facts as they exist. The sound sense of the most civilized peoples has, however, shown itself, especially in the wake of the tragic experiences of the recent world conflicts; specifically, it has revealed itself in recognizing the dictates of *recta ratio* as imperative law, not only for the internal government of a State but also in international relations. The thesis of the unlimited arbitrary will of the State, although still taught in many schools, has already been abandoned in the most advanced constitutions and in the programs of international organizations, even though such programs have, to date, been only partly realized. For instance, the *Universal Declaration of Human Rights*, adopted by the General Assembly of the United Nations on December 10, 1948, rightly asserts that "recognition of the inherent dignity and of the equal and inalienable rights of all members of the human family, is the foundation of freedom, justice and peace in the world."

If, as several signs indicate, the human race is evolving towards a unitary juridical order in spite of all the obstacles which make this progress slow and laborious, it is due to the common longing for peace and to the increasingly widespread belief that an enduring peace can be founded only on a law imposed by reason—a law of justice and of freedom. Otherwise, if we had to accept the dogma of the unlimited sovereignty of each State, the world would be condemned to perpetual instability and virtual anarchy.

This dogma, which excludes any duty on the part of the State to respect certain principles, has been properly altered so far as the internal order is concerned, that is to say, in relations between the State and the individuals who compose it. The constitutions of the more advanced States have admitted and formally sanctioned the principle that the State must recognize the fundamental rights of its citizens and that such a recognition constitutes a legal limitation on its own freedom of action. This does not mean that the concept of sovereignty has been abandoned, only that it has been corrected in the sense that sovereignty is no longer to be understood as absolute power. A similar rectification is needed in regard to relations between States. Here also, sovereignty must be understood in the sense of "constitutional sovereignty," that is to say, confined within certain limits and subject to conditions which, because of their universal application, imply no diminution of one State in relation to others. It is a matter of applying to international relations those principles enunciated in the theories of natural law which have already been incorporated in the constitutions of many States. All through human life, individuality must be tempered by sociability. Even as the individual is obliged to recognize that he belongs to a society of his fellow men, which safeguards and even reinforces his natural and rational rights, so the State must recognize that it forms part of an international or interstate order based on respect for the fundamental rights of man. This respect constitutes an indefeasible obligation for each State as well as for the interstate order. No State can claim to be recognized *de jure*, if in its internal order these rights are violated (though we may allow the possibility of a partial, *de facto* recognition, subject to adjustment later on a more real and sound basis).

It is a very old error, refuted long ago by Plato but still not wholly eradicated, to put one's faith in things perceived by the senses rather than in the universal ideas which transcend them. This fundamental error reappears in many forms even in the domain of the juridical sciences. Many jurists regard as "real" only those imperatives emanating from States or visibly existing authorities, and not those emanating from reason or from human nature. Yet even those who, in compliance with this preconception, deny natural law, implicitly admit the imperatives of logic and of grammar and frequently also of morality, although these imperatives have never been decreed by any government or any parliament.

Through this regrettable prejudice, certain schools have remained deaf to the substantial agreement of countless thinkers who have affirmed in the name of reason the validity of the supreme ideals of mankind.

The idea of the necessity of a society of the human race appeared in the philosophy of the Stoics, and was nobly expressed by Cicero in the well-known passage: "Nec erit alia lex Romae, alia Athenis, alia nunc, alia posthac, sed et omnes gentes et omni tempore una lex, et sempiterna et immutabilis continebit." Similar passages can be found in Seneca ("Aliquod esse commune jus generis humani. . . . etc.") and in a later age in Dante Alighieri ("totum humanum genus ordinatur ad unum"), and in Francisco de Vitoria ("totus orbis aliquo modo est una res publica"). Many other philosophers, too, while employing different methods in their proofs, agree in their conclusions, all of which support the postulate of "one great city of the world" (Vico), or "civitas gentium maxima" (Wolff), or "Weltrepublik" (Kant).

Between the realm of arbitrary will and the realm of reason there are no intermediate solutions. If through an antiphilosophic prejudice—the error of which has been demonstrated by epistemological criticism—we reject the universal truths dictated by reason and refuse even to listen to the "heavenly voice" of conscience, if we place faith only in the arbitrary decisions of governments and accept as valid every manifestation of their ambulatory will, construction of a juridical organization of the human race will be as fruitless a task as would be an attempt to erect a building on shifting sands.

The thesis propounded by certain ancient writers: "exeundum esse e statu naturae," is erroneous if taken literally, in that it seems to imply the hypothesis of a primitive extrasocial state, which has never really existed; but it expresses a truth if we understand it in its deeper meaning as an affirmation of the requirement of reason that individuality must be tempered by sociability. This requirement holds not only for individual persons but also for States; and, as membership of a State does not diminish but confirms a man's intrinsic dignity, so the participation of a State in the universal society is not a diminution but rather an affirmation of its authority in accordance with its real nature. All this is subject, of course, to the condition that the State, as well as the society of States, acknowledges and gives effect to those rights rooted in human nature which are summed up in the idea of justice. This idea is a real category (*a priori*) of the mind and is not undetermined or undeterminable, as some have claimed; rightly understood, it contains precise prescriptions which are valid as norms for all intersubjective or social relations. This does not mean that errors are any less possible in this domain than in every other, since human reason is fallible and is frequently led astray or darkened by passion. But it is the business of philosophers to point out the right road.

Above all, justice demands that the human being be acknowledged and treated by all others as endowed with liberty, that is, with a natural right, in regard to which a perfect equality reigns among all men. In accordance with the same idea of justice, the various forms of human activity must have a corresponding number of specific applications of this fundamental right—which is freedom harmonized and elevated to the universal—with regard to the possibility of coexistence (freedom of thought, of speech, of work, of assembly, association, etc.).

In conformity with this, it is necessary to determine the functions of the State, whose duty it is to confirm and protect the validity of those rights as a first and unchallengeable condition of its existence, the primary and immanent justification of its activity, the limit and essential condition of its legitimate authority over individuals. Justice thus manifests itself in its various forms (distinct from, though always coherent with, one another), such as political justice, economic justice, educational justice, international or cosmopolitan justice, and all those forms of justice concerned with industrial organization, social assistance, compensation and reparation.[2]

Up to the present time these principles have been applied very imperfectly, especially in the international sphere. Even the United Nations Organization is not exempt from grave defects. It has solemnly asserted in its Charter, and more fully in the Universal Declaration of Human Rights, its purpose of "reaffirming faith in fundamental human rights, in the dignity and worth of the human person"; but it has not hesitated to welcome States which manifestly disregard these principles both in their internal government and in their relations with other States. Furthermore, the Charter, while affirming that "the organization is based on the principle of the sovereign equality of all its members," grants, with evident contradiction, a privileged position to certain States, while relegating others to a condition of permanent inferiority. It is a contradiction which is all the more unjust in that among the privileged States are some which show no respect for human rights, while in the second category are others which do respect them.

It would be vain to search the Charter for a direct appeal to natural law, the logical prerequisite of a universal society of States. Natural law would consecrate the unity of the human race and thereby impose on every State the categorical duty to adhere to a just international organization. The Charter wrongly makes such adherence optional. Here, too, the root of the error lies in the confusion between liberty and arbitrary choice, and disregard for the fact that liberty can subsist only when it is in harmony with reason and the law of reason.

A perfect international organization ought to include all existing States (either at their own request, or even *ex officio*), not conferring equal powers and equal functions on them all, but rather making a distinction between legitimate or "just" States and those which are despotic, and granting only to the first the power of participating in debates and voting. A just regard for the personality of individuals as well as for States would, at least for discussions of major importance, require a twofold approval: the majority of the States and the majority of the populations they represent. This, of course, would always be subject to the principle that only legitimate or "just" States should be allowed to vote.

Questions of detail can be left open to discussion. What is important is that we should not confuse accidentals with essentials; the only essential is that the world should be governed according to the dictates of reason, not according to the blind impulses of passion. We therefore repudiate those doctrines which, by proposing a false concept of liberty, end by legitimizing every possible aberration.

We can all clearly see how not only justice and peace but the very existence of the human race is today imperilled by the arbitrary will of a few, to which these false doctrines lend support.

We are not prophets nor do we know what ordeals the world will have to undergo, but we are confident that good will finally prevail over evil and right over force; for, if through supreme misfortune justice were to perish, it would not be worthwhile (here we repeat the words of Kant) for men to live on the earth.

(Salzburg, 1962)

NOTES

1. LASSON, *Prinzip und Zukunft des Völkerrechts* (Berlin, 1871). Lasson's ideas are discussed in DEL VECCHIO, *Studi su la guerra e la pace* (Milano, 1959).
2. For these concepts see DEL VECCHIO, *Justice* (Edinburgh, 1952).

THE UNITY OF THE HUMAN MIND AS A BASIS FOR COMPARATIVE LEGAL STUDY

IN THIS GRAVE HOUR IN THE HISTORY OF THE WORLD THE significance of a meeting of jurists coming from so many countries cannot escape anyone. If there is hope (and hope itself is a duty) that mankind can escape the awful fate which its technical progress may be reserving for it, such hope can rest only on the development and consolidation in humanity of a common moral and legal conscience. Our attendance here proves our desire to work to that end. The ideal which animates each one of us is justice, that justice without which States would be, as St. Augustine said, *magna latrocinia.* I am sure that I express the thought of all Italian jurists in greeting with a fraternal spirit our colleagues from other countries and in voicing the hope that our labors may contribute not only to a better mutual knowledge but also to a strengthening of those bonds of human solidarity which attain their most certain and solemn confirmation in law.

Many years have passed since the International Philosophical Congress at Heidelberg in 1908, when attempting to delineate the "Idea of a Science of Universal Comparative Law," I expressed the conviction that to grasp the reasons and aims of this science it would be necessary to refer to the principle of the real unity of the human mind. This principle is the implicit presupposition and logical foundation of all our comparative researches, including those which seek to understand single institutions or particular subjects. As the logicians teach us, there is no possible comparison between totally heterogeneous things, comparison being the observation of what is similar and what is dissimilar in the same class or kind of objects.[1] Even the perception of different degrees within the same series involves reference to a unity of measure. Comparison can only begin from the basis of a homogeneity of the object, which subsists and which reaffirms itself throughout its various manifestations. Comparative legal study presupposes the idea of law, though it neither contemplates this idea *sub specie aeterni* nor analyzes it in the abstract. Rather, it considers law in the concrete, in its manifold realizations as an element or fact of experience.

It has been debated whether the idea of law represents a true and proper category (that is to say, a necessary truth) or an empirical concept based solely on particular and relatively accidental observations. Critical analysis of knowledge shows the first theory to be the sounder. I am not so Platonic as to hold that every generic notion to which our intellect tends constitutes an absolute universal endowed with a transcendental reality of its own; I do not hold that besides the horse there is "horseness." Admitting, however, that there are *a posteriori* notions which are derived in some way from the senses, it must not be forgotten that these also imply a relationship with the mind or spirit which apprehends them; remember the "nisi ipse intellectus" of Leibniz. There are, moreover, concepts which the mind draws from itself, and these bear characteristics of universality and necessity which experience cannot give us. One of these concepts is law, understood as a *pure form of intersubjectivity*, according to which the subject must recognize in others his own quality as a subject. In this way, and only in this way, can we explain how law unfailingly manifests itself—with more or less clarity—at all times and in all places wherever human life exists, so that the field of comparative legal study is in fact as large as that of the history of man. Law always and everywhere reveals itself as a coordination between person and person, as a limit of reciprocal activity and as a series of rights and correlative obligations. The formal nature of this schema allows it to include a great variety of content while remaining unchanged and unchangeable. Only a superficial and erroneous observation can lead to the mistaken thesis that in law everything varies, forgetting or not recognizing that uniform and constant element through which and only in relation to which is there any sense in speaking of variability.

This is not all. Even if variations in the content of law can indeed be conceived, in theory, as being infinite (saving only the formal schema of juridicity), an objective examination of all known legal systems reveals a striking number of coincidences and identities. The protection of the person and the limitation of his arbitrary free will, through regard for his coexistence with other persons, are fundamental points which recur in the institutions of all peoples. Differences on these points are secondary and often only apparent, since they result from the necessity to attain, by the means available in each case, an identical end. Without superfluous quotation we can summarize the unanimous conclusion of all the most comprehensive and careful studies on this subject: the greater part of legal principles and institutions form a common inheritance of all humanity at all times.[2]

More precisely, we can assert that a substantial concordance exists not only from the static but also from the dynamic point of view, that is to say, that there are uniform tendencies in the development of the systems of various peoples, so that, in general, each of them passes through the same phases. Not that the immense panorama of legal history is lacking in individual characteristics and even deviations, regressions and anomalies. But we can still perceive the general tendencies of development; this is all the more true in that history itself proves that sooner or later these deviations and involutions are destined to disappear, as the disease of an organism cannot last forever but must be resolved in some way, by life or death. The only difference here, of course, is that the death of a people is a very rare occurrence.

It is therefore possible—and here is one of the tasks confronting the science of universal comparative law—to distinguish and to systematize the various phases of juridical evolution. This must be done without distorting reality. The peculiarities of phenomena observed in different peoples must be respected and we must avoid that excessive "historical systematicism," prompted by ideological preconceptions, which vitiated the old philosophy of history (not excluding the work of Vico, for all its genius). Thus, for instance, the duration of the various phases in the historical development of law cannot be established *a priori*, as it depends on particular circumstances in the life of various peoples. What is important is that, with respect to the over-all course of juridical phenomenology, we should describe in order the modes of development of the successive transitions and establish the types resulting therefrom. The history of any particular system naturally follows a chronological order, but our design must be metahistorical because, in the description of any particular phase, we can and must include instances offered from different chronological epochs by peoples who were or are in that phase.

To admit the essential identity of the mind in its constitutive forms, and in the laws and tendencies of its development, is to recognize that no exclusion, either of epoch or of race, is justified if we are planning a program for the science of comparative law. Inquiries limited to a few systems or institutions can be useful and sometimes valuable, but they must always be considered as fragments with respect to the more general design.

We do not condemn those limitations of the field of inquiry which are imposed by the practical necessity to restrict our work according to our individual strength and the brevity of life. What is to be condemned is the prejudice that only certain systems of law are "worthy" of study and that, therefore, comparative study must be limited to them. This prejudice in both ancient and modern times obtained such currency—despite the contrary attitude of some broad-minded thinkers, such as Leibniz, Feuerbach and Amari—that only recently has it become possible to effectively establish the science of universal comparative law. Let us mention with due honor the names of Maine, Post, Kohler, Lambert, Wigmore, and Gutteridge.[3]

The work that has been accomplished in this relatively short time is far from small; yet much remains to be done. One of the difficulties is that the various legal systems often possess very different structures and modes of expression, so that, to make them comparable, it is necessary, in a sense, to reduce them to the same denominator. There are, for instance, systems in which the legislative form predominates, and others in which much room is given to custom, even in advanced phases of civilization and in fundamental matters, such as the constitution of the State itself. There are systems which contain precise, even if only partial, declarations of the so-called general principles of law, and others in which such principles are merely understood, leaving it to interpreters, and in particular to the judges, to deduce them from their own conscience or from the spirit of existing laws. It has further been observed that each legal system has certain "implicit premises," which, even if not formulated, are important for a proper understanding of the system and its component parts.[4]

Thus, by assembling and comparing the different data, the science of universal comparative law is able to discern, even in institutions geographically and chronologically remote, that basis of humanity which is common to them and which becomes ever more evident with the progress of evolution, as rationality, implicit from the beginning but in the first phases almost buried in extrinsic and accidental elements, gradually reveals and affirms itself and progressively transforms itself into uniform general principles. The spontaneous convergence of developments is gradually facilitated by the increased possibility of mutual borrowings and derivations among different systems. Comparison effectively shows both the identity of the psychological origin of law and its communicability from one people to another.

The science of universal comparative law is not and cannot be a mere catalog or inventory of laws which have existed or exist, at every time or in every place. Although it collects all historical elements which have a legal significance, unlike history it places them in an order of development of the human mind, which is substantially an order of values. Far from equating primitive juridical institutions with those more rationally evolved, it makes evident their respective inferiority and superiority or, as one might say, their varying degrees of humanity. It is true that phenomena of regress occur in the vicissitudes of the life of peoples and that barbaric forms sometimes reappear among so-called civilized countries, as has recently happened; but it is also true that the most effective criticism of these forms is the demonstration that they belong to an historical phase already past. Human conscience almost inevitably reacts against these anachronistic *monstra legum*, through the unconquerable and always reviving strength of reason, which like ". . . the bough, when the wind rushes by, / Bendeth its topmost leaves and then is raised / By its own virtue, and once more springeth high."[5]

Therefore, the science of universal comparative law is more important, both theoretically and practically, insofar as the systems of law to which it refers are more perfect and advanced. By displaying the highest points attained by juridical thought, namely, the laws which are the richest in rational and human content, this science becomes a guide to further progress and offers a model for further improvements and reforms. It is, therefore, an efficient instrument for the progressive unification of the positive law of the various countries. This goal is far off, yet it is clearly perceivable from the steps already made in its direction. The United Nations Organization is still imperfect and of uncertain stability (it does not at the moment [1950] include that nation which was the teacher of law to all others, and which, as was said by the Secretary-General of this Congress, Professor Elmer Balogh, is "the second Fatherland of every jurist");[6] yet one cannot but recognize that it represents a great attempt to approach that ideal of the political coordination of mankind, seen as such by ancient philosophers and which today more than ever is felt as a vital need by the most enlightened minds of every country.

Nor should we overlook the many particular agreements, concluded with increasing frequency not only between single countries but also among large groups of countries, to create uniform law for specific matters of common interest. Finally, there is the important fact that in the internal law of civilized countries the juridical value of the human being, without reference to his nationality, has been recognized, so that in the more advanced countries the difference between citizens and foreigners in matters of private law has been reduced to a minimum. The recent world conflagration and the present uneasiness have prevented further progress in this matter, and have even caused some regress; but if reason prevails over madness, and the love of peace and justice over the savage instincts of plunder and domination, we can surely expect that after overcoming today's crisis, as others have been overcome in the past, humanity will resume its upward march towards a society of free and equal nations. This will not be the monarchy conceived by Dante, but will fulfill that same need of supernational unity which inspired the poet's great design. Even today his maxim is valid, and it remains eternal: "Totum genus humanum ordinatur ad unum."[7] And the Bible, as Dante himself recalls, says: "Omne regnum in seipsum divisum desolabitur."[8]

(Address delivered at the closing session of the Third International Congress of Comparative Law, London, August 5, 1950)

NOTES

1. Cf. WUNDT, *Logik*, 4 Aufl. (Stuttgart, 1920), II Bd., p. 369; III Bd., p. 62.

2. DEL VECCHIO, "Sull'idea di una scienza del diritto universale comparato" (1908) and "Sulla comunicabilità del diritto" (1938), both repr. in *Studi sul diritto*, Milano, 1958, vol. I.

3. On the beginnings and progress of studies in comparative law, see: F. POLLOCK, *Essays in the Law* (London, 1922), ch. I, "The History of Comparative Jurisprudence"; H. C. GUTTERIDGE, *Comparative Law* (Cambridge, 1946; 2 ed. 1949), esp. ch. II; C. W. WESTRUP, *Introduction to Early Roman Law—Comparative Sociological Studies*, vol. IV (London-Copenhagen, 1950), pp. 185-201; DEL VECCHIO, the essays *cit. supra* n. 2.

4. See, *inter alios*: T. ASCARELLI, *Premesse allo studio del diritto comparato*, in *Saggi giuridici* (Milano, 1949), p. 10; DEL VECCHIO, *General Principles of Law* (Boston, 1956).

5. DANTE, *Paradiso*, XXVI, 85-87.

6. Italy was admitted to the UN on Dec. 14, 1955.

7. DANTE, *Monarchia*, L.I, C.V (VII).

8. LUKE, 11, 17; MATT., 12, 25.

EVOLUTION AND INVOLUTION IN LAW

I.—MEANINGS OF EVOLUTION

ALL THE WRITINGS OF FLAMINIO MANCALEONI ON ROMAN LAW are familiar to Romanists, but one essay in particular, although bearing on Roman law, has much wider significance than the others. This is his introductory lecture of 1920 on "Regressive Evolution in Legal Institutions."

This lecture is particularly valuable in that it is a considered critical reaction against a tendency prevailing at that date—and still strong today—to regard the life of law as a continual, uninterrupted, and necessarily *progressive* evolution, such as is seen, or imagined, in organic nature.

Even in the study of the organic world and of all physical reality, evolution is merely a hypothesis and a regulative principle providing a context for the unification of certain experiences. It is not, nor should it be, held as a dogma, for there are also instances of a contrary process which must be interpreted according to an opposing concept called *involution*. This can be observed in social phenomena, including positive law, as well as in the field of biology.[1] Long before the conception of the theory of evolution in its narrow sense, Nicolo Cusano spoke both of an *evolutio* and an *involutio* in mathematics; and Leibniz described death as an "involution" of the organism.[2]

Students of social life and history often refer to involution, decadence and regression but more with respect to customs, to learning and to the fine arts than to law. Yet even in law, the idea of indefinite progression is a mere abstraction, and the real life of laws and institutions displays as many phenomena of regression or involution as of progression or evolution.

Evolution, in the most general sense, simply means the continuity of a process. We could go further and consider evolution as synonymous with mere becoming. That is the first of the seven meanings which Rickert observes in the concept of evolution.[3] The second is synonymous with change and would exclude mere repeated becoming. These two meanings, however, seem too vague and indeterminate, and really are outside the concept of evolution, which signifies something more than the "eternal becoming" of Heraclitus. We conceive of a development or a process of formation only when we think of the different parts which succeed one another as constituting a single whole (Rickert's third concept). But the unity of the process, in relation to the whole, implies a direction toward an end (fourth concept). In relation to the end, a scale of values is then constituted, that is to say, an evaluation of the different degrees (the fifth concept, which, according to Rickert, goes beyond the purely scientific role of history). The ascending series of values, necessarily successive in time, accounts for the idea of progress (sixth concept). Finally, the supreme value realized in the process may be conceived as the cause of the process itself, so that one is but the product of the other (the seventh concept).

The history of thought shows many and various applications of these concepts. Schelling, for instance, interpreted the products of nature "als verschiedene Stufen der Entwicklung einer und derselben absoluten Organisation," and states that "die Natur als unendliche Produktivität eigentlich als in unendlicher Evolution begriffen gedacht werden muss."[4] In relation to historical and social phenomena, we may record among the advocates of "spiritual" evolution the names of Lessing, Herder, Kant, Fichte, and particularly Hegel, for whom evolution had an essentially logical and dialectic meaning; others, particularly Spencer,[5] supported evolutionism in the physical sense, but Spencer's terminology is ambiguous, as he himself partially recognized.[6] More recently, Bergson has tried to elaborate a new theory of evolution, conceiving the development of life as an "endless creation"; according to this theory intelligence is only an "aspect" or a "product" of the unity of the organic world in its infinite development.[7] The theory of evolution, understood in different ways, generally dominated the philosophy of the last century, and its practical importance was made manifest in its many applications in all the sciences. Yet, if the concept of evolution has helped to explain many aspects of phenomenal reality, it has also, because of the ambiguity and ineptness of its formulations, been the cause of errors. The dogmatic misapplication of these formulations has sometimes led to the discarding of Being in exclusive favor of Becoming and at other times to a sort of fatalism, causing us to pay little heed to the fundamental role of the psychological elements, especially the will, in the production of historical events. Philosophical criticism must denounce and correct these errors, while retaining the idea of evolution as a principle of research, within its own limits of reality.

II.—EVOLUTION AND THE LIFE OF LAW. POSSIBILITY OF REGRESSIVE EVOLUTION

The historical vicissitudes of law have been interpreted according to the standards of the evolutionary concept both in its biological or naturalistic and in its spiritual or dialectic sense, and sometimes with a certain fusion or confusion of these meanings.[8] The historical school of jurisprudence was at first strongly influenced by Schelling's philosophy, and then by Hegel's; later it, or its successors, adopted an avowedly positivist or out-and-out materialist standpoint, discarding its cloak of idealist formulae. In this second sense, the concept of evolution in law found vigorous expression, especially in the work of Jhering. Although referring particularly to Roman law, Jhering has stated in the first chapters of his *Geist des römischen Rechts* certain general criteria for interpreting the life of juridical institutions. The formation and modifications of these institutions were to be regarded as organic development, whence arose the possibility—indeed the necessity—of an anatomical and physiological consideration of law. Jhering remarked on the sometimes slow, sometimes rapid process of formation and transformation of juridical institutions, which do not all have the same "plasticity and mobility" (*Bildsamkeit, Beweglichkeit*).[9] He also observed how, within a single system, evolution may proceed at varying speeds in its different parts. He did not, however, expressly treat the phenomenon inverse to evolution, which is also found in history and which should be similarly referred to the analogy of observable organic life.[10]

Mancaleoni has quite justly pointed out[11] that even in biology, "the theory of evolution rests upon the consideration of two movements: the progressive, which produces the birth and the development of organized beings, and the regressive, which produces the disappearance of organs and species, leaving traces in the atrophied organs of living beings, and in the fossil testimony of paleontology." The same phenomenon occurs and must occur in the field of law: "The path of law is likewise strewn with institutions which grow up by differentiating between themselves and ascend by integrating, amplifying, reinforcing their functions, and with institutions which wither and decline or die, sometimes violently through a revolutionary crisis, more often slowly, like natural death through organic exhaustion." This provokes another pertinent remark, which is that we should not neglect "the relics and the dead remains, as if there were little to gain from the study of what is no longer of practical effect," for "in those relics and dead remains are found the reasons which explain why many things now alive will perish in their turn, fulfilling the progressive role of death, to which Auguste Comte attributes the merit of renovating the social tissues." Hence the necessity of studying regressive evolution, or involution, even in law.

III.—PERMANENCE AND MUTABILITY OF LAW. INCREASE, DISINTEGRATION AND ARRESTED DEVELOPMENT IN LEGAL SYSTEMS

The matter regulated by law is the whole of human life, since there is no activity in any system or any epoch which is not juridically qualified as licit or illicit, as deserving respect or opposition. In its concrete determinations, while the logical pattern of legality or illegality remains immutable (immutable whatever the content may be), law reflects all psychic motives and all elements of reality in their relation to human activity, since law is the resultant of all these factors. Hence the perpetual flow of law in its positive expression and hence the possibility of various degrees of spiritual development in law and juridical customs which may correspond to harmonious and elevated civilization or to blind and violent barbarism. In effect, the manners of life and hence also the modes of law are infinite . . .[12] All human aspirations, conceptions, and passions, insofar as they possess historical consistency, make themselves felt in the form of law. Since these same sentiments and the same passions continue to appear in various guises in the human psyche, it is always possible for laws to take shape in accordance with the most varied mental outlooks, including those which are thought to belong characteristically to ages now long past. Thus Bodin wrote: "Humana Historia, quod magna sui parte fluit ab hominum voluntate, quae semper sui dissimilis est, nullum exitum habet."[13] "Si quis historicorum, non poetarum excutiat intelligentiam, profecto iudicabit parem esse in rebus humanis, atque in omnium rerum natura conversionem: nec aliquid sub sole novum esse."[14] Without going so far as to assert the existence of laws of history, of cycles or predetermined periods, we must admit on the basis of experience that, like individual life, the life of peoples is subject to alternations.[15] Periods of economic prosperity are followed by periods of depression, which can be followed by phases of new prosperity. Just as an individual's virtuous actions may be succeeded by others that are blameworthy, so also in the history of peoples we observe that after phases of rigid and austere habits decadence and corruption sometimes ensue. We remember the loosening of morals, perhaps under Oriental influence, which was one of the causes, and possibly the most important, of the ruin of the ancient Roman State. Dante criticized the degeneration in Florentine customs after the time of Cacciaguida. In the history of letters and of the fine arts flourishing periods of classical perfection are followed by periods of sterility, mediocrity and bad taste. Why cannot something similar occur in law, if law is linked in its positivity with all the other aspects and phenomena of human life?

That even the most complex and powerful juridical structures are subject to decay and destruction is demonstrated by historical fact.[16] This usually happens through a slow process of erosion or involution; in such a case we have the phenomenon of organic decadence, which because of its slowness may escape superficial observation. But a sudden and violent suppression can also occur, as when a State is conquered and destroyed by another. The cases of disappearance or, better, violent transformation, in which, as the poet puts it, "kingdoms and empires collapse like old stage-sets,"[17] do not require specification. Some analysis is necessary, however, to appreciate the process of disintegration or degeneration through which a juridical institution gradually ceases to exercise its function. This phenomenon of gradual atrophy may affect a whole system, for reasons of a general character, but more often it is seen in single institutions which for various causes gradually lose their reason for existence. We then speak of involution or regression in the strict sense.

A legal system may be compared to an organism, because its parts tend to compose themselves in coherent unity, all serving to regulate the life of the system, which in every moment of its history is necessarily linked and convergent upon determined ends.[18] Hence the perpetual labor of jurisprudence to coordinate and harmonize the existent rules with those continuously arising to supplement them from the perpetual flow of social life. This organic character, in a certain measure, belongs also to the separate parts of one system. We may observe the natural growth of an institution of public or private law, just as we may observe the physiological development of the various parts of the human body. But it is possible that some parts may develop more and others less; arrested development or atrophy of single organs is possible without necessarily implying that the same happens in the remaining parts. Furthermore, it is possible (both in the biological and in the social sense) to have phenomena of hypertrophy, that is to say, excessive growth of an organ or of part of it, which may constitute a danger and an injury to the whole organism, although, regarding that organ alone, it should be described not as involution but as evolution.

To leave metaphor, the development of certain juridical institutions does not always mean real growth or progress for the whole system of which they are parts; and, conversely, the regression of some may signify the progressive development of others, and even of the whole system. Thus, the gradual transformation and final extinction of the institution of slavery meant in reality the reinforcement and extension of the right of personality according to the principle of the natural liberty and the juridical equality of men. Similarly, the decadence and the gradual suppression of feudalism meant the creation of a new and more solid political state-structure (the so-called modern State).

All law is a complex system of values which are functions of one another, sometimes positive, sometimes negative. More specifically it may be said that every legal system represents an attempt to reconcile the value of order and the value of liberty. To secure a greater measure of one of these values, the other, to the degree that it stands in opposition, must be limited. Such tempering happens in many different ways in the changing life of peoples. There can be no absolute criterion in these matters when we are seeking to understand historical reality in its effective causes and its own relativity. The decadence or involution of certain institutions corresponds to the disappearance of the real causes which brought them to life; whence the apparent return to a phase already past. We say "apparent" since a real return to what belonged to past ages, with all the age's concrete characteristics, has never taken place, nor could it. The past is in a sense irrevocable. There may be analogies or imitations of past phenomena but never true reproductions.[19] History does not repeat itself even in the field of law; and all that happens in the world really happens only once.

IV.—EXAMPLES FROM ROMAN LAW

The history of Roman law in its complex vicissitudes offers us, as Mancaleoni remarks, "cases of regression of some single characteristic of an institution; cases affording opportunity to study a category of connected parallel regression in different institutions; and cases of the regression and the complete disappearance of a whole juridical institution." At times, there may even occur "a complex progressive evolution of an institution as such, accompanied by the regression of some of its characteristics." Naturally the search for these partial involutions is more difficult, as Mancaleoni notes, just as microscopic anatomy is more difficult than macroscopic anatomy. Evaluation is hard to carry out, because the apparently regressive transformation of an institution often corresponds to progression in a broader order. Mancaleoni cites a typical example in the *lex Poetelia,* which marked the decline of the institution of *nexum,* and therewith marked the decline of all proceedings against the person of the debtor. On the other hand, this law made possible the affirmation and perfection of the principle of attaching liability to the debtor's property. There are many cases of such intertwining of regression and progression and it is prudent to refrain from hasty judgments on their merits. Thus, the regression of *manus* and tutelage of women corresponds to a new organization of the family institution in relation to the State. "The functions of the agnatic family, whose peculiar organs were *manus* and tutelage, are assumed by other institutions: the State performing the political functions, the cognatic family those of a domestic nature."[20] So, too, the decadence of the ancient *jus Quiritium* was an index of its inability to cope with new social factors which developed under the more ample and elastic forms of praetorian law. Legislative organs likewise had to transform themselves, since, as Bonfante wrote, "the work of assemblies is not suited to the mainly nonpolitical task of developing private law."[21] The Praetor "in fact usurps the legislative functions so that he becomes the classic organ of evolution of Roman jurisprudence."

It is important to study the survivals which in each phase of history represent the fragmentary record of earlier periods, namely, the "institutions smitten by regressive evolution." These surviving elements may sometimes exercise an attenuated function; even names borne by institutions often contain the memory of a dead element.[22] For the most part, the decadence of an institution can be perceived in its gradual failure to exercise its real function. One indication of this is (as Bonfante noted) the multiplication of exceptions or of particular legal institutions, which little by little exhaust the principles and institutions which were originally fundamental, until these finally become a dead letter, in total contradistinction with actuality. Not every law, even if formally in force, is a living part of a juridical organism. As Jhering said, "Laws can be enacted, even in a short time, in great numbers . . . Laws may be heaped up as clouds in a troubled sky, but if they pass as rapidly as those clouds and leave no trace, they are not true products but the dross and chips which fly off as history takes form. The productivity of legal history has for its object the evolution of the juridical organism, and this is not achieved in what that organism consumes, but in what it digests."[23] The loss of an institution's real efficacy may occur, as we have already indicated, as much by atrophy as by hypertrophy. Mancaleoni cites two examples from Roman history: "When the Senate acclaims a single orator who explains the imperial will, and it has no other form of spontaneous deliberation, its legislative power is extinct." "When Caracalla gave citizenship to all the inhabitants of the Empire, he marked the fall of the *civis* and the rise of the *subditus*." Rightly, Mancaleoni observes that an institution may lose its functions either by having them assumed by other existing or new institutions or by virtue of the institution itself assuming other functions of restricted or inferior nature; or, finally, when differing institutions are absorbed or fused, with resultant exhaustion of some or all.[24] Examples of all these types appear in the history of Roman law.

The regressive evolution of an institution is typically perceived in the form of desuetude, and also in the numerous artifices of juridical technicality (for instance, in fictions, exceptions, amendments by way of restrictive and extensive interpretation). A vast work of this kind was achieved by Roman jurisprudence, when little by little the rigid scaffolding of the ancient *ius civile* was destroyed and, freed from its archaic formulations, the law was adapted to the new conditions of life. As a conclusion of his study, Mancaleoni holds that two principles may be enunciated: first, "an institution which has reached the full extent of its progressive evolution, obedient to the necessity of transformation, must regress"; second, "on account of the irreversibility of evolution and hence also of involution, it is impossible to retrace one's steps; a vanished institution cannot reappear nor can a surviving element begin again to develop and resume its lost function."[25]

V.—THE SENSE OF HUMAN HISTORY; PROGRESS AND REGRESS

When we contemplate these facts in their perennial multiplicity—the continuous evolution and involution of juridical institutions and their parts, with their almost infinite series of intersections and complications of progress and regress, the birth and cessation not only of institutions but of entire States—we may wonder whether human history has a well defined meaning, or whether it consists, rather, of an endless labor of construction and destruction, fated to recommence in perpetuity, like that of Sisyphus.[26] To dispel this doubt it is not enough to note that many prejudices and errors handed down by the laws of an earlier age have been corrected in later history, for such aberrations belong not only to the origins but sometimes occur where previous civilizations were immune (thus, for instance, Graeco-Roman antiquity did not know the laws against witchcraft which shed so much blood in the Middle Ages). No conquest has ever been made by human thought, even in the field of law, that can be considered definite and irrevocable.

The human race constitutes an ideal, not a real, unity. Its various parts comprise distinct organisms, each of which has its own life, which is complicated and at times hindered by minor organisms which grow within it like (if the comparison is permissible) germs in the human body. The various groups have histories distinct though sometimes intercommunicating. They develop in an asynchronous manner, so that one cannot attribute to all peoples living in a given period a common type of civilization. In each people, and in each institution of its legal system, movements of development or evolution alternate with others of regression or involution. This complicates the lines of any picture which purports to represent in a unitary way the life of the human race.[27] To speak generically of progress under these circumstances, as if it expressed a constant and uniform reality, is so contrary to the data of experience as to merit the criticism of many modern writers[28] and the sad irony of Leopardi in the famous passage of *Ginestra*.[29]

Do these facts, we may ask, take all value from the idea of

progressive evolution, or is it simply a matter of determining more exactly, and more critically, the meaning of that idea? We should note, first of all, that it is necessary for us to achieve, in our minds, a certain unity with respect to the events of history (which is one of the meanings of the word "evolution"). Frequently, the sequence of successive phenomena undeniably represents an organic growth, that is, a true and proper development, through which these phenomena attain an end which comes to be recognized as virtually determined from the beginning. With respect to regressive evolution or involution the process is inverted.[30] The teleological principle can be applied in both cases to indicate the unity of a process and to render it intelligible. However, it would not be correct to deduce from the existence of two antithetical tendencies that they necessarily have equal efficacy, and thus can neutralize each other and make real progress impossible. This would betoken simple prejudice or a very superficial view of reality, as if, from observation of the tossing sea and the alternating winds one were to conclude that no vessel could ever achieve its destination. The data of experience, rightly interpreted, lead us to a very different conclusion.

Regressions in law are often such only in a relative sense; they mark the death of an institution only to make room for one which answers better to the new conditions of life. Even the collapse and disappearance of an entire State or Empire may in reality signify the recomposition of the same elements in a more advanced form; so that it is not so much a death as a rebirth.[31] In the eventide of Graeco-Roman civilization, the advanced civilization of the Northern coast of Africa disappeared but its heritage was gathered in and later gave life to a new civilization. Mazzini said: "The peoples are like workers in the immense factory of humanity, like instruments of labor who can, their work done, fall or expire, but they leave its fruits to the entire species."[32] Persecution of the followers of a faith, religious or national, even when it has apparently succeeded in its purpose, has often rather served to miraculously strengthen that faith and carry it to triumph. The history of Christianity affords a superb example; and political history (particularly that of Italy) confirms Mazzini's doctrine that nations cannot be founded without martyrs.

VI.—IMMANENT FINALITY AND AWARENESS OF ENDS

Philosophical consideration has shown that, far from there being an exact correspondence between the motives and the effects of human activity, there is a very great excess of the latter over the former. Egotistical motives not infrequently serve as an instrument for achieving higher ends. This is a manifestation of that recondite entelechy, or intrinsic finality of history, which Vico called "Providence" and others have defined as "heterogenesis of ends" or "the secret artifice of nature." Kant, moving from the consideration that man has a tendency toward sociability and also a tendency toward isolation, added that but for the antisocial tendency ("not commendable *in se,* but nevertheless producing the resistance which everyone necessarily encounters in reaching his egotistical aspirations"), spiritual gifts would never blossom.[33] Nature should, therefore, according to Kant, "be thanked for incompatibility, for the rivalry of ambitions, for the insatiable craving to possess and to dominate." The function of war, the greatest expression of antagonism among men, may even be to achieve union among peoples: "All wars are attempts (not in the intention of men but in that of nature) to create new relations between States and, through reciprocal destruction and mutilation, new political bodies, which in their turn cannot maintain themselves without passing through similar revolutions, until a state of things is achieved which, in the fashion of a civil community, can stand by itself."[34]

By these standards, many superficial evaluations of progress and regress in history should be re-examined. The decline of certain institutions and even the disappearance of entire States may assume a significance analogous in physical life, particularly in the vegetable world, to that of the alternation of the seasons, where decay is an intermediate phase before a further reflorescence. It is true that decay of social and political institutions is nearly always accompanied with suffering and with the death of individuals and of peoples. Does this signify perhaps that men, or peoples, are but blind instruments to achieve certain designs of nature? And that all the events of history are not only causally determined but equally justified, as means suitable to a pre-established end? Such fatalism or absolute finalism, which would abolish every distinction of values in the acts of men, does not correspond, we believe, to the thought of Kant and, in any case, it is unacceptable. Because human history has generally a meaning and an end, and profound tendencies, as well as superficial motives, operate in that direction, it does not follow that there are no adverse tendencies, or that they will soon be overcome. Deviations and aberrations are possible in history, as in individual life. Even in biological organisms, which by definition imply an entelechy, teratological formations (monsters and freaks) can be found, representing unsuccessful attempts of nature to achieve her ends.

With respect to human history, another observation may be made. The knowledge of their own ends which individuals and peoples acquire in the course of evolution becomes a factor in evolution itself, that is, it helps in general to guide it more directly toward those ends. Partial deviations and regressions tend to become less frequent as in our spirit there develops an awareness of the goal of the movement of history. *Ducunt volentem fata, nolentem trahunt.*[35]

Such a philosophical consideration of history neither supplants nor excludes that more strictly scientific consideration which consists in gathering as completely as possible and ascertaining as exactly as possible human facts.[36] Philosophical constructions in these matters must be largely heuristic, and always require the ultimate confirmation of events. They make possible a more profound vision of historical data—even in the connections that are most distant and inaccessible to the common view—but they do not free us from the need for minute research, just as in the physical world the use of the telescope does not exclude chemical and microscopic analysis. In no case can the reality of experience be strained to fit a preconceived design. To do so would be to fall again into the errors which discredited the old philosophy of history.

For this reason, we must avoid confusion between explanatory inquiry, intent upon comprehending the course of human vicissitudes (whether in the strictly historical sense or in the "metahistorical" or philosophical sense) and the ethical or deontological inquiry which responds to an entirely different requirement of our spirit; this we must avoid even if we can imagine a final meeting of these different considerations in an absolute unity, such as is the unity of the spirit from which they move.

VII.—THE SCALE OF VALUES AND THE SUPREME CRITERION OF JURIDICAL VALUES

We must ask if it is possible to establish a criterion for a scale of values, that is, a measurement in the light of which progress and regress can be determined. Too often such evaluations are entrusted merely to individual sentiment, so that the same fact may be described in diverse and even contradictory ways; think of the various evaluations which, according to his political predilections, each individual can make as to the relative value of liberty and order. However difficult the solution may be, the problem is essentially philosophical and consists precisely in the determination of an ideal principle, universally valid, by which to judge the degree of justice in the juridical and political formations which the flow of history presents in changing forms. . . Philosophical analysis has here a wide field for study, and we dare not assert that it has surmounted all difficulties, even those concerning law, or that it has sufficiently illuminated all aspects of the subject. Nor is it to be thought that to have established a principle, however just, is enough to make clear the manner of its application to particular matters. A civil or penal code, however perfect it may be, does not dispense with the work of judges who must interpret and apply it.

If, however, the philosophical elaboration of fundamental principles is the subject of argument in the schools, those same principles are alive and active in common consciousness. This is a comfort to those who labor in this field, as well as a guideline toward the correct solution of the problem. Thus, with regard to law, even in the common consciousness the passage from extermination of vanquished foes to their preservation, even in a state of slavery (*servus quia servatur*), thence to the mitigation and abolition of slavery itself, appears not as simple mutation but as real progress. Such examples do not prove that common consciousness suffices in itself to establish the entire scale of values and to resolve the grave questions continuously presented by the complexity of reality, but they do prove that the thought of the philosophers and jurists has a real basis in our human mind (Vico). The error most to be avoided is the confusion of the scale or order of values obtainable by deduction with the series of degrees in empirical reality; as if it were certain, *a priori,* that history develops with mechanical rigidity, ascending from low to high in each period and in each place. All dogmatism or apriorism must be excluded when the task in hand is the collection of the data of experience.

That collection is still far from complete and may never be completed, because many peoples have vanished leaving little trace, while others are not yet born. The human world is perhaps still young, and it is possibly not too audacious a paradox to say that we live in prehistoric times and that true history has not begun.[37] However that may be, we should be cautious in affirming or denying the existence of historic laws which could only be definitively ascertained on the basis of more experience than we now possess. Nevertheless, with all due caution and reservations, it seems logical to conclude that the aptitudes innate in the human mind and in nature have undergone a certain development, in their juridical manifestations, through varied and not always progressive changes.[38] In other words (to adopt a suggestive idea of Vico's which anticipated the results of modern research) just as in theoretical science the knowledge of truth has advanced, even though subject to periods of splendour and periods of obscurity, so too the principles of law, implicit in human nature as ideal vocations, are being historically realized by countless efforts, often painful and not always successful. Here too light alternates with shade, progress with pause and regress.[39]

VIII.—ETHICAL ASPECT OF THE PROBLEM. CONCLUSION

A final aspect of the problem must still be briefly alluded to. Belief in the possibility and necessity of progress (in the ethical or deontological sense) has in itself an ethical value. The unity of our spirit makes it impossible to work toward a certain end without thinking that this end can and must be achieved, even if only in the distant future and through the work of later generations. The determination of any supreme value, including that of law, implies for our conscience the duty to cooperate in its fulfillment; hence also the confidence that it is not unattainable. That does not mean that any mere wish or Utopian dream may legitimately take the place of well-founded foresight, or that the obstacles which hinder the realization of an ideal must be ignored. But, when the ideal is rightly perceived and rationally demonstrated, the vision of the distance separating us from its achievement does not free us from the obligation to advance as near to it as possible. The difficulties, however grave, which stand in the way should at the most only compel us to postpone beyond this mortal existence the hope that the goal will be finally achieved. In this sense, sadness and even pessimism so far as individual life and goals are concerned may go hand in hand with the trustful serenity of the just and wise man who "lives in eternity."

It has been said of ancient history that the prophets of ill events were often their makers.[40] Similarly, and perhaps for better reason, the assertion of a progressive advent of justice, or of a greater future perfection of legal institutions, can have a practical value and contribute to that perfection. Objective examination of the ups and downs in the history of law cannot and must not extinguish our faith in justice as a supreme human ideal. Even in face of events which represent a setback or a deviation, that ideal remains unshaken as a criterion of value; without it, deviation would be meaningless. Even if contradicted by empirical facts, this ideal does not lose its ethical and deontological truth. These contradictions between "is" and "ought to be" can be neither permanent nor general. The reality of "this civil world" arises from the human spirit, which engenders and contemplates ideality; some meeting between the *ordo idearum* and the *ordo rerum* there must be.

Examined as a whole and not in its separate moments, the development of historical events cannot but confirm, even if slowly and imperfectly, that ideal which represents the true sense, the deep reason, and the final aim of the development. In the over-all economy of nature all decadence and regression has in itself the promise of a revival or a resurrection. It is true that this revival is never a mere return to the past, which bears within itself something irrevocable, but the memories and the relics of what has already been attained are reliable signs of future possibilities. Not even the catastrophical view of a probable end of our world would allow us to exclude the possibility of new development of the universal spirit; we must remember Vico's brilliant idea that infinite worlds are perhaps born from time to time out of eternity.[41] It is not in us to conceive the total disappearance of being, the complete death of the spirit.

The mission of philosophy is to elevate us above contingent details, to look at principles and ultimate ends. The facile laughter of the vulgar, who are interested only in the tangible things of the hour (which to them is the only science), must not deter the philosopher from fulfilling his proper task. Even if ignoble passions lead men to attack and oppress one another, jeopardizing the achievements of civilized humanity and darkening the clearest truths, and even if the fundamental rights of man consecrated in solemn legislative texts are once again denied and violated by monstrous aberrations in the shape of law (*monstra legum*), we must still philosophically affirm as always and absolutely valid the ideal of freedom, order and peace (in a word, of justice), both within the State and between States. The more gravely that ideal is violated, the loftier (we must believe) will be its reassertion.

Lux in tenebris lucet. Even in the deepest gloom there is a spark which is not extinguished, and the darkest night is followed by the brightest dawn.

Regress, or involution, will never be the last word spoken, as long as there exists a human spirit which in its nature is capable of the infinite.

(1938)

NOTES

1. See, in general, DE GREEF, *Le transformisme social* (Paris, 1895), P. II; DEMOOR, MASSART, VANDERVELDE, *L'évolution régressive en Biologie et en Sociologie* (Paris, 1897); LALANDE, *La dissolution* (Paris, 1899); RICHARD, *L'idée d'évo-*

lution dans la nature et l'histoire (Paris, 1903), p. 284 *et seq.* Regarding law, see R. von MAYR, *Entwicklungen und Rückschläge in der Rechtsgeschichte* (Prague, 1909), p. 54: "Die Rechtsgeschichte muss das Recht als einen lebendigen Organismus betrachten . . . der in seinen Erscheinungen die Gesetze der Abstammung, der Entwicklung und des Rückschläges aufweisen muss."

2. LEIBNIZ, *Principia Philosophiae*, § 76: "Sunt enim evolutiones, et accretiones, quas generationes appellamus; quemadmodum involutiones, et diminutiones, quod mortem vocamus." On the use of the terms "evolution," "Entwicklung," etc., cf. EUCKEN, *Geschichte der philosophischen Terminologie* (Leipzig, 1879), pp. 82, 187, and EISLER, *Wörterbuch der philosophischen Begriffe* (4 Aufl., Berlin, 1927-1930).

3. RICKERT, *Die Grenzen der naturwissenschaftlichen Begriffsbildung* (Tübingen, 1902), p. 472 *et seq.*

4. SCHELLING, *Erster Entwurf eines Systems der Naturphilosophie* (1799; in Sämmtl. Werke, I Abth., Bd. III, Stuttgart, 1858), p. 33. Cf. *id.*, *Von der Weltseele* (1798; *ibid.*, Bd. II), p. 348. *Id.*, *Einleitung zu dem Entwurf eines Systems der Naturphilosophie* (1799; *ibid.*, I Abth., Bd. III), p. 287.

5. SPENCER's teaching on evolution is connected with that of DARWIN; but Spencer's first statement thereof (*The Development Hypothesis*, 1852; repr. in *Essays*, vol. I) preceded the publication of D.'s *Origin of Species* (1859). S. extended the hypothesis of evolution from the field of biology to philosophy and knowledge in general, giving much space to psychology, sociology and ethics. Alongside of evolution, he admitted also as universally valid the opposite principle of "dissolution" (*op. cit.*, P. II, ch. XII).

6. On the uses of the word "evolution" in Spencer, cf. LALANDE, *Vocabulaire technique et critique de la Philosophie* (Paris, 1926), s.v. "Evolution," where five meanings are distinguished. Cf. *id.*, *Evolution, révolution, involution* (in "Atti del Cong. int. di Filosofia, Roma, 1946," vol. II, Milano, 1948, p. 499 *et seq.*) On cosmic and biological evolution in general, and social evolution in particular, see ANGIULLI, *La Filosofia e la scuola* (Napoli, 1888), pp. 251 *et seq.*, 311 *et seq.*, where Spencer's theories are particularly discussed. Cf. CANESTRINI, *La teoria dell' evoluzione* (2 ed., Torino, 1887)); A. CONTI, *La dottrina dell' evoluzione e le scienze* (Sassari, 1885); G. CALDERONI, *L'evoluzione e i suoi limiti* (Roma, 1906); DELAGE et GOLDSMITH, *Les théories de l'évolution* (2 éd., Paris, 1920); NIGRIS, *L'evoluzione* (Roma, 1935). See also, on the philosophical aspects of

Darwin and Spencer, HÖFFDING, *History of Modern Philosophy* (Eng. trans., London, 1900), vol. II, pp. 434-485.

7. BERGSON, *L'évolution créatrice* (Paris, 1907; 36 éd., 1930), esp. p. 114. We need not here examine whether B.'s system, defined by himself as a new spiritualism, is not rather a refined materialism. On the relation of B.'s theory of evolution to those of Schelling and Spencer, see LOSACCO, *Schelling* (Milano, 1914), p. 119 *et seq.*; HÖFFDING, *La philosophie de Bergson* (Paris, 1916), p. 89 *et seq.*; SERINI's Introduction to the Italian ed. of B. (*L'evoluzione creatrice*, Milano, 1935), p. 42 *et seq.*

8. BLUNTSCHLI, *Die Entwickelung des Rechtes und das Recht der Entwickelung* (in *Gesamm. kl. Schriften*, I Bd., Nördlingen, 1879, pp. 44-55); MERKEL, *Ueber den Begriff der Entwicklung* (in *Fragmente zur Sozialwissenschaft*, Strassburg, 1898, pp. 36-44); *id., Ueber den Begriff der Entwicklung in seiner Anwendung auf Recht u. Gesellschaft* (*ibid.*, pp. 45-68); ZANI, *Il diritto secondo la legge di evoluzione* (Mantova, 1881); FISICHELLA, *Evoluzione e diritto* (Catania, 1884); COGLIOLO, *Saggi sopra l'evoluzione del diritto privato* (Torino, 1885), p. 25 *et seq.*; KOHLER, *Die Entwicklung im Recht* (in "Zschr. f. d. Privat-u. öff. Recht der Gegenwart," Bd. XIV, 1887, pp. 410-418); POST, *Studien zur Entwicklungsgeschichte des Familienrechts* (Oldenburg, 1889), and other works; D'AGUANNO, *La genesi e l'evoluzione del diritto civile* (Torino, 1890), esp. p. 118 *et seq.*; LETOURNEAU, *L'évolution juridique dans les diverses races humaines* (Paris, 1891); G. CIMBALI, *Diritto ed evoluzione* (1891; in *Saggi di Filosofia sociale e giuridica*, Roma, 1903, pp. 43-81); HILDEBRAND, *Ueber das Problem einer allgemeinen Entwicklungsgeschichte des Rechts u. der Sitte* (Graz, 1894); NEUKAMP, *Einleitung in eine Entwicklungsgeschichte des Rechts* (Berlin, 1895); F. LUZZATTO, *Osservazioni sopra la dottrina dell'evoluzione in relazione alle scienze sociali e giuridiche* (in *Saggi di Enciclopedia giurid. e Filosofia del diritto*, Roma, 1896, pp. 133-174); PICARD, *Le droit pur* (2 éd., Paris, 1908), p. 227 *et seq.*; DE LA GRASSERIE, *Les principes sociologiques du droit civil* (Paris, 1906), p. 285 *et seq.*; TANON, *L'évolution du droit et la conscience sociale* (3 éd., Paris, 1911), p. 105 *et seq.*; von MAYR, *Entwicklungen u. Rückschläge in der Rechtsgeschichte*, *cit.*; WIGMORE, *Planetary Theory of the Law's Evolution* (in "Evolution of Law Series," vol. III, Boston, 1918, pp. 531-541); *id., Problems of the Law's Evolution* (in *Problems of Law*, New York, 1920, pp. 1-61); ORESTANO, *Filosofia del diritto* (Milano, 1941), p. 313 *et seq.* See also, on the evolution of law and

of particular legal institutions, the writings of various authors collected by KOCOUREK and WIGMORE in "Evolution of Law Series," vols. II and III (Boston, 1915-1918).

9. JHERING, *Geist des römischen Rechts auf den verschiedenen Stufen seiner Entwicklung,* I T. (5 Aufl., Leipzig, 1891), p. 66.

10. On this analogy, see esp. the work of DEMOOR, MASSART, VANDERVELDE, *cit. supra*, n. 1. Like Jhering, ARDIGÒ, who has systematically developed the concept of evolution or "natural formation" in application to social and juridical life, does not seem to have given due place to the opposite phenomenon of involution. Cf. ARDIGÒ, *Sociologia*, C. II, § IV; in *Op. filos.*, vol. IV, 3 ed., Padova, 1908, pp. 96-97, and *ibid.* § III, p. 96.

11. MANCALEONI, *L'evoluzione regressiva negli istituti giuridici* (in "Studi Sassaresi," Serie II, vol. I, 1921).

12. "Humani juris condicio semper in infinitum decurrit, et nihil est in ea, quod stare perpetuo possit" (*Cod.* 1.17.2.18). Cf. AULUS GELL., *Noctes Atticae*, XX, 1. On the mutability and relativity of law, see DEL VECCHIO, *The Formal Bases of Law*, pp. 8 *et seq.*, 25 *et seq.*, and the writings there cited. Cf. also CARDOZO, *The Nature of the Judicial Process* (New Haven, 1928), pp. 26-28.

13. BODIN, *Methodus ad facilem historiarum cognitionem* (Parisiis, 1572), p. 14. On Bodin see DELVAILLE, *Essai sur l'histoire de l'idée de progrès jusqu'à la fin du XVIIIe siècle* (Paris, 1910), p. 132 *et seq.*

14. BODIN, *op. cit.*, pp. 470-471 and 480. Cf. SENECA, *Epist.*, CVII, 8: "contrariis rerum aeternitas constat." The seeds of this doctrine may be found in *Ecclesiastes* 1, 10-11 and 3, 1-15.

15. "All the works of man must bear the imprint of man's weakness and must be forever subject to continual change." A. DE GIULIANI, *Saggio politico sopra le vicissitudini inevitabili delle società civili* (1791; ed. B. Croce, Bari, 1934, p. 41).

16. Among the writers who have mentioned (in most cases, only incidentally) this phenomenon, is TAPARELLI: "Society can present itself in three states: progress, or immobility, or decadence" (*Saggio teoretico di Dritto naturale appoggiato sul fatto*, 4 ed., Roma 1928, vol. II, § 1585; cf. §§ 1587, 1592, 1624, 1634). PROUDHON (*De la justice dans la Révolution et dans l'Eglise*, nouv. éd., Bruxelles, 1898, T. III, p. 272 *et seq.*) particularly notes "la régression de la Justice, c'est à dire, dépravation de la société, et par suite décadence."

17. CARDUCCI, *A Vittore Hugo*. On the perishable nature of States, and of all human things, we may recall DANTE, *Parad.*, XVI, 76-79, and TASSO, *Gerus. Lib.*, XV, 20.

18. This is not to say that a legal system is a unity in the biological sense. On the contrary, it depends on factors which are essentially spiritual ("because men made it with intelligence"—VICO) and by these factors it is modified and developed. The "organism" is a *logical* organism.

19. Cf. DEMOOR, MASSART, VANDERVELDE, *op. cit.*, *supra*, n. 1. at p. 218 *et seq.*, p. 314: "Il est toujours possible d'appliquer à des formes sociales nouvelles l'étiquette d'une institution définitivement abolie, mais, ce qui est impossible, c'est de faire revivre l'institution même, dans un milieu radicalement transformé." TARDE (*L'opposition universelle*, Paris, 1897, p. 301 *et seq.*; cf. *Les lois de l'imitation*, 2 éd., Paris, 1895, p. 410 *et seq.*) particularly stresses the "irreversibility" of social facts. Regression is not a return to what existed before. "Le dépérissement et la mort des langues, des religions, des constitutions, des arts, ne sont pas l'inverse de leur naissance et de leur croissance" (*L'oppos. univ.*, p. 449). Cf. DE GREEF, *Le transformisme social*, *cit.* n. 1, p. 473 *et seq.*; WORMS, *La sociologie* (Paris, 1921), p. 87 *et seq.*, who, however, makes some reservations. With special regard to law, R. von MAYR (*Entwicklungen u. Rückschläge*, *cit.*, pp. 28-29, 33, 44) holds that institutions of a past age can return to life, but for purposes other than their original purpose, and thus with certain intrinsic differences; there is, in such a return, an "aüsserer Parallelismus" and an "innere Divergenz" (*ibid.*, p. 48).

20. MANCALEONI, *op. cit.*, pp. 8, 9, 10-11, 22.

21. BONFANTE, *Storia del diritto romano* (3 ed., Milano, 1923), vol. I, pp. 258, 259; cf. p. 265.

22. MANCALEONI, *op. cit.*, pp. 14, 15.

23. JHERING, *Geist des röm. Rechts*, I T., p. 69.

24. MANCALEONI, *op. cit.*, pp. 19, 20, 21.

25. *Ibid.* p. 29; see also p. 12. This agrees with the observations of TARDE and others, *cit. supra*, n. 19. Cf. also DE FRANCISCI, *Storia del diritto romano*, vol. I (2 ed., Milano, 1939), p. 74.

26. "La justice, et, plus généralement, la morale doit être conçue comme un devenir. Rien n'autorise, *a priori*, à affirmer que ce devenir soit un progrès, et un progrès ininterrompu." LÉVY-BRUHL, *La morale et la science des moeurs* (3 éd., Paris, 1907), p. 219.

27. On decadence and regression in human societies, see (in addition to works already mentioned): NOVICOW, *Les gaspillages des sociétés modernes* (Paris, 1894), p. 331 *et seq.*; FREE-

MAN, *Social Decay and Degeneration* (London, 1921); COOLEY, *Social Process* (New York, 1925), p. 153 *et seq.*; HUIZINGA, *La crisi della civiltà* (Ital. ed., Torino, 1937); BRUCCULERI, *L'involuzione della civiltà* (2 ed., Roma, 1939). On the contrasting doctrines of "perennial deterioration" and "perennial improvement" in human history, we may still refer to C. BALBO, *Meditazioni storiche* (3 ed., Firenze, 1855) IV, p. 58 *et seq.* According to CROCE, "decadence is an eternal moment of progress itself" (*Il concetto di decadenza*, in *Orientamenti*, 2 ed., Milano, 1934, p. 83).

28. WORMS, *Philosophie des sciences sociales* (Paris, 1903), T. I, p. 151 *et seq.*; CHIAPPELLI, *Nuove teorie sul progresso civile* (in *La crisi del pensiero moderno*, Città di Castello, 1920), p. 206 *et seq.*; DUPRÉEL, *Deux essais sur le progrès* (Bruxelles, 1928), p. 111 *et seq.* Cf. BAGEHOT, *Physics and Politics* (2 ed., London, 1873), p. 41 *et seq.*; M. NORDAU, *Der Sinn der Geschichte* (Berlin, 1909), p. 357 *et seq.*; G. SOREL. *Les illusions du progrès* (4 éd., Paris, 1927), ch. V. Cf. C. GRAY, *Realtà e trascendenza nel progresso del diritto* (Milano, 1943), C. V-VII.

29. "Or tutto intorno
Una ruina involve . . .
Dipinta in queste rive
Son dell'umana gente
Le magnifiche sorti e progressive."

30. Thus, e.g., DE GREEF considers the "lois sociologiques, *progressives* et *régressives*" (*Les lois sociologiques*, 3 éd., Paris, 1902, p. 165 *et seq.*); cf. his *Le transformisme social*, *cit.*, p. 435 *et seq.*

31. And philosophy, art and religion may advance in periods of political regression. Cf. OZANAM, *Du progrès dans les siècles de décadence* (Paris, 1852).

32. MAZZINI, *Storia della rivoluzione francese di T. Carlyle* (in *Scritti ed. e ined.*, vol. IV, Roma, 1881), p. 278.

33. KANT, *Idee zu einer allgemeinen Geschichte in weltbürgerlichen Absicht* (1784), *Vierter Satz.*

34. KANT, *op. cit.*, *Siebenter Satz.* Cf. *Der Streit der Fakultäten* (1798), II Abschn., § 7.

35. SENECA, *Epist.*, CVII, 11.

36. Cf. KANT, *Idee zu einer allg. Gesch.*, *cit. supra, Neunter Satz, in fin.*

37. Cf. PETRONE, *La storia interna ed il problema presente della Filosofia del diritto* (Modena, 1898), p. 59 *et seq.* We cannot tell how those "who will consider the present time as ancient"

(DANTE, *Parad.*, XVII, 120) will judge us, or how still more remote ages will judge them.

38. DEL VECCHIO, *The Formal Bases of Law*, Part III, ch. VIII, esp. p. 326. *Philosophy of Law* (Washington, 1953), p. 406 *et seq.*

39. The fact of pauses or "historical intermissions" is not contrary to the notion of evolution, if understood in its generality and not measured by the individual life. Cf. G. TREZZA, *Il Darwinismo e le formazioni storiche* (in the vol. ed. by E. MORSELLI, *C. Darwin e il Darwinismo nelle scienze biologiche e sociali*, Milano, 1892, p. 109 *et seq.*).

40. E.g. by KANT, *Der Streit der Fakultäten*, II Abschn., § 2 (ed. Cassirer, *Werke*, Bd. VII, p. 392).

41. VICO, *Principj di scienza nuova*, L.I., *Del metodo* (ed. Nicolini, P.I, p. 187).

THE *HOMO JURIDICUS* AND THE INADEQUACY OF LAW AS A NORM OF LIFE

I.—THE FIGURE OF *HOMO JURIDICUS* AND ITS POSSIBLE MEANINGS

THE ECONOMISTS HAVE CREATED A HYPOTHETICAL FIGURE OF *homo economicus*, to express graphically the fundamental theorems of their science, that is, they have postulated a man governed in all his actions exclusively by the motive of economic interest. Although they admit the obvious, that in real life the economic motive is complicated by other motives, yet, they say, such a conceptual abstraction makes it possible to determine what in any given circumstances would be the behavior of an individual animated by this motive alone. By a similar hypothesis one might create other abstract figures each determined by a single motive, for instance, *homo religiosus*, *homo moralis*, and so on. So long as we avoid the error of confusing these hypothetical figures with reality and the error of giving them all an equal normative value, such abstractions may be of some scientific use. We may, then, ask ourselves: can we construct the image of *homo juridicus* and if so, what will be his outlines and his meaning?

A little reflection shows several possible meanings of the term. It might mean the man who *ex hypothesi* always keeps within the limits of the law and thus violates no legal rule, or the man who exercises to the utmost all the rights to which he is entitled, giving up none of the legal powers attributed to him by the rules which apply to him, or it might mean the man who dedicates himself to the defense of the law, that is to say, to preventing or opposing violations of legal rules. In all these cases, law is assumed to be the fundamental motive of human action, but the variety of possible application of the concept shows what we propose now to explain, namely, that law, in itself, is not sufficient to regulate life. A study of *homo juridicus* will also give us the opportunity of determining the essential characteristics of law in comparison with other rules of social life and with the laws of reality.

Some fifty years ago two great German jurists, Jhering and Kohler, held a dispute over Shakespeare's character, Shylock. Jhering, in accordance with his theory that we must always fight for our rights, because by so doing we help to safeguard the legal order in general, saw even in the odious character of Shylock a sort of champion of Venetian law, in the sense that when Shylock demanded that the law uphold him, his right became identified with that of the Venetian republic. The artifice of the judge who, while admitting Shylock's legal right to cut away a pound of living flesh, prevented him from availing himself of that right, was considered by Jhering to be contemptible.[1] Kohler, on the contrary, praised the wisdom of the judge who consciously violated the letter of the law to make way for a new and more humane rule and to prevent a substantial injustice.[2] Both authors agreed (as is evident to any modern jurist) that Shylock's demand should have been rejected by the judge, because the terms of the agreement were contrary to the principles of the legal order and to good morals, and the agreement was therefore void. But if according to the law of Venice at the time the agreement was valid (as the judge in Shakespeare's play held it to be), could the judge by an obviously sophistical subterfuge frustrate the law and so deprive Shylock of his right? That is the point on which Jhering and Kohler differed. However, setting aside this question of the powers of the judge in the application and interpretation of the law, we note that Shylock is a typical *homo juridicus* in one of the senses we have indicated; he is the man who insists on his own rights to the utmost, refusing to be restrained by any moral or other rule differing from the legal rule.

Yet it is clear that, even admitting the validity of the agreement and hence of Shylock's right, he could, without violating any legal rule, have renounced the exercise of this right. His right was a faculty—not a duty. The problem of how to behave towards his debtor was not one to be solved with respect only to his legal right, since it is juridically indifferent whether a creditor enforces his claim in court, or compromises it, or even lets it fall by renunciation or by prescription.

II.—THE JURIDICAL IMPERATIVE; ITS HYPOTHETICAL AND CATEGORICAL CHARACTER

It is true that every rule of law has imperative character, even if this does not appear from the grammatical form or the superficial meaning of the rule itself. So-called permissive rules, when they do not imply a permission to claim something from another person (who is thus potentially bound, that is, subjected to a conditional imperative), form exceptions to or limitations upon other more general rules and thus contribute towards determining their meaning; an absolutely permissive rule, standing by itself, would have no meaning in law. Further, a legal imperative, in comparison with a moral imperative, is peculiar in that it creates an obligation between one subject and another to whom is attributed the power to claim fulfillment of the obligation. This is the characteristic which St. Thomas Aquinas called *alteritas* and which is indicated in modern language by the term "bilateral" in contrast to the unilateral character of morals.

While these points are well settled, we must pause for a moment over another aspect of the logical nature of law, namely, the hypothetical or conditional character of the juridical imperative. Some jurists, for instance, the late Giovanni Brunetti, have tried to show that alongside the imperative legal rules there exist so-called final, or defining, rules establishing the correct procedure towards a given end, and that these rules are merely facultative and not obligatory.[3] Brunetti quoted two articles from the Italian Civil Code: Art. 371, which reads, "Within five days of the birth, notice of the birth shall be given to the registrar of civil status"; and Art. 401, which reads, "Requests for the rectification of the registers of civil status shall be laid before the court . . ." "Obviously," Brunetti commented, "in the first case there is a real obligation and in the second there is no obligation, because there is no duty to request rectification of the registers."

Our teachers commonly make a similar distinction, between dispositive rules, which are said to be binding only subject to the will of the parties, that is, provided there is no agreement to the contrary, and taxative rules, which are said to be binding absolutely. Here again, as in Brunetti's examples, there is an attempt to explain a difference which certainly does exist between types of rules but, in our opinion, it has another foundation and must be explained in another way.

Every juridical rule is in a sense hypothetical or conditional, in that it is applicable only in certain circumstances of fact as defined by the rule itself. The rule being in its nature general, it must begin by determining in what sort or series of cases it can and should be applied. Many legal rules, especially those which are of negative tenor and are accompanied by penal sanctions, presuppose nothing more than the existence of a physical subject, irrespective of particular conditions. The duty not to kill or steal applies to everyone. More numerous, however, are the rules which presuppose not only physical existence but also certain other conditions of fact. These conditions are sometimes of a physical nature and independent of human will (for instance, the attaining of a certain age may give rise to the obligation of presenting oneself for military service), and sometimes they consist in manifestations of the will of the subject addressed or of another person. Relationships founded thus conditionally on a manifestation of will, especially of the will of the subject himself, form a great part of the web of actual juridical life, but we must guard against the error of attributing to the legal consequences of an optional manifestation of will a character equally optional. The structure of the rule is imperative and obligatory even when it has among its presuppositions of fact a manifestation of will which is not made obligatory by some previous rule.

This concept corresponds to that which Grotius expressed in the words: "Quod initio est voluntatis, posterea fit necessitatis." Every one is free, for instance, not to marry, but, if one marries, the resultant legal obligations are not optional in character. Liberty to make contracts and testaments (within the limits set by law) does not prevent such juristic acts from having their own *virtus obligandi*, that is, from creating obligations of imperative character. We need not here enter into the classic debate whether this imperative character depends only upon the authority which makes the rule or upon the will of the subject; it reduces itself to the problem of the State-character of the law, and the true solution of this problem (as we have tried to show elsewhere) critically reconciles the reasons behind both points of view.

As to the hypothetical or conditional character of the legal rule, it should be observed that this character does not exclude imperativeness, as Zitelmann thought when he set up against the imperative theory a counter theory according to which law consists only of hypothetical judgments. Later, Zitelmann himself recognized that, in spite of this, every juridical proposition contains an imperative element, since the connection between the factual premise and the legal consequence is the object of an act of will through which the connection is imposed.[4] Some, however, perhaps through confusion with the familiar Kantian distinction, which has quite another meaning, have been led to think that the concept of the hypothetical imperative deprives law of all categorical validity inasmuch as the legal imperative is (so they say) subordinated to premises of contingent character and, in particular, to the will of the subjects to whom it refers. Some have even carried this view to the extreme conclusion that the debtor is legally free not to pay his debt if he prefers to submit to forced execution, or even that anyone may commit a crime if he is willing to suffer the penalty. This would place an infinite gulf between law and ethics; there would be no difference between these cases and cases where the law expressly refers to the free will of the parties, as in matters of contract.

We must reject this conception and affirm (even if we thereby force words a little) that law has both a hypothetical and a categorical character. First of all, many legal imperatives have the physical existence of the subject as their sole conditional premise. This is practically equivalent to an unconditional assertion of the imperative, since the imperative can obviously refer only to existent and not to nonexistent subjects. The general duty which is summarized in the words *neminem laedere* is categorical in that it does not depend on the will of the subject but is imposed on him in such a way that he cannot evade it. Here there is no difference between the moral and the juridical imperatives, for all that the one has for its particular characteristic the establishing of a relationship among several persons; the categorical character is exactly the same. In relations between persons, the law by means of its imperatives establishes a series of limits, that is, a sphere within which the subject has the faculty of acting. Then, within the ambit of this sphere, a further distinction is made by which some, though not all, optional acts create new obligations for the subject himself and for other persons when they are performed. But this does not mean that these obligations, although in a sense conditioned, do not have a categorical validity. In the sense that they are binding not only if the subject wills them but even if he afterwards changes his will, they do possess categorical validity.

III.—ETHICAL RULES (MORAL AND JURIDICAL) AND TECHNICAL RULES (NOT BINDING IN THEMSELVES)

This is the fundamental difference between moral and juridical rules on the one hand and, on the other hand, those rules which are commonly called technical and which really establish merely hypothetical imperatives without any categorical character. These rules simply signify that if we wish to attain a certain end it is necessary to act in a certain way, and they leave open the question whether we have a duty, or a liberty, to act in that way or to have that end in view. The field of these rules is as vast as the field of human knowledge. Every scientific fact can be converted into a technical rule. Once it is ascertained that a certain effect naturally follows on a certain cause (this is the procedure typical of science), we can immediately deduce the rule that in order to attain that effect it is necessary to put that cause into action. But we still remain outside the ambit of both law and morals, for it must yet be determined whether the intention of bringing about that effect as the end of our action is or is not in conformity with ethical norms.

When Kant, in his *Grundlegung zur Metaphysik der Sitten*, distinguishes the hypothetical from the categorical imperative, he does not mean to attribute to the former the meaning of an obligation subject to a condition, that is, a duty valid under certain factual circumstances. He wishes merely to indicate a relationship between means and end, irrespective of the ethical value which the intention of achieving this end (and hence the corresponding activity) may have.[5] This corresponds precisely to the concept of a technical rule as elaborated in subsequent investigations, such as the lucid exposition of Korkounov.[6] The hypothetical imperative in the Kantian sense, that is, the technical rule, entirely excludes the question of the goodness or the lawfulness of an action. When in its application something is described as "good," this does not mean good in the moral sense but simply "suitable" or "efficacious" in relation to a supposed purpose. We speak of a good gun, meaning that it answers the marksman's purpose, even if that purpose is illegal or immoral. Kant himself removes all doubt on this point when he calls hypothetical imperatives "*Imperative der Geschicklichkeit*" (imperatives of fitness) and adds, "Whether the purpose be reasonable and good is not in question here but only what is necessary to achieve it. The prescriptions employed by a doctor to restore a man to health and those employed by a poisoner to kill him have equal value in the sense that in both cases they serve to carry out their intention."[7] One could not ask for greater precision, and it is a deplorable error of jurists to confuse the Kantian doctrine of the hypothetical imperative with the doctrine of the conditional (and in a quite different sense hypothetical) character which is proper to legal rules.

It is true that technical rules are often juxtaposed to moral and legal rules in such a way as to create apparent confusion. When the end conditionally assumed by a technical rule happens to be one which is prescribed as obligatory by an ethical rule (moral or juridical), the technical rule itself appears to acquire a certain ethical character. The rules of hygiene are typical. So far as they simply state the effects of certain circumstances or certain actions on physical health, they are of a technical nature, but they acquire ethical significance as well insofar as the preservation of health is conceived as a duty.

This duty, however, cannot be inferred from the simple causal nexus, which is all that is supplied by the technical rule; its foundation must reside in a consideration of the order of values. Under certain conditions—for instance, in the case of danger to one's country—both morals and law may command disregard for the laws of hygiene so that, even at the risk of damage to health, a higher end may be attained. The coincidence between the dictates of ethics proper and those of hygiene is accidental and must not mislead us as to their different logical nature.

In social relationships the observance of the technical rules of the various arts and professions is often assumed as the content of moral and juridical rules. Morality commands us, in general, to devote study and sincere effort to all we undertake; it condemns laziness, inconstancy and negligence, and it also imposes on us an over-all respect for the sentiments and tastes of our neighbors. Thus, if we grant that the techniques of language, of poetry, of the arts, and so on, have definite rules which correspond to the nature of the procedure of these subjects, the infringement of these rules through ignorance or carelessness will seem to be reprehensible as being contrary to morals. A man who in speaking or writing makes mistakes in grammar, or who disregards the rules of meter in poetry, or who performs badly any work which he undertakes, incurs a certain blame not only from the technical point of view but also from the moral. Yet here, too, these modes of appreciation are not to be confused. Their difference is shown by the fact that the mere transgression of technical rules is never in itself sufficient to justify moral condemnation. For moral judgment we must weigh all the elements that constitute the personality of the subject, his possibilities and his intentions in the concrete circumstances in which he is placed; no one would think of blaming a child who makes pictures not in conformity with the rules of drawing, or an inexpert swimmer who jumps into the water to save others in danger of drowning, or, in general, anyone who breaks technical rules when to do so is the only way to give effect to a laudable intention.

In legal matters, especially in contractual relations, the observance of technical rules is usually presupposed. One who entrusts to a sculptor the making of a statue, or to a lawyer the conduct of a case, or to an engineer the construction of a bridge, assumes that the person to whom he entrusts the work and who undertakes to execute it binds himself to respect the rules of the art or profession in question. This therefore becomes an integral element of the contract, and, if the technical rules are violated through the fault of the professional, he will justly be held responsible by the other party to the contract. Here there is a real rapprochement between legal and technical rules, yet the two kinds of rules are still intrinsically distinct. Technical rules are not in themselves obligatory in the proper sense; the sculptor who makes an ill-shaped statue for his own pleasure, the engineer who constructs strictly for his own use an insecure bridge over a stream on his own property, the accountant who neglects his own books, commit no infraction of the law. Obligatory character is, however, given to technical rules as soon as the activity to which they correspond is made the content of a contractual relationship, so that the other party may demand their observance.[8]

IV.—SO-CALLED CUSTOMARY RULES

Human life presents countless forms of obligation: sometimes typically moral, sometimes typically juridical, and sometimes mixed, representing an intermediate or transitional form. This is a difficulty which has to be faced by anyone who wishes to classify the various species of norms, and it has led to a variety of conflicting doctrines which are often far from adequate for the multiple and mutable social reality. Nevertheless, the task of assembling and logically defining the typical forms of ethical norms must not be abandoned. They do not always present themselves clearly in the empirical world; and they admit of a series of accentuations and attenuations, but this is not peculiar to this particular field of study. In natural science the vegetable and animal kingdoms are not separated by a clear line and among the various species there are often intermediate grades. It is characteristic of empirical reality to particularize the universality of concepts into a myriad of always new and always different cases, which commonly contain an element never completely reducible to pure conceptual schematism. But since we cannot reason, or even think, outside of concepts, we must make the continual effort to understand reality in universal logical forms.

Here we are not concerned with explaining the genesis of phenomena according to the laws of physical reality, among which the law of causality holds a sovereign and unassailable position, but to penetrate into that other world which is made up of deontological or ethical values. Any principle of this nature can be conceived and placed in one of two universal and logically distinguishable forms, according to whether it applies to the consciousness of one subject or to relations between several subjects. Hence the distinction between morality and law; hence the proper characteristics of these two essential forms of ethical valuation with respect to which we may say that in the realm of abstract logic *tertium non datur*. But empirical reality, which reveals these forms concretely manifested with varying historical content, also discloses phenomena which generically reflect the ethical (or deontological) valuation without being clear as to whether this valuation is of moral or juridical form. In human societies there is often a diffused sense of obligation, which emanates not only from the subjective consciousness but also, in a vague way, from centers of social organization, and it is from such centers that there arises an uncertain and imperfect power of claiming on the part of others. This is typically found in primitive ages, when only so-called indeterminate custom (combining both morality and law but not differentiating between them) prevails, but even when in the course of time the differentiation is made there remains in the social milieu a sort of gray zone, a series of duties which are partly of moral and partly of juridical character.

This is the world of custom, in which the so-called sanction of public opinion holds sway. In this zone are legal rules which have either lost or are losing their juridical quality and are assuming a merely moral character (remaining, that is, unilaterally entrusted to the individual), and also moral rules which are tending to acquire juridical character and to become enforceable in bilateral form. In this intermediate zone there are many and sometimes conflicting currents. The complication is increased by the fact that such rules and valuations do not always express a state of mind common to the whole society but may emanate from only one part of it (for instance, from one of the so-called social classes, or from a particular organization, even one not formally constituted); and sometimes they purport to apply throughout the whole society, sometimes only to a particular section. The sentiment of honor assumes different forms for the "common people" and for the "upper classes." The rules of custom may be in harmony or in conflict with those of the legislature and even with those of morality in the strict sense. If, while remaining contrary to legislative enactments, they acquire enough vigor and a sufficiently juridical aspect, we are then confronted with one of those contradictions between different juridical orders which constitute what is called "the crisis of the State." If, on the other hand, they are essentially individual sentiments and appreciations, they represent a particular morality, which may very well be in disagreement with the prevailing moral ideas, since the moral system, like the juridical, is historically subject to contradictions and crises. Nor (as we have already observed) can we exclude the possibility of an intermediate condition which oscillates between these extremes, a kind of state of suspension which can be protracted for a long time, inasmuch as historical processes in this field are very slow.

Should we then admit a third form of ethical valuation in addition to morals and law? No, because obligatory character cannot logically be other than subjective or intersubjective. We may recognize in the empirical world an oscillation or fluctuation between these terms, but it would be incorrect to abandon them as insufficient. It is precisely because we take them as our fixed points that we are able to recognize the flow of intermediate manifestations.

In its most general sense, custom is not a species of rule but denotes the fact of observance of any kind of rule. Positive legal rules are "encustomed" (as Vico said), that is, they are translated into customs. So, too, are the precepts of morality insofar as they are actually received and observed. Those who treat custom as a norm *sui generis* are mistaken; they are misled by the fact that in real life we find norms in operation which are not well distinguished and oscillate between the moral and the juridical. By taking custom as a reflex of deontological valuations which are still indistinct, it is possible to admit its existence as something particular without destroying the fundamental bipartite division of ethics. We must of course bear in mind that not only mixed or indistinct norms but also those which are definitely moral or juridical can equally have their reflex and their actual existence in custom.

V.—THE PROBLEM OF RELIGIOUS RULES

According to a widespread theory, proposed *inter alios* by Vanni and Gény, side by side with moral, juridical and customary norms there exists a separate category of religious norms, founded on the relationship between man and the divine, from which are derived certain precepts for the duties of man toward God, toward himself and toward other men.[9]

Religious rules, however, insofar as they direct human actions, necessarily take the form either of morality or of law, according to whether they create duties in the subject toward himself or duties in the subject toward other subjects to whom is attributed a corresponding power of claiming. We have, therefore, not another species of norm but a foundation *sui generis*, metaphysical and transcendental, for a system of rules for conduct which is erected out of morality and law in certain of their relations to one another. Believers attribute to their own moral and juridical duties a new and higher sanction so far as the realm of the other world is concerned. This "other world" is represented on earth by the priests of their Church, but not even ecclesiastical authority can regulate the behavior of anyone except by adopting the form of subjective dutifulness or of intersubjective dutifulness. And this, in turn, means adopting the form of morality or of law.

If an ethical system founded on a religious basis constitutes a complete organization in itself and, upheld by the preponderant social will, inspires and effectively regulates the life of a people, it identifies itself, on its juridical side, with the State-order. That is to say, it itself constitutes the State, which is in such a case called a theocratic State. This has occurred in various historical epochs. If, on the other hand, a religion, even though translating itself into a system of norms and acquiring a certain degree of positivity, finds that it must coexist with a different legal order based on the State, there is established between the two systems a series of relationships and contacts which may take the form of a pacific *modus vivendi*, or of friction, or even of open conflict. History offers a rich and varied collection of illustrations. But from the logical aspect it is not apparent why rules based on a theological assumption should be designated differently from rules which rest on any other foundation. Whatever be the content of the ethical principle, it cannot avail to direct action except in the form of morality or of law. When we are studying and classifying the various systems of morality and of law, we must distinguish theological from lay, rational or naturalistic morality and theocratic or sacerdotal from laicized law, but these internal distinctions in the two fundamental categories do not warrant the invention of a third category which is neither morality nor law.

To be properly studied, the intimate relationship between a believer and the divinity would require *inter alia* a study of the various creeds. Generally speaking, however, we may say that in the highest forms of religion the believer finds the principle of divinity deep in his own consciousness; therefore, in following its rules he does not find himself confronted by an extraneous subject. Thus the practical decisions inspired by faith generally assume the pure form of morality. However, it is different with those religions that are characteristic of primitive peoples, in which the divinity (or the divinities) assumes a corporeal form which contraposes itself as an extraneous and more powerful object to the personality of the subject. Here we can conceive of a sort of intersubjective relationship between the individual and his God, a relationship which—although in a metaphorical and often quite fictitious sense—may have the formal characteristics of juridicity. Yet even in this case it is difficult to conceive that the rules for action which have a theological basis are absolutely *sui generis*.

Nevertheless, the problem of the relationship between man and the divinity in which he believes does present particular difficulties, and it may be that in certain forms of religion this relationship does impose certain peculiar characteristics on the structure and formulation of precepts for conduct.

VI.—MORALITY AND CUSTOM

Many writers have tried to classify the various types of norms for conduct but seldom on clear logical foundations. The main source of confusion lies in the concept of "norms of custom," the ambiguity of which we have already noted. Within this group subdistinctions are often made between various species, between rules of propriety, of decency, of decorum, of social tact, of courtesy, of etiquette, and of ceremony, for instance.[10] Some writers, however, treat all these as "norms of usage" and distinguish them from "norms of custom."[11] Thus, among the Germans there are those, like Wundt, who distinguish *Brauch* from *Gewohnheit* and from *Sitte*.[12] Many subdistinctions are made by Jhering[13] and Spencer,[14] who, almost at the same time but independently, are credited with having first explored this subject scientifically. But, rather than follow them into particular subdistinctions, we should examine generally the attempt of these authors to separate these species of norms from moral norms. It is admitted, for instance by Vanni, that they imply a judgment of approbation or disapprobation and, like moral norms, determine sentiments of sympathy and benevolence toward others, but it is asserted that "while the judgment which follows upon the violation of a moral norm concerns the good or bad will of the doer, the judgment of an act with reference to custom concerns only his behavior, that is, the outward form of social relations."[15] It is often said that these norms are of lesser importance than the norms of morality.

This way of stating the problem is incorrect insofar as it rests upon a belief (often tacit) that morality consists only of a few general and immutable precepts. This belief leads to other misconceptions concerning the relationship between morality and law.

In a strictly logical sense, the term "moral" must be understood simply to import "dutifulness"—the quality of being a duty—and this quality may be expressed in universal and absolute as well as in particular and relative norms. Law can be similarly expressed in principles of universal character as well as in contingent and particular rules. The relativity and the mutability of morality more readily escapes examination because, moral rules not being generally codified, their changes and variations in application develop almost imperceptibly. But it is incontrovertible that alongside absolute morality there exists a positive and variable morality (parallel to positive law) which is subject to the mutable flux of history.

It is the task of morality to serve as a directive to life at every moment of each subject's activity; it must, therefore, consider all of a human being's real energies and aptitudes and all his possible ends, and then establish among them a hierarchy of values. It cannot leave uncertainties; it must in all circumstances indicate to the subject the course to follow, what he must do and what he must refrain from doing. Hence its consistently imperative form, which definitely does not admit the category of the merely permissible. Thus, while founded essentially on a few supreme principles, like the Gospel's "Do not unto others what you would not have them do unto you," it follows that morality by its nature must be translated into an extensive series of precepts concerning diverse matters and conditions of life. It follows, too, that morality in its historical and positive existence takes shape in different groups of rules, applying not only to the various relationships of life but also to the various strata of society even within the same nation. It is scarcely necessary to observe that differences in morality exist between nations according to their degree and form of civilization; the danger is rather that we may forget the profound similarity which underlies the apparent differences.

We must thus concede that not all the precepts which comprise the moral system of a people have equal importance. The rigor of Stoicism, which would oppose all gradation, has rightly been refuted. For instance, between the moral precepts which impose on us the duty to respect the life of our fellow creatures and those which impose the use of certain forms of courtesy there is a vast distance. But, if we had to admit that solely for this reason these norms had a different logical structure and that only the former belonged to morality, why should we have to regard as equally juridical the fundamental laws of the constitution of the State and the detailed rules governing the contract of agistment or creating trivial petty offences? In law, too, there are rules which apply only to certain, often narrow, classes of persons, such as the royal family or members of a particular profession, and similarly there can exist moral rules which have force only among particular social classes or apply only to a limited set of relationships.

VII.—MORALITY AND LAW

In conclusion, we hold it possible to maintain that all the so-called norms of propriety, decorum, courtesy, ceremony, and so on, are (leaving aside the few which impose juridical duties) properly of a moral nature, that is, they are particularizations, albeit partial and minute, within the category of duty in its subjective form. It is not correct to say that judgments concerning transgressions of these minor or complementary moral norms[16] regard only facts or external behavior and not the state of mind of the transgressor. We do not blame physical facts but the mental character which they reveal.

The only difficulty still to be met is the measure and manner of exigibility appropriate to such norms. As a rule, as every man is expected to do his own moral duty, so he can expect that others will do theirs. In all human societies there is at least a diffused sort of expectation, reflected in public opinion, that every one will act in conformity with the commonly accepted morality (positive morality). This is expressed not only in judgments and valuations but in definite reactions, considered to be morally justifiable, against those who do not conform. A rich man who has refused charity to the poor will probably be treated with less benevolence if he happens to fall into poverty, and *vice versa*. One who is courteous to all will usually be treated with courtesy, and so on. But this sort of exchange or correspondence of treatment is not to be confused with exigibility in the juridical sense, which consists in the possibility of claiming and enforcing, usually by a judicial process, a certain performance by another person, so that, in short, to a duty there corresponds a right. The indirect or vague forms of expectation and, in a wide sense, of exigibility, which with their corresponding reaction are encountered in the social field in respect to moral duties, never attain the precision which is proper to law. They cannot attain it, without the transformation *ipso facto* of the moral duty into a legal duty. In the same way, and for the same reason, a transition may be observed in the opposite direction. When juridical duties lose their precise character of exigibility, that is, when they no longer form the basis of a potentially enforceable claim on another person, they cease to exist as legal duties and, if they remain part of the regulative system at all, remain only as moral duties.

If a distinction between law and morality is to be made, it does not rest on any difference in their foundation, since both spring equally from the same human spirit and are but different, yet equally necessary, modes of directing its activity. In their origin both contain an ideal element of absoluteness and in their practical application an element of relativity. Each regulates the whole of human action and neither limits itself to one aspect thereof, such as the physical or the psychological, because human action necessarily partakes of both the physical and the psychological. Both comprise positive and negative determinations: that is, they impose both acts and forbearances. No action (using the word in its wildest sense) escapes ethical valuation in both of these forms; in other words, no action is morally or juridically irrelevant, and here we must bear in mind that the mere quality of "lawfulness," which imposes a duty on others to respect—that is, not to obstruct—one's act, is something which is juridically relevant.

The two forms of ethical valuation are closely related; each is an inseparable part of the same regulative system of conduct, which would be incomplete if it contained only moral or only juridical determinations. There would be a contradiction if it were impossible for the subject to perform his moral and his legal duties simultaneously. The pretended contradictions which philosophers like Fichte have denounced are simply resolved by observing that the freedom given by law to perform or not to perform certain moral duties does not in any case imply an obstacle to their performance. Rather, it only proves that law possesses a different function from morality. There can be a true contradiction, not between morality and law as part of the same system, but between systems, that is, between different ethical criteria, but each of these criteria is necessarily translated internally into moral and juridical determinations which are consistent with one another.

VIII.—THE INSUFFICIENCY OF LAW AS A RULE OF LIFE, THE NECESSITY OF PERFECTING IT IN THE LIFE OF THE SPIRIT

To illustrate the concepts which we have expressed schematically, we might say that law represents the social profile of ethics, or its intersubjective articulation, or even, as has been said, the "connective tissue of society," and go on seeking similar more or less happy metaphors. Systematic strictness, however, is perhaps worth more than any strained comparison or flower of speech. What is important is that law is necessary but insufficient by itself to direct human action. The duties which it imposes absolutely, representing a limit as against others, are always confirmed under another aspect by morality, which could not permit their violation without nullifying the same ethical system of which it also forms a part. Within this limit, however, that is, in the sphere of freedom which law allows to every subject, the intervention of morality is required for that further determination without which action would lack a proper guide and a safe orientation. What use man is to make of the freedom left to him by law, law does not say. For instance, law fixes the obligations that are derived from a given manifestation of will in the field of contract, but whether or not it is reasonable or prudent to make a particular contract would be a vain question to put to any code. Only morality, which takes into account all the ends of life, subordinating the lower to the higher, dominates the existence of the person in its entirety and helps to solve the ever new problems which confront him.

The man who never fails in any legal duty (*homo juridicus* in the first sense of the term) may be poor in wisdom and humanity. Such an image does not constitute an ideal of great value. Law often abstains from imposing restraint on certain actions not because they are worthy of approval but because the restraint would be even more reprehensible; an occasional transgression of the duty of temperance is a lesser evil than would be the empowering of one man to impose on others a fixed measure for their eating and drinking. But in this and all similar cases the mere lawfulness or juridical "freedom" is far from commensurate with full ethical value; it implies no more than the condemnation of the violation of that freedom by others (*sub specie alteritatis*). Thus we see how grave an error lies in the belief that it is always morally allowable to avail oneself of every legal right.

These considerations do not diminish the ethical value of law, which still remains a supreme human ideal; they simply define its functions and its nature. In all cases, law must be respected; an offense against law is *a fortiori* an offense against morality, and this is in itself sufficient to show how law truly stands at the apex of human values. But the mere non-violation of the ethical principle in this specific form of intersubjective relations is not the same as positively putting it into effect in its concrete entirety. We might here apply (though not quite in the usual sense) the familiar saying that law represents an ethical minimum.

The same considerations lead us to reject the view that in every case it is right and praiseworthy to enforce one's legal rights to the limit. The figure of *homo juridicus* in this sense does not represent a true ideal, and those who take him for such once again confuse the proper nature of law with that of morality.

Finally, we cannot admit as a sufficient ideal of life even the fight against legal wrong, which corresponds to the third meaning of the term *homo juridicus*. It is true that, besides the duty not to break the law, there exists the highly moral duty to co-operate in its defense against violations by others; the modes and limits of such defense must, however, be fixed not on the basis of an oversimplified formula but with regard to all the guiding forces of life, and only morality conceives these in integral fashion. Besides directly combating the wrongs done by others (which is the specific task of certain officers and organs of the State), we must also practice good in other ways, each fulfilling practical and constructive duties in the field of action allotted to us. An individual who followed an abstract program of upholding every legal right might still dissipate his activity indefinitely and neglect his proper business in life. Such a one could not be pointed to as a model, if only because his contribution to the effectiveness of the law would probably be less than if he observed the maxim of *suum agere*. There may be something noble, but there is also something pitiable and even comic in the enterprise of Don Quixote, who wanders across the world in defense of rights he imagines to have been violated and who thinks that he is serving justice when he frees from their guards the robbers whom he meets on his way.

A fundamental precept of ethics is that, within the limits of our existence, we ought to acquit ourselves of our duties toward ourselves, our families, our country and humanity in general, developing our innate spirituality for the greatest universal good. Into this program there enters that sacred form of activity which is the fight against injustice, but this task must be tempered and harmonized with the others; it cannot be isolated and converted into an exclusive precept implying the abandoning of all other duties . . .

Only through an illusion produced by bad logic can one presume to regulate human life completely in the form of morality alone or of law alone. The attempt to solve all the practical problems of life by the sole, eminently moral, rule of neighborly love ("Love your enemies") clashes with the necessity of determining the proper limits of reaction against attack, whether between individuals or between nations. Even if it were morally laudable always to forgive any offense against ourselves (which is at least doubtful), it would be wrong and ethically reprehensible to allow others to be offended with impunity when we could defend them. A moral system must be complemented by a juridical system.

Similarly, the attempt to regulate life by law alone appears on analysis to be untenable. It is impossible, without forcing the proper order and structure of ethical precepts, to reduce them all to a function of intersubjective relationships, or to describe them all under the species of sociality. It is necessary that the subject should find in his own conscience a rule which, moving *ex interiore homine*, guides him to the solution of the doubts and problems of life, pointing out in every case the path of duty: and this is the form of morality. Law and morality join in their extrinsic manifestations, since they have a common root, but neither can do without the other, or replace the other, without deforming the complex and living harmony of human and social activity.

What is important to bear in mind is the common deontological character of law and morality, which affirms and maintains itself in spite of the specific differences of their formulations and because of which, both categories equally transcend the law of physical nature . . .

(Paper read at the Sorbonne, Paris, at the second session of the Institut International de Philosophie du Droit et de Sociologie Juridique, Oct. 1, 1935).

NOTES

1. JHERING, *Der Kampf um's Recht* (14 Aufl., Wien, 1900), pp. 58-61; cf. *ibid., Vorrede*, p. xi.

2. KOHLER, *Shakespeare vor dem Forum der Jurisprudenz* (Würzburg, 1883; 2 Aufl., Berlin, 1919); *Nachwort zu S. vor dem Forum der Jurisprudenz* (Würzburg, 1884).

3. G. BRUNETTI, *Norme e regole finali nel diritto* (Torino, 1913), p. 89.

4. ZITELMANN, *Irrtum und Rechtsgeschäft* (Leipzig, 1879), pp. 208, 222; *Internationales Privatrecht* (Leipzig, 1897), I Bd., p. 43 *et seq.*; *Ausschluss der Widerrechtlichkeit* (in "Arch. für die civ. Praxis," Bd. 99, 1906), p. 3 *et seq.* [The English reader may recall Mr. Justice Holmes' theory of contract as creating merely conditional liability. See *The Pollock-Holmes Letters*, 2 vols., Cambridge, 1942, Index, s.v. "Contract."]

5. KANT, *Grundlegung zur Metaphysik der Sitten*, II Abschn. (ed. Vorländer, p. 36 *et seq.*). Cf. *Kritik der Urteilskraft*, Einl. I (ed. Vorländer, p. 7 *et seq.*).

6. N. M. KORKOUNOV, *General Theory of Law* (Boston, 1909), p. 41 *et seq.* Cf. also (although his conclusions are unacceptable) A. RAVÀ, *Il diritto come norma tecnica* (Cagliari, 1911).

7. KANT, *Grundlegung, ed. cit*, p. 37.

8. Rules merely arbitrary, like the rules of games, have in themselves no obligatory character, but they can acquire such character indirectly through being made the object of a convention or an agreement, even tacit, between the players. Where there is no agreement to observe the established rules, everyone is free to invent and experiment with different rules.

9. VANNI, *Lezioni di Filosofia del diritto* (Bologna, 1904), p. 64: GÉNY, *Science et technique en droit privé positif*, vol. I (Paris, 1922), p. 45 *et seq*. Cf. GROPPALI, *Istituzioni di scienza generale del diritto* (Bergamo, 1921), pp. 22-25, and, for the opposite view, BARTOLOMEI, *Lezioni di Filosofia del diritto* (5 ed., Napoli, 1933), p. 127.

10. See VANNI, *op. cit.*, p. 66. STAMMLER, in his essay, *Die Theorie des Anarchismus* (Berlin, 1894), and subsequently in his larger works, placed, alongside of law, the other rules of social life as *Konventionalregeln*. Cf. *Lehrbuch der Rechtsphilosophie* (3 Aufl., Berlin, 1928), § 37; *Wirtschaft und Recht* (4 Aufl., Berlin, 1921), § 23 *et seq.*; *Theorie der Rechtswissenschaft* (2 Aufl., Halle, 1923), § 14. So M. E. MAYER, in *Rechtsnormen und Kulturnormen* (Breslau, 1903), p. 17, uses the term *Kulturnormen* to include all species of nonjuridical rules. F. STOERK, in *Völkerrecht und Völkercourtoisie* (Tübingen, 1908), p. 151, discussing the concept of *comitas* or *courtoisie* in international law, reduces it to custom or *Verkehrssitte*.

11. E.g., BARTOLOMEI, *op. cit.*, p. 127 *et seq*.

12. WUNDT, *Ethik* (4 Aufl., Stuttgart, 1912), I Bd., p. 131 *et seq*.

13. JHERING, *Der Zweck im Recht* (4 Aufl., 1905), esp. II Bd., K. IX, p. 257 *et seq*.

14. SPENCER, *Principles of Sociology* (London, 1876-1896), esp. Vol. I, Pt. IV, *Ceremonial Institutions*.

15. VANNI, *op. cit.*, p. 67.

16. On the term "complementary ethic" see the observations (not altogether acceptable) of JHERING, *Der Zweck im Recht*, II Bd., p. 261.

TRUTH

IN MORALITY AND LAW

INTRODUCTION

THE PROBLEM OF TRUTH HAS MANY ASPECTS. IN THIS ESSAY, the epistemological aspect will be treated summarily. Our aim is not so much to examine what truth may be as to consider the rule which imposes on all the duty to tell what they believe to be true, or at least not to lie and not to deceive. This simple rule, which in the abstract is recognized by everyone, raises many difficult questions in its application. We are not always obliged to express our thoughts in words; in many cases both morality and law consider secrecy to be permissible and even obligatory. In other cases, however, reticence is not permitted, nor is dissimulation, which is often equivalent to deception. Up to a point, the law of war admits the use of stratagems to deceive the enemy, but certain kinds of deception are forbidden. It is disputable whether in a trial the parties and their representatives are or are not bound to tell the whole truth; whether such an obligation exists in commerce or whether it is lawful for the vendor to praise his wares without disclosing their defects; whether the pretenses which may be useful and customary in politics and diplomacy are justifiable. Such questions have both a moral and a juridical aspect, and the answers do not always coincide. Here is a broad field for investigation. Many opinions have been pronounced, and monographs have been written on particular points, but it does not appear that the question has ever been treated systematically as a whole. To do so is the purpose of this brief essay, which certainly cannot presume to exhaust the subject . . .

I.—INTELLIGENCE AND TRUTH IN GENERAL

To know means to aim at truth and to attain it. What then is truth? Is it within us or outside us or is it both at the same time? Knowledge implies a relationship between a subject and an object, but does this relationship concern only the individual subject or does it concern the universal subject which is identical in all individuals? Acceptance of the latter answer would suffice to justify us in saying that there are truths which are necessary and "objective," in Kant's sense of "universally valid." But objectivity can also be understood in a fuller sense as ontological contact or real equivalency between intelligence and being in itself—*adaequatio intellectus et rei*, as St. Thomas defined truth. "Dicitur enim *intelligere* quasi *intus legere*. Nam cognitio sensitiva occupatur circa qualitates sensibiles exteriores; cognitio autem intellectiva penetrat usque ad essentiam rei. Obiectum enim intellectus est *quod quid est*."[1]

It is difficult to deny that there exists in us at least a glimmer of the absolute. Even Kant, after excluding the absolute from theoretical reason, readmitted it in the practical reason. The supreme ethical (moral and juridical) and theoretical (logical and mathematical) truths, innate in our mind with the characteristics of necessity, eternity and universality, afford us a kind of guarantee that we are not mere ephemeral appearances bound to the changeable and deceptive impressions of the senses, but substances which participate in the absoluteness of being in general. Without this, the most profound and indestructible beliefs and aspirations of our mind would remain inexplicable. Therefore, ancient and modern attempts (as by Condillac and, later, by Taine[2] and others) to explain knowledge in a purely mechanical manner, using only the data of the senses, have failed and must fail.

We need not here make a detailed examination of doctrines concerning the intellect: for instance, the Aristotelian distinction between the poetic or active intellect (νοῦς ποιητικός) and the pathetic or passive intellect (νοῦς παθητικός), which for centuries has been the subject of comment and dispute. In modern philosophy, intellect has often been contraposed not only to sensibility and intuition but also to reason, where intellect (*Verstand*) is understood as the faculty of forming concepts and judgments, and reason (*Vernunft*) as the supreme unifying power of thought according to principles (ideas). But there still survives, even among philosophers, the use of the word "intellect" in a wider sense, to designate cognitive power in general, the "thinking function of the mind" (Bain), including "the powers known as Perception, Memory, Conception, Abstraction, Reason, Judgment and Imagination."[3]

On occasion an attempt has also been made to distinguish between intellect and intelligence (which are commonly considered as synonymous), by defining intelligence as intellect in action. So St. Thomas: "Hoc nomen *intelligentia* proprie significat ipsum actum intellectus, qui est intelligere . . . Sic ergo intelligentia ab intellectu non distinguitur sicut potentia a potentia, sed sicut actus a potentia."[4] Taking intelligence in the absolute sense, Boethius asserts that it is an attribute of God rather than of man.[5]

However limited, relative and deficient it may be, nevertheless within us there is an aptitude and an inclination toward truth. The founder of modern philosophy did not err in his remark that the soul thinks continually, since even in the subconscious and in dreaming a certain psychic activity continues to function. "Mens semper actu cogitat"—later psychological studies have confirmed this saying of Descartes. "What," he asked himself, "am I? A thing which thinks. And what is a thing which thinks? It is a thing which doubts, which intends, which conceives, which asserts, which denies, which wills, which refuses, which imagines and feels."[6] This variety of psychological phenomena does not preclude their fundamental unity. Their division or classification is of secondary importance. There cannot exist, in the concrete, an intelligence without will or a will without intelligence.

We can go even further and admit (contrary to the opinion of Descartes) that premonitions, or inferior forms of intelligence are found in all the animal kingdom. Animals are not "pure automata," as Descartes asserted; they have, if not an "intellectual soul," at least a "sensitive soul," according to the Aristotelian division adopted by the Scholastics. Perhaps even this distinction is too absolute, since the senses and the intellect are not two separate worlds. And, although the superior faculty of reason belongs to man alone, we may still hold (according to a thesis maintained ever since Plutarch) that between the psychic faculties of man and those of animals there exists only a difference of degree . . .

Some, like Maeterlinck, have claimed to see "proofs of intelligence" even in plants, especially in flowers, and claimed that "chaque fleur a son idée, son système, son expérience acquise qu'elle met à profit."[7] We cannot, however, truly attribute intelligence in the proper sense of the word to that which lacks consciousness and self-reflection.[8] But neither can we be satisfied by a purely mechanical explanation of nature, especially of organic nature, which is the realm of teleology. The correspondence of means to ends and the constant effort to make these proportionate to one another (which is what life consists in) represents a "realized harmony" (better, a harmony in course of realization), analogous to the activity of thought. In exploring nature, we discover reflected therein the laws of our own mind, as if nature were the mirror of our mind, or our mind the mirror of nature. Even in its rigidly mechanical aspect, that is to say, in its dead parts, nature presents itself to us in terms of intellectuality, as (in a phrase of Hegel's) "the cadaver of intellect." True, the stars move according to mathematical laws; yet there is in nature a life, that same life which breathes in us, and its manifestations bear the same ideal imprints which we encounter as data *a priori* in our consciousness. Subject and object are in some way refractions of an absolute unity. In this sense we can repeat with Spinoza, "Ordo et connexio idearum idem est ac ordo et connexio rerum."[9] The essence of things coincides with thought objectively understood; it is, in short, the Platonic Idea.

II.—THE DUTY OF TRUTH. ITS LIMITS AND EXCEPTIONS. (SECRECY, MENTAL RESERVATION, DISSIMULATION AND SIMULATION, AND CONNECTED QUESTIONS)

The inclination toward truth which is innate in our mind is not only a psychological and epistemological datum; it is also an ethical principle, a moral requirement. We have the duty of seeking truth and, insofar as we can, of respecting it and conforming our activity to it.[10]

Obviously, this duty falls in a special manner on those who are dedicated to the study of science and philosophy, whose mission is summed up in the precept, *vitam impendere vero*.[11] But it is a duty incumbent on all, whatever their condition and circumstances.[12] No ethical system worthy of the name is possible without this precept, which is inseparable from the fundamental precepts of charity and justice. The commandment of the Old Testament, "Thou shalt not bear false witness,"[13] has, like the other commandments, not only been accepted but fruitfully developed by Christianity. Christianity has extracted from it a series of commands and prohibitions that have in common a fundamental respect for truth. By including among the sins against the Holy Ghost that of contesting the known truth, Christian ethic has lent a new consecration to this principle. Even in the most precise philosophical language we could not define the offense knowingly committed against truth more exactly than as a sin against the Spirit.

In contrast with the clarity and simplicity of this principle, which translates into imperative form the intellect's natural vocation, are the difficulty of applying the principle in social life and its all too frequent transgressions. If the human mind were to exercise itself only upon natural phenomena and upon its own inner self, the ethical problem of truth would not be so difficult, because in this case the only pertinent moral precept would consist in the duty to live as a thinking being, that is, to develop and refine one's intelligence in conformity with its nature. Every man has the duty to attend to his own education and, in certain cases, to that of others. In order to fulfill their own ends, those who have the ability ought to engage in creative work, whereby they not only develop their own minds but contribute to the development of minds in general. So far, however, as the activity of thought is considered in its individual aspect alone, that is, simply in itself and with regard to nature, the mind can indeed err and be deceived, but it cannot deceive; therefore, this is the field rather of psychology and logic than of ethics.

The question becomes more complex when we consider intelligence in its social aspect, that is to say, as a means of communication with others. Communicability is an essential characteristic of thought, especially in its higher forms; insofar as it raises itself above the senses, the activity of the spirit takes on dialectical and abstract forms which are necessarily common and intelligible to any thinking subject. The fact of thought gives rise—at least potentially—to an intersubjective relationship. Not without reason did St. Thomas teach that *veritas sive veracitas* is connected with justice and is, indeed, a *pars iustitiae*, since it too, in its manifestation, is *ad alterum*.[14] Every man has the duty to be truthful to others—"ex honestate unus homo alteri debet veritatis manifestationem"—if only because living together, which is imposed on man by his social nature, would be impossible without mutual trust. The words of Aquinas adopt a phrase of Aristotle but they also anticipate certain arguments of Grotius and Kant and other modern doctrines. "Quia homo est animale sociale, naturaliter unus homo debet alteri id sine quo societas humana servari non posset. Non autem possent homines ad invicem convivere, nisi sibi invicem crederent, tamquam sibi invicem veritatem manifestantibus. Et ideo virtus veritatis aliquo modo attendit rationem debiti."[15]

Potential communicability does not, however, prevent thought from being concealed or dissimulated or even falsely presented. This may be done for various reasons, not all equally blameworthy. In some cases, to set limits or restraints on the knowledge of truth may not only be ethically permissible but even a duty. Here lies a sort of contradiction: while faithful and complete manifestation of thought is the fundamental rule which binds our consciences and renders society possible, while the search for truth and its diffusion should be promoted, while lying must be opposed by every means, yet many evils would result and social life would be made unduly difficult if everything that every man knows and feels were immediately laid open to all other men, without regard to times, modes and circumstances. We must ask: Is the duty of truthfulness absolute and unconditioned, or is it subject to exceptions and limitations, and, if so, how are these to be determined?

In the field of ethics, one duty can be limited only by another duty. And, however fundamental be the duty of sincerity, there are other duties which also impose themselves upon our conscience. There can be no irreconcilable contradiction in this matter, since ethics, like life itself, rests upon a single foundation. But for this very reason, duties must be considered in the concrete and not in their abstraction, which would set them in opposition to one another as irreducible entities. Charity, for instance, must be limited by justice. No duty is more sacred than that of beneficence, but (St. Augustine well asks) would it be permissible to rob the rich in order to give to the poor? Or to suppress or forge testaments, so that inheritances should go to charitable rather than to unworthy men? Clearly, not.[16]

The duty to tell the truth does not exempt us from our duty to respect the rights of others, nor does it justify rashness, presumption and arrogance.[17] There is an ideal sphere of personality which must be respected no less than the material sphere; there is a right to honor as there is to physical integrity; there is an intellectual property no less deserving of protection than property in the material sense. All this lays the basis for a system of limitations upon the arbitrary communication of truths; nevertheless, if in many cases it makes silence a duty, it does not thereby necessarily make lying permissible.

Not all truths are suitable to all men.[18] For instance, in dealing with children and young people we rightly keep silent about those aspects of the sad reality of human affairs which they could not properly understand and which, imparted too early, would disturb the healthy development of their minds.

Such is the weakness of human nature that truth imprudently revealed makes for enmity, as the Latin poet observed,[19] arousing in ill-disposed minds inappropriate and dangerous reactions. The divergence of ideas and feelings among men, particularly on certain issues, is and has always been so grave that conflict and even violence will inevitably erupt if a certain restraint is not observed both in the expression of one's own opinions and in inquiring into those of others (always provided that such expression or inquiry is not required by some special duty). This reflection, which is dictated by prudence (and prudence, rightly understood, is also a fundamental virtue), takes specific form in morals as a complex of rules for right living and good manners.[20] We should remember, however, that, carried beyond a certain point, caution and reserve can easily degenerate into hypocrisy and disloyalty.[21]

In many cases secrecy is permissible and sometimes it is obligatory, especially in matters which have been confided to us with the understanding of secrecy.[22] To deny this would be to deny the obligatory force of agreements, unless it were to be held wrong to receive any confidence. And this has never been maintained by anyone. Particularly rigid and absolutely unbreakable is the obligation in the matter of religious confessions, which would lose their *raison d'être* if they were not held secret. But even apart from cases where secrecy bears this sacred character, it can be required because of special ethical or technical exigencies, as in certain professions.[23] Compassion may suggest concealment (usually only temporary) of painful truths,[24] and protection of legitimate interests may require that information not be communicated save at certain times and to specified persons.

From the withholding of a known truth to its dissimulation is a brief and sometimes almost inevitable step. This is apparent even in the teaching of those who most violently denounce lying and champion truth at any cost. St. Thomas, for instance, teaches that we are not always obliged to reveal our mind to others and that "etiam in doctrina multa sunt occultanda, maxime infidelibus, ne irrideant," according to the text "Nolite sanctum dare canibus."[25] And, in recalling a passage from St. Augustine,[26] he even goes to the point of admitting that sometimes "licet veritatem occultare prudenter sub aliqua dissimulatione."[27] Authoritative modern writers on morals have sought to justify "equivocal or ambiguous expression, with a double meaning, one true and the other false, when the questioner has no right to a precise answer."[28] They also in fact permit, in certain cases, mental reservation, that is, the limiting of the sense of words according to the understanding of the speaker, when there is a just cause for concealing the truth and the truth might be inferred from the words used.[29] These are delicate arguments which rightly perplex the theorists and in practice give rise to many doubts. Yet how, it is asked, could the obligation of secrecy be maintained if it were not permissible to use an ambiguous expression such as "I do not know" with the unexpressed reservation "in such a way that I can tell"? Cardinal Massimi has observed that "it would sometimes be at least a partial revelation of the secret to say 'I cannot say'; the listener should know once for all that the words 'I do not know' may legitimately hide 'I cannot say'."[30] Nevertheless, such mental reservation has something unseemly about it and as far as possible it should be avoided.[31]

Lying is, in principle, deserving of condemnation and it is condemned, even in its mildest forms, even if it violates no duty other than that of veracity.[32] This is because the easily formed habit of lying degrades man and leads him astray.[33]

There is only one type of case in which there are exceptions to this general precept, just as exception to the prohibition of killing or wounding can be made when such action is the only means of defending oneself or others from wrongful violence.[34] The criminal or the madman who threatens our life or the life of another frees us, by his act, from our duty to treat him with truth even as he frees us from our duty to respect his life.[35] Any cunning or deceit becomes permissible for lawful defense and the cleverness shown in such a crisis, even though it may involve lying, may not only be blameless but even a matter for admiration. We recall the wise man who, while making astronomical observations on top of a tower, was confronted by a madman who threatened to pitch him down; the wise man declared that he was capable of something much more difficult, namely, jumping from the bottom to the top, and with this subterfuge succeeded in descending unharmed and so escaping from danger.[36] This category of exceptions must, however, be kept strictly within its proper limits, lest observance of the general rule against lying be made to depend simply on the utility of avoiding inconvenience, which would destroy the validity of the rule.[37]

It may happen that a momentary deception corresponds to the vital interest, and thus to the profound and real will, of the person deceived. The moral justification then consists (as in the juridical institution of *negotiorum gestio*) in the subsequent ratification which can be legitimately presumed from the beginning. Thus, for instance, praise has been accorded the quick wit of the theater manager who, when a fire broke out behind the scenes, told the audience that the performance was being suspended for another reason, and so succeeded in clearing the theater without the panic which would have ensued had he told the truth. But this sort of infraction of the duty of sincerity can be allowed only within very narrow limits; we must consider, *inter alia*, that the use of such means implies a certain moral weakness in those for whose advantage it is employed, and with the progress of moral education such exceptions should tend to disappear.[38]

III.—DECEPTION IN WAR—STRATAGEMS

The use of tricks to deceive the enemy is generally admitted in the juridical theory and practice of war. War is made not by arms alone but above all by intelligence, which, in the supreme effort belligerents make to overcome one another, becomes fertile in every kind of invention. Polyaenus in his *Stratagemata* (2nd century A.D.) cited some nine hundred stratagems; by how much could this number be increased today?

The deceits which even savages employ in hunting animals —matched only by the tricks used by certain animals to obtain food or to escape from danger—are multiplied and infinitely refined when it is a question of attacking, or defending oneself against, other men. From the moral point of view it is deplorable that so much study and ingenuity should be devoted to the art of injuring our fellowmen, yet it is also true that without the powerful stimulus of war many inventions, even in the field of industry and the arts of peace, would never have appeared or would have appeared much later. (This is not to claim that technical advantage, however great, can compensate for moral evil, which is absolute and therefore incommensurable.)

Simulation and dissimulation are so involved in the technique of warfare that they could not be abolished unless war itself were abolished. As Paulsen wrote, "eine Kriegführung mit offenen Karten ist eine schlechthin unmögliche Sache."[39] Artifices for deceiving the enemy become ever more various and ingenious, since their effectiveness lies in their novelty and in the difficulty of discovering their secret. Tricks which seemed ingenious in ancient times, like the Trojan horse, might make modern strategists smile.

St. Thomas recognized that in war "insidiae ordinantur ad fallendum hostes,"[40] and in general he did not deny their lawfulness, since, as St. Augustine had already observed, "cum aliquis iustum bellum susceperit, utrum aperta pugna, utrum insidiis vincat, nihil ad iustitiam interest."[41] Yet even war has laws which should not be transgressed; thus, according to an ancient opinion, also in St. Ambrose, "foedera etiam inter hostes servanda."[42] Finally, also according to St. Thomas, not all the deceits of war are lawful but rather only those which consist in hiding one's real plans from the enemy. Vittoria, *inter alios*, referred to this doctrine when he reconsidered the problem which had been discussed by St. Thomas, whether every simulation is a sin.[43]

Even in our rapid survey we must not omit the name of the man who in his political teaching so emphasized deception that his name itself has become synonymous with cunning and duplicity. Macchiavelli, starting from a pessimistic view of human nature and paying scant regard to ethics, asserted that, "it is necessary for [the Prince] to be a great simulator and dissimulator; and so simple are men and so obedient to present necessities, that he who practices deception will always find those who will let themselves be deceived."[44] In particular, he declared that "the use of deception in war is a glorious thing," but in developing his argument he somewhat tempered this by adding, "I do not mean that there is glory in the fraud which leads you to break a pledge given or a pact made; because, although this may sometimes win you a kingdom, it will never give you glory."[45] Machiavelli's teaching, however, stands as a document of little ethical sensibility, which exposed the practices of his time but did not serve to correct them, nor did it help, as the author had hoped, to promote the welfare of Italy.

The treatment of this question by Alberico Gentili deserves mention. First of all, he observed that "in bello gerendo aliquid est, quod eius omnes partes pervadit: dolus et stratagema,"[46] but (proceeding in a way not substantially different from St. Thomas) he set himself to distinguish *dolus bonus* from *dolus malus* and to mark out the limits of *dolus* permissible against an enemy.[47]

Until quite recently, later teaching on the law of war likewise progressed along the line of distinctions and limitations, admitting certain kinds of deception (ambushes, feigned attacks or withdrawals, tricks of various kinds to obtain information about the enemy, diffusion of false reports, etc.), but excluding others as contrary to the law of nations and to military honor (violation of the pledged word, the use of alien flags or military uniforms, etc.). And in modern times positive rules have been laid down to similar effect.[48] Doubts and uncertainties are not lacking,[49] however, and the possibility always remains open that the established rules may be violated in practice by the use of deceptions which go beyond the limits of "lawful deception." It is clear that this conception is valid only insofar as we admit, under certain conditions, the lawfulness of war; if the lawfulness of war were denied, there would be no more right to deceive in war than to kill or to wound.

IV.—DECEPTION IN GAMES

Far less important but still deserving mention as a means of illustrating our argument, is the fact that in many games it is considered permissible (not without a certain analogy with war) to use deceit in order to win.[50] So long as he does not violate the rules of the game, each player may use his ingenuity to delude his opponent by misleading him as to his real intention. So-called "feints" are allowed and are praised as proof of skill (in fencing, football, etc.), and so, in games of pure intelligence like chess, are "traps," where the deceitful offer of an apparent gain results, if accepted, in a loss. How is this to be justified ethically? Are not such deliberately deceitful actions contrary to the fundamental duty of sincerity and loyalty?

A first and partial justification can quite easily be found if the deception is reciprocal. Further, these deceptions always presuppose respect for the established rules of the game and are thus practiced within the limits of a certain legality.[51] This lends them the character of *dolus bonus* and distinguishes them from the act of the player who cheats by distracting his opponent's attention in order to surreptitiously move a piece on the board. But what is most important of all is that, within the limits mentioned, the right of mutual deception is agreed on in advance by the players, so that they may test their ingenuity against each other. Thus they impliedly renounce the right to complain if defeated. "Nemo videtur fraudare eos, qui sciunt et consentiunt."[52]

Here, too, simulation and dissimulation constitute an exercise of intelligence which psychologically may attain a high degree of refinement but which ethically remains confined within strict limits.[53] Neither morality nor law allows the complete abandonment of the fundamental rule of respect for truth, even where partial exceptions seem to be tolerated. And it is obvious that the very possibility of deception depends on the credibility of assertions, and thus on the general effective vigor of the rule.

V.—THE LEGAL OBLIGATION OF TRUTH, ESPECIALLY IN CIVIL CASES*

From what has been said it is evident that respect for truth is a fundamental ethical principle which finds application not only in morality but also in law; these two normative categories have the same source and hence a necessary mutual coherence. However, while in morality the principle presents itself immediately in its absolute value—as a categorical imperative which has only minimal exceptions or limitations—in law the obligation to speak the truth assumes a precise form, with civil or penal sanctions attached, only in a determinate class of cases, namely, where lying or reticence constitutes an unjust harm to others. This follows from the proper nature of law, which in the sphere of the personal liberty of each subject allows not only such acts as are prescribed by morality but also some which are contrary to morality, so long as they do not disturb the sphere of competence of other subjects. To take an obvious example, the man who drinks to excess violates the duty of temperance. But he is not exposed to legal sanctions so long as his drunkenness leads to no disturbance or offense. So, too, the *miles gloriosus* who in his boasting claims for himself prowess beyond the truth deserves moral reproof, but he is not guilty under the law, nor is the hunter who presents as his own catch the game he has bought in a shop.

*[In this section Professor Del Vecchio's illustrations are mainly drawn from Italian law.]

But if the false assertion of nonexistent qualities or merits has the aim and effect of inducing others to contract a definite obligation, the party deceived has legitimate grounds for seeking annulment of the contract and, where the necessary elements are present, even more serious consequences may follow.[54] To protect the public faith, the law punishes the man who wrongfully wears in public the uniform or insignia of a public office, or of a political, administrative or judicial corporation, or of a profession for which a special State qualification is required, or who wrongfully wears in public an ecclesiastical habit, and likewise one who arrogates to himself academic dignity, rank, titles, decorations, etc. The reasons underlying such rules, which are found in the laws of all nations, are evident. The false appearances created by such abuses directly affect social relations, setting a snare for those who are deceived by them and prejudicing the rights of those who legitimately possess title or rank and can claim that the value of their title or rank is thereby diminished.

However, although artifices aimed at deception are in principle condemned not only by morality but also by law (remember the maxims: *fraus omnia corrumpit*; *malitiis non est indulgendum*), there are many cases in which the law permits, within limits, simulation and dissimulation, that is, it recognizes them as capable of producing certain effects, for the protection of the good faith of third parties, for the certainty of juridical relations, or for other reasons.[55] This topic is one of the most discussed in juristic science, and it was especially the subject of much discussion before the new Italian civil code was adopted. The code laid down certain rules which correspond, substantially, to what had been worked out by doctrine and judicial decision, and which also draw upon the general principles of law.[56] Where a conflict exists between an apparent (simulated) juristic act and the real intention (dissimulated) of the parties, the latter is rightly held to prevail, provided of course that it has a legitimate object and possesses all other essential requisites (*plus valere quod agitur, quam quod simulate concipitur*). The simulated act produces no effect between the parties themselves, but they cannot plead its falsity against third parties in good faith, who can acquire certain rights even under a simulated transaction.

Legal science and technique have worked out various rules in these matters, some of which have subtle distinctions. In Italian law, for instance, if a minor incurs an obligation by falsely declaring himself to be of age, he has the right to ask for annulment of the obligation—the law's protection in his favor extends even to a case of simulation. If, however, he has concealed the fact of his minority by "trickery," for instance, by producing a false birth certificate, he loses this right. Thus is applied, but only up to a point, the old maxim: *Nemo auditur turpitudinem suam allegans.*[57]

Quite different from simulations are the so-called legal fictions which are found in both ancient and modern systems and are known to every lawyer. These are merely technical means for formulating legal rules and making them applicable even when some of the elements normally required are lacking. By feigned equivalence between the existence and the non-existence of a specified fact we obtain an abbreviated and simplified expression of rules which could have been formulated differently and more appropriately to their real object. Such fictions (called by Jhering "technische Notlügen") are not meant to deceive and do not offend truth, save in a relative sense, just as dramatic spectacles, sham battles in military maneuvers, or the attachment of false limbs to the human body, do not offend truth.[58] Generally speaking, alterations or artificial imitations of reality, if openly declared and accepted as such, are not in themselves to be censured; they constitute a sort of secondary truth, relative or conventional and not devoid of merit when used for legitimate ends.[59] Of course, such artifice must find a limit in real needs and must cease when these cease. This holds also for legal fictions, which in their beginning exercise a sort of provisional function in the evolution of law, facilitating the introduction of new rules under the appearance of maintaining the old. In this sense, as Jhering observed, fictions have been and still can be useful instruments of legal progress, and it would not be reasonable to propose, *ex abrupto*, their abolition until they can be replaced by specific new legislation which will better meet the same needs. We should not ask a man who walks with a crutch to throw it away before he is able to walk without it.[60] The gradual elimination of fictions from the field of jurisprudence is, however, an ideal to which legislators and jurists ought to aspire, and in the more advanced systems this has already been achieved.[61]

So closely allied to legal fictions as sometimes to be confounded with them are presumptions *juris et de jure*, that is, presumptions which do not admit of proof to the contrary. These assume that something must always be held to be true which, although probable, might in some cases not correspond with fact, for instance, *pater is est quem nuptiae demonstrant* or *res judicata pro veritate habetur.* These are commonly justified by the need for assuring the stability of legal relations and of preventing litigation from continuing indefinitely. These are weighty reasons, yet such presumptions (unlike those *hominis* and *juris tantum*) are an impediment to the free search for truth and should be reduced to the indispensable minimum.[62]

The ethical principle which demands respect for truth assumes special importance and gives rise to special problems in the field of legal procedure. Since judicial activity, civil as well as penal, has as its first duty the ascertaining of the truth (which is an obviously necessary prerequisite for the right application of the law and thus for a just decision), one can well understand that the obligation of truthfulness is rigorously prescribed, with the severest sanctions prescribed for infractions, for those who, as witnesses and experts, concur in informing the judges of the facts on which the judgment turns.[63] To emphasize and render this obligation more solemn, modern legal systems, like those of ancient times, require witnesses and experts to swear an oath which involves not only their legal responsibility but also their religious conscience.

The same obligation does not exist, or is not asserted with the same rigor, for the accused in a criminal case or for the parties in a civil case. The questioning of the accused, like that of the witnesses, aims at discovering the truth. But the principle that the accused must be allowed the fullest liberty to defend himself makes it impossible to punish his lying or his silence by legal sanctions (save where he falsely states or denies his own identity). It is left to the judges to determine the credibility of his assertions.[64]

However, even in this field, there are exceptions and limitations which show how the duty of telling the truth must be harmonized with other duties which also have ethical value. Thus, except in special cases, the nearest relatives of the accused need not testify, since to imperil the accused would disturb their consciences. The expert is bound to secrecy, save insofar as the parties wish to take cognizance of his expert knowledge. Modern legislation guarantees respect for professional and official secrecy and for the secrecy of political and military intelligence, the disclosure of which might injure the State.

All the foregoing constitutes a restriction on the principle of the right and the duty to speak the truth on every occasion, but this protection of secrecy is in many cases founded on serious ethical reasons and its abolition would disturb the ordered development of civil life. It should be further kept in mind that silence is not to be confused with lying. However, in a future and better order of society the disappearance of many of the present restrictions on the free communication of knowledge can be conceived of as desirable.*

Some observations may be added on matters which particularly concern the forensic profession. Since the objective of advocate and judge alike is to realize justice, there should be collaboration between Bench and Bar. An advocate falls short of—indeed betrays—his mission if he upholds his case by sophisms and false proofs; he sacrifices thereby both truth and justice. An honest advocate will not hesitate to refuse to undertake a case when he does not believe that it can be supported by serious and well-founded arguments.[65] On the other hand, we must remember that the reality of social relationships is often complicated, and that it may be useful and necessary, even for the sake of justice, to look at a case from both sides. Opposite interpretations and opposite opinions can be held

*[A discussion of the question as to whether and how far the parties to a civil action are under legal obligation to speak the truth has been omitted. See the Italian version of the present essay in DEL VECCHIO, *Studi sul diritto*, II, pp. 213-217, with notes citing works on this question in Italian and other legal systems. The Anglo-American approach is different: if a party chooses to give evidence on oath, he is bound by the full obligation of the oath.]

with equally good faith. It is a vulgar error to hold that the complications of social life are deliberately created by the advocate; they arise from the very nature of things and the nature of the human mind, which displays itself in an infinite variety of changing events which are often, in their concrete forms, unforeseen and unpredictable even by the legislator . . .[66]

VI.—BAD FAITH IN BUSINESS DEALINGS

The duty of reciprocal good faith also obtains as the fundamental principle in contractual relationships.[67] Conflicting interests may tempt the contracting parties to mutual deception, but such impulses are held in check not only in morality but also in law, which declares void (more exactly, voidable) any dealings tainted by fraud. The oft-cited maxim "circumvenire se invicem naturaliter licet contrahentibus" is to be restrictively interpreted;[68] in its generality it is very far from reflecting the actual rules of either Roman or modern law. Modifying the ancient, strict *ius civile*, the Roman praetor introduced measures against fraud, in the *actio* and the *exceptio doli*, and such measures were further perfected by the jurists. In the contract of sale the rule that came to prevail was that the seller was liable if in bad faith he suppressed the defects of the thing sold.[69] Cicero's treatment of the topic in *De Officiis* shows the progress made by Roman jurisprudence.[70]

In this matter, as in others, we must not confuse the rules of law with those of morality, even though they share the same root. Morality, referring directly to the conscience of the subject, repudiates lying as such. The aim of law is to establish limits in interpersonal relationships; law thus forbids only such departures from the truth as result in injury and offense to others. In the new Italian Civil Code fraud is cause for annulment of a contract when the deception employed by the one party is such that, had it not been for the deception, the other party would not have entered into the contract. If the deception were not such as to determine consent, the contract is valid, even though without the deception it would have been concluded on different terms. But in such an event the party in bad faith is liable for damages.[71] It is worth noting that fraud within the meaning of the section does not require the use of words; it may consist in keeping silent concerning that which should have been disclosed.[72]

This does not mean that all reticence is unlawful and that, for instance, the seller must point out the less advantageous aspects of his wares.[73] As always in law, it is a question of limits. Exaggerated praise of one's wares is not fraud in law, nor are the flattery and suggestions of commercial publicity, nor, in general, are such artifices as could not deceive a person of ordinary prudence. Law does not protect foolishness beyond a certain point, and it presupposes in those whom it protects a certain degree of diligence. No legal system could survive without some co-operation from the intelligence of individuals. The co-operation required may, however, vary a great deal, since it necessarily depends on the age, circumstances and education of the persons concerned. Where normal capacity is entirely lacking, as with young children or the insane, legal protection takes the form of recognizing their incapacity and therefore their inability to bind themselves. In other cases it opens the way for the investigation of possible defects of consent.

The battle against bad faith develops in various ways in the different fields of law and in different historical epochs. The development which took place in Roman law, particularly regarding the law of contract, is characteristic. In accord with the principles of Christianity, which influenced both Roman law and all later systems, canon law attributed great importance to the idea of good faith.[74] One may say that the advance of law is shown by its increasing regard for the fundamental duty of honesty, especially in contracts. Examples appear both in legislation and judicial interpretation, wherein we can see increasing preoccupation with what Ripert has called "the moralization of contracts."[75]

Abuses in this matter have occurred in every age,[76] and the continuous efforts of both legislation and jurisprudence to eradicate them suffice to indicate the gravity of this chronic social evil. In a time not far distant from our own, the growth of commercial competition and a relaxation of ethical conscience connected with the prevailing materialistic and utilitarian opinions increased the frequency of such abuses. Herbert Spencer, in an essay in the *Westminster Review* in 1859,[77] sketched from factual evidence a gloomy picture of the deceptions practiced by merchants. He attributed them to an exaggerated esteem of and desire for wealth. The evil was so widespread that in certain branches of trade even upright men could hardly avoid it, since they had to meet the competition of the less scrupulous. The argument was: "The honest man must fail. Deceit, within limits, is the lesser evil." In 1893 the *Economic Review* published an essay on the same theme,[78] citing cases where shop assistants had been dismissed because they would not lie to the customers, and giving the answers of businessmen to such questions as: "Is it permissible to deceive the public as to the true quality of merchandise? Is it difficult to apply the principles of truth and justice in business?" The answers revealed all too clearly (as Sraffa observed) that "business men, relying on the convenient, and brutishly interpreted, theory of the struggle for existence, tend to justify, as a necessity, deception, dissimulation and lying in their relationships with customers."[79] Other jurists spoke out against such methods. Brugi, for instance, wrote: "We have today come to admit, particularly in commercial contracts, a deplorably wide range for untrue assertions which would fall into the Roman category of *dolus malus*."[80]

A salutary reaction against such abuses was not long in appearing, and in recent decades both law and public opinion have treated with increasing rigor infractions of the fundamental principles of ethics which had previously been wrongly tolerated, as if these principles were not valid in law as well.[81] Such principles have inspired the most recent Italian civil and criminal laws for the protection of industrial property and inventions from dishonest competition and fraud. They are laws which are broad in their terms and severe in their sanctions, and they are applied daily in judicial decisions which emphasize their real significance and fulfill the judicial duty of harmonizing law with morality.[82] Professional associations, too, by exercising their disciplinary powers are co-operating to the same end.

VII.—CRIMES OF DISHONESTY

We shall not enter that vast field in which offenses against truth assume their gravest forms, such as crimes against public faith, swindling, and the like. What we have said elsewhere is sufficient for condemning *a fortiori* such acts. In these cases there is not only conscious alteration of the truth and, according to the canon law definition of *dolus*, a "deliberata voluntas violandi legem" (*Cod. iur. can.*, 2200), but actually a "machinatio ad circumveniendum, fallendum, decipiendum aliquem adhibita." Here we meet wrong in a typically satanic form, which neither law nor upright conscience can justify or pardon, that fraud which, in Dante's phrase, "taints the whole world."[83] Whether the penalties hitherto imposed for such crimes are really just and adequate, whether they could not be replaced or reinforced by other provisions more effective for the reparation of the social and individual harm inflicted, is a question beyond the limits of the present discussion; it involves the foundation of punishment in general.[84] In such crimes the wickedness of the intention is often accompanied by a remarkable expenditure of intelligence. If we contemplate the ingenuity of counterfeiters or the complicated schemes of certain swindlers, we can easily accept the statistical evidence that crimes of fraud are more frequent where culture is more developed, while crimes of violence are more characteristic of primitive societies.[85] The development of social life multiplies, if only through improved means of communication, the possibilities of crime in its more refined forms. There is no discovery or invention which has not soon been put to profit for questionable ends. The increase in "crimes of intelligence" is a shadow darkening the development of civilization, and proves that intelligence and culture, unguided by ethics, are not sufficient by themselves.

The motive for fraud is usually the desire for gain (which in turn may arise from various passions) or the desire to free oneself from more or less heavy burdens, such as tax liabilities. When such burdens are felt as excessive, fraud, although still subject to punishment, generally appears more excusable, and persons who would be incapable of other crimes sometimes indulge in crimes of fraud.[86] But even in such cases, where the tax burden may be truly inequitable, there is no ethical justification for fraud. Justification arises only where burdens are imposed by an entirely unlawful authority which is maintaining itself by violence and threats (to the point of extortion and blackmail); here the victim may even defend himself by deception, for it is as licit *repellere vim dolo* as *vim vi.* Thus argued the ancient philosophers in discussing the problem of whether promises made to robbers and pirates are binding.[87]

The study of typical fraudulent criminals shows that in their psyche, besides material interest, another motive is sometimes active: namely, the desire to assert their intellectual superiority over those whom they deceive.[88] With moral restraints removed, the success of the trick brings the trickster a joy (not unmixed with cruelty) similar to that of the hunter who sees the game fall into his trap.[89]

The contest between the evil arts of the impostor and the sincerity of the honest man can be an unequal affair when the latter's good faith has little experience and shrewdness accompanying it. Hence the need of aid and preventive vigilance to protect the inexperienced. According to a widespread belief, every man should be advised to exercise not only prudence and caution but even a certain cunning (*dolus bonus*) as defense against the cunning of others; thus, the proverbs, "A trompeur, trompeur et demi" (cf. "A avocat, avocat et demi"); "Knavery is the best defence against a knave," etc.[90] But these maxims should not be accepted without reservation, because in general it is not permissible to requite evil with evil or to set lies against lies.

VIII.—RECAPITULATION AND CONCLUSIONS

Our summary observations have shown the complexity of the question. Let us recapitulate and clarify the fundamental concepts, so that we may then draw our conclusions.

The divine gift of intelligence distinguishes and ennobles our nature, instilling in us a vocation for truth which is not only an indestructible psychological tendency but an ethical law and a supreme duty. Valid for every man, whatever his station in life or degree of education, is that categorical imperative which Manzoni expressed in the words, "The holy Truth never betray."[91] To serve truth at any cost, to seek it with no matter what toil, to love it for itself and not for the advantages it may bring—that is our mission, and in fulfilling it we feel we are transcending the miseries of our ephemeral life, entering the eternal kingdom of the Absolute, and so making ourselves worthy of the immortal stamp within us.[92]

From this ethical principle issue many consequences, including the duties to cultivate and develop our intellective faculties, and to recognize in others the spirituality which is theirs, and the right to demand equal recognition from them.

To live with truth and according to truth means, in substance, to respect the Spirit. We must continually keep in mind this fundamental rule and its derivatives as a guide and criterion for action. But are these sufficient to indicate clearly what is permissible and obligatory for each man? If we could answer "yes," the ethical problems, both theoretical and practical, with which life continually confronts us would not be so delicate or so difficult.

The respect owed truth clearly excludes lying. But it does not exclude silence,[93] which often indicates greater virtue than speech, even as a means of searching for truth in our own consciousness, since "in interiore homine habitat veritas."[94] We should regard truth as a goal to be attained by intense and constant study rather than as a possession to be passively retained. We should strive towards the Absolute but not regard as absolute our every state of mind or opinion. Granted that he who sincerely expresses a feeling or thought of his own does not sin against truth, since (as St. Augustine wrote) "non omnis qui falsum dicit mentitur si credit aut opinat verum esse quod dicit,"[95] but this simply proves that *non mentiri* is not enough and that it must be supplemented by the requirement of consideration and reflection, and hence a certain discretion in speech.[96]

Men are naturally reluctant to impart truths regarding themselves which they fear may injure their reputation or their interests,[97] but they are less circumspect regarding the affairs of others. It is not easy to follow the right course in either case, but, speaking generally, to correct these egoistic tendencies, ethics would in the first case counsel frankness tempered by prudence and in the second case reserve, which might even go as far as secrecy.

The most difficult questions arise in the case of relationships with persons who do not observe the same fundamental rule of respect for truth. May cunning be opposed to cunning and deceit to deceit? Can such means be employed not only against *dolus* but against violence and threats by the other side? The answer cannot be absolutely negative, just as the use of force in legitimate defense is not to be condemned outright, but the use of such means must be held strictly within the limits necessary for the just protection of one's own rights or those of others (*moderamen inculpatae tutelae*). Not even in war, where deception is permissible, can we admit that it should go to the point of fraud or perfidy. Such means degrade their user. In every contest an open defense is often the most effective, and human ingenuity has a vast field in which to exercise itself—allowing for concealment in certain cases—without tainting itself with treachery. In the last resort, it is better to succumb in purity and with honor than to survive at the price of guilt and shame.

The ancient (but non-Roman) maxim, *non servanti fidem* (or *fidem frangenti*) *fides non est servanda,*[98] cannot be accepted as generally valid,[99] except insofar as it may be reduced to the much simpler maxim, *inadimplenti non est adimplendum.*[100] He who does not fulfill an obligation cannot claim fulfillment from the other party, but this does not imply a reciprocal lack of faith, because the breach is on one side only—the other cannot break what is already broken. The reason for this rule is objective rather than subjective and the rule does not necessarily presuppose the bad faith of the party who has not fulfilled his obligation.

With some reason, it has been asserted that whoever acts in a certain way toward others legitimizes, under similar circumstances, an equal action by them toward him. But this juridical theorem (to which Kant attributed the same validity as to the laws of mechanics)[101] is limited in the field of law in that lawfulness and unlawfulness are determined in relation to the conditions appropriate for each person, and, as these conditions are almost always different, the equation in practice loses much of its value. Moreover, it is not true that law always allows unlawfulness to be met by unlawfulness (which would thereby cease to be unlawful). He who commits a crime may not have, in the abstract, the right to complain if the same crime be committed against him, but this subjective consideration does not objectively justify (save in special cases) the transgression of legal rules, even against the one who has transgressed them. Moreover, not all that is allowed by law is equally allowed by morality, which as a rule forbids returning evil for evil.

Still less can we approve those doctrines which advise men in general, and politicians and diplomats in particular, to use cunning or plain deceit to attain success for their plans. Machiavelli is the typical example, but he had precursors among the ancients[102] and has had followers in quite recent times.[103] To Louis XI of France is attributed the maxim, *Qui nescit dissimulare, nescit regnare.* (Actually it is probably of earlier origin and it certainly has counterparts in many languages.)[104] Against this teaching, which would exempt rulers from the obligation of fidelity, it has been rightly observed that because of their greater dignity this obligation is even more incumbent on them than on any other person. "Fidem si grave est privatis fallere gravius est Principi ratione dignitatis."[105]

Violation of the fundamental laws of ethics is not legitimized because it has some supposed public interest as its goal. Devious paths rarely lead to high goals and the apparent success of deceitful arts is almost always illusory and transient. States are maintained and become enduringly great through the moral virtues of the governors and the governed. Duplicity and corruption may enjoy brief triumphs but in the long run they lead to certain ruin. There is no real discord between politics and morality,[106] because morality, although opposed to fraud and lying, recognizes shrewdness as a virtue necessary in private affairs and still more in affairs of State.

There are many obstacles in the path of truth, and the problem remains difficult even if we set aside its epistemological and ontological aspects (*quid est veritas*?) and consider only, or mainly, its moral and juridical aspect. By this we refer not so much to the objective value of our cognitions as to the power of communicating to others that which we believe to be true. Spinoza's "in libera republica unicuique et sentire quae velit, et quae sentiat dicere licere"[107] meets an aspiration of our mind but in its absoluteness it is not accepted by any legal system. In developing his notion, Spinoza himself recognized the legitimacy of certain limitations. Criticism of unjust laws and proposals for their repeal should be permitted to citizens, but no State allows insults to magistrates and incitements to violation of the laws so long as these remain in force.

There are, however, so many intermediate forms and degrees, not easy to define, between simple criticism and instigation to rebellion, between absolute license and extreme severity, that the field for dispute and for opposing tendencies both in the theory and the practice of politics is a very broad one. There can be and have been errors in both directions, but if we look at political history in general, they have more often consisted in excessive restrictions on the freedom of thought and speech. To win a freedom unfettered by unjust restrictions —when legal action is not possible—history solemnly affirms the natural right of revolution.

In the face of just or unjust checks and impediments which in social life oppose the communication of (what is believed to be) the truth, in the face of the net of lies and deceits which incessantly threatens us, the task of the man who wishes to "live truthfully," as duty commands, is much less simple than it may seem. It involves a struggle which requires firmness and courage. What above all things ennobles a life is to keep faith with the known truth, to profess it without hesitation or compromise—no matter what the temptation to do otherwise —and he who in the last resort will sacrifice his very life in testimony of his faith transcends his mortal nature and attains its highest consecration.

But uprightness of purpose should not be blind. Veracity, like charity, should be illumined by the intellect.[108] When upholding our ideas (better, before upholding them), we should think them through and clarify them, and we should not forget the respect which is owed to the ideas of others when honestly professed. Fanaticism and superstition, the source of many of the most atrocious and bloody crimes of mankind, cannot be justified simply by pleading the good faith of their followers. Our conscience, if we but listen to it, warns us of our own fallibility and we are never quite sincere if we attribute to ourselves an absolute power over our fellow men.

Words spoken rashly or under the influence of passion cause pain and harm not only to ourselves but also to others, and so offend against the laws of charity and justice. The love of truth does not exempt us from observance of these laws; rather does it impose on us respect for them, since they are themselves the most certain and unshakable truths. The love of truth must be strengthened and supported by vigilant reflection and by a measure of self-criticism; only then will it really guide us to the fulfillment of all our duties.

Thus we can overcome and adjust the discord which sometimes arises between sincerity and intelligence. Neither is sufficient in itself. If we were asked whether the polished skill of the swindler were more to be admired than the innocent simplicity of his victim, we should not hesitate for a moment to give first place to ethical value and put moral excellence above intellectual (for, as Kant recognized, the only absolutely good thing in the world is the good will),[109] but the antithesis between the two terms is largely fictitious, and the conflicts between them are sporadic and unessential. The powers of heart and intellect are profoundly linked and cannot, save briefly, be developed separately. Wickedness is at bottom a sort of foolishness and goodness a form of intelligence. The so-called inventions of fraudulent men are but petty applications of the great inventions of others. The mind, in order to create, has need of that serenity which is produced only by the loftiness and purity of the aim to which it is directed. "Les grandes pensées viennent du coeur."[110] Scientific discoveries have commonly been made by those who were exploring the secrets of nature for the good of all and not for the purpose of deceiving their neighbors. Only ideas springing from disinterested love, not subtle trickeries, have brought into the world great and lasting things and supported humanity on its weary road.

The same conclusion presents itself in the oft-discussed relationship between culture and morality. Education alone is not enough to guide the will rightly, and where the will is evilly disposed or dominated by passion, education can even facilitate the execution of evil schemes.[111] Some crimes are committed only by persons of a certain degree of education. The opinion that vice and crime depend solely upon ignorance (*omnis peccans est ignorans*), literally interpreted, is untrue; but it becomes true in a deeper sense if ignorance is taken to mean the lack of that spiritual light which cannot be automatically produced by a superficial culture or a smattering of school-learning and which is often seen in persons of little education. The ways of Heaven, as Descartes observed, are open to the unlearned.[112]

Here too, reality is complex, and deviations and irregularities are always possible. Generally speaking, however, education is not only directly opposed to those forms of aberration or delinquence which are founded on prejudice and superstition; it also corresponds to and is accompanied by moral progress.[113] The methodical application of the mind to the knowledge of truth is also a means of purifying the spirit. Therefore constancy in the search for truth is held to be a virtue in itself, and if we look, not at the wiseacres or the half-educated, who have ill digested the little they have learned and are often presumptuous and importunate, but rather at the truly great scholars, we rarely find them lacking in modesty and humanity.

To ascend from the particular to the universal, from the contingent to the eternal, is the procedure we must follow to fulfill our mission in conformity with the true nature of our being. This applies both to knowledge (science and philosophy) and to action (morality and law). To live in eternity, *habitare mente in coelestibus* (in the beautiful words of the liturgy), is the final goal in which all the aspirations of the intellect and the heart are satisfied, since in the end (to paraphrase Vico) *verum et bonum convertuntur.*

(Dedicated to Roscoe Pound, 1967)

NOTES

1. ST. THOMAS, *Summa Theol.*, 1a, q. XVI, art. I; q. XXI, art. 2; *ibid.*, 2a 2ae, q. VIII, art. 1.

2. H. TAINE, *De l'intelligence* (Paris, 1870; 11 éd. 1906).

3. A. BAIN, *Mental and Moral Science*, P. I (London, 1884), p. 2.

4. *Summa Theol.*, 1a, q. LXXIX, art. 10.

5. BOETHIUS, *De consolatione philosophiae*, V; cf. ST. THOMAS, *loc. cit.*, ad sec.

6. DESCARTES, *Méditation seconde* (*Oeuvres*, 1904, vol. IX), p. 22.

7. M. MAETERLINCK, *L'Intelligence des fleurs* (Paris, 1915), p. 52. According to BERGSON, we should admit the existence of a "conscience végétale," albeit "endormie" (*L'évolution créatrice* [19 éd., Paris, 1916, p. 122]). A. SGANDURRA,

L'anima delle piante (Genova, 1941) and G. BONI, *L'essere nella spontaneità creativa e nella riflessione razionale* (Roma, 1953), p. 573 *et seq.*, also speak of "intelligence in vegetables."

8. On this almost all the greater naturalists agree. Cf. the botanist P. BACCARINI, in "La Lettura," XIII, 1913, pp. 1111-1116; he admits, however, that "all the development and all the acts of plants are perfectly fitted to their purpose, as are those of animals." On the analogies between vegetable and animal life, see also G. HABERLANDT, *Ueber Bewegung und Empfindung im Pflanzenreich* (in "Scientia," II, vol. III, 1908, pp. 290-300); cf. BERGSON, cit. *supra* n. 7, p. 115 *et seq.* Among the great naturalists, perhaps only F. DELPINO attributed to plants psychic faculties, using the term in a very wide sense (see his lecture: *Il passato, il presente e l'avvenire della Psicologia*, in "Ann. della R. Univ. di Bologna," 1888-89, esp. p. 42 *et seq.*). A certain *rapprochement* among the various realms of nature, in the direction of a general psychism, is suggested also by the investigations of the Indian scholar J. C. BOSE, *Response in the living and non-living* (2 ed., London, 1910). L. CIPRIANI has similarly maintained that "the study of plants reveals, no less than the study of animals, the essential characteristics of biological psychism" (*Psicobiologia: storia e dottrina*, in "Parapsicologia," II, 1956 No. 1, p. 38).

9. SPINOZA, *Ethica*, P. II, Prop. VII.

10. "La verite générale et abstraite est le plus précieux de tous les biens: sans elle l'homme est aveugle; elle est l'oeil de la raison. C'est par elle que l'homme apprend à se conduire, à être ce qu'il doit être, à faire ce qu'il doit faire, à tendre à sa véritable fin." ROUSSEAU, *Les rêveries du promeneur solitaire*, Quatrième promenade (*Oeuvres compl.*, Paris, 1853, T. I, p. 417). "To know truth and not make one's actions conform to it is a crime which heaven and earth condemn." MAZZINI, *Doveri dell'uomo*, § I (in *Scritti ed. e ined.,* ed. Daelli, XVIII, p. 5). "Truth is the beginning of morality." ROSMINI, *Principi della scienza morale*, C. V, art. V (in *Op. di Fil. mor.*, I, Milano, 1837, p. 100).

11. JUVENAL, *Sat.* IV, 91. ROUSSEAU adopted this maxim as his motto, though he confessed that he never succeeded in living up to it (see *op. cit. supra*). According to FICHTE, the scientist who is conscious of his mission must be able to say to himself: "Ich bin ein Priester der Wahrheit; ich habe mich verbindlich gemacht, alles für sie zu thun und zu wagen und zu leiden" (*Ueber die Bestimmung des Gelehrten*, Vierte Vorlesung).

12. Even among primitive peoples, the duty of not telling lies is generally felt and, as a rule, respected; lying and bad faith are al-

lowed by some peoples only in particular cases, especially in relations with outsiders. See E. WESTERMARCK, *The Origin and Development of the Moral Ideas*, II (2 ed., London, 1917) chs. XXX-XXXI, pp. 72-136. JHERING's assertion that falsehood came before truth (*Der Zweck im Recht*, 4 Aufl., Leipzig, 1904-5, II Bd., p. 477) is a paradox which conflicts with all the data of psychology and history, and with J.'s own doctrine. See *infra*, n. 15.

13. *Exodus*, 20, 16. Cf. *Psalms* 5, 6; *Prov.*, 12, 22; *Ecclesiasticus*, 20, 26 *et seq.*

14. *Summa Theol.*, 2a 2ae, q. CIX, art. 1 and 3.

15. *Ibid.*, art. 3, ad 1. See also 2a 2ae, q. LXXX, art. un., c: "Ad hoc debitum pertinet quod homo talem se exhibeat alteri in verbis et factis, qualis est. Et ideo adjungitur justitiae veritas." This concept seems to be the basis of the maxim "pacta sunt servanda." Cf. CICERO, *De off.*, I, C. 7 ("Fundamentum autem est iustitiae fides, id est dictorum conventorumque constantia et veritas") and GROTIUS, *De jure belli ac pacis*, Proleg. § 15 and L. II, C. XI, §§ 1-4. We recall MONTAIGNE, *Essais*, L. I, ch. IX ("Nous ne sommes hommes, et nous ne tenons les uns aux autres, que par la parole" [This sentence first appears in the 1588 edition of the *Essais*.]) and L. II, ch. XVIII ("Le premier trait de la corruption des moeurs, c'est le banissement de la vérité") and KANT's doctrine of the impossibility of erecting falsehood into a universal rule (*Grundlegung zur Metaphysik der Sitten*, II Abschn., ed. Vorländer, p. 46; cf. I Abschn., p. 21 *et seq.*). G. D. ROMAGNOSI (*Instituzioni di civile Filosofia ossia di Giurisprudenza teorica*, in *Op.*, ed. De Giorgi, III, P. II, § 2973, p. 1746) insisted on the law of "reciprocal exercise of veracity and loyalty." L. TAPARELLI (*Saggio teoretico di Diritto appoggiato sul fatto,* 4 ed., Roma, 1928, I, § 366 and cf. § 370) says that the duty of veracity is "the first external bond of society," while lying "uproots every seed of society, making impossible the co-operation of minds." The fundamental importance of veracity as a condition of social life is recognized even by those who maintain a relative, rather than an absolute, ethic, e.g. JHERING, *Der Zweck im Recht*, *cit.*, II Bd., p. 472 *et seq.*

16. ST. AUGUSTINE, *Contra mendacium*, C. VII, 18.

17. PASCAL, *Lettres à un provincial*, XI, in *Oeuvres*, Paris, 1877, T. I, p. 113.

18. As was recognized by the Pythagoreans: Μὴ εἶναι πρὸς πάντας πάντα ῥητά. Cf. G. TAURO, *Il silenzio e l'educazione dello spirito* (Milano, 1922), p. 275.

19. "Veritas odium parit," TERENCE, *Andria*, I, 1, 68. Cf. PASCAL (*Pensées*, Art. II [V], 8): "Dire la vérité est utile à celui à qui on la dit, mais désavantageux à ceux qui la disent, parce qu'ils se font haïr." LEOPARDI (*Pensieri*, I, in *Op*., ed. Le Monnier, vol. II, p. 109) bitterly noted that "the good and generous are hated, because they are usually sincere and call things by their right names." ERASMUS in his *Praise of Folly* (*Stultitiae Laus*, 1511) observed that truth is hateful to all, and especially to princes, who for that reason prefer the company of flatterers and fools to that of philosophers.

20. G. DELLA CASA, in chapter XI of his famous *Galateo* (1554; ed. Firenze, 1940, p. 43; cf. p. 77) recommends that one should not speak of "things very contrary to the time and to the persons who are listening, even of things which, in themselves and said at the proper time, would be good and sacred." He advises that "one should defer to the opinion of others in things which matter little." These are precepts less noble than convenient and conducive to quiet living; to conceal one's own thought and one's dissent may often be permissible, but sometimes it amounts to deceit and cowardice. Yet Della Casa (ch. XIII) took a stand against lying, where other writers, especially in the 17th century, permitted dissimulation and hypocrisy, according to the maxim: "Qui nescit fingere, nescit vivere." See, e.g., T. ACCETTO, *Della dissimulazione onesta*, 1641, C.V (ed. Firenze, 1943, p. 61): "It is sometimes allowed to change cloaks . . . not in order to inflict but in order not to suffer harm." Accetto is one of the more moderate of these writers, in that he tries to reconcile feigning with honesty. On Della Casa and Accetto, see the Introductions by P. PANCRAZI and G. BELLONCI to the editions cited; see also B. CROCE and S. CARAMELLA, *Politici e moralisti del seicento* (Bari, 1930), esp. p. 301 *et seq*.; cf. A. NICEFORO, *L'io profondo e le sue maschere* (Milano, 1949), esp. p. 42 *et seq*.

Admirable in their psychological subtlety, but not wholly worthy of ethical approval, are the precepts of B. GRACIAN (*Oraculo manual y arte de prudencia*, 1647) and those attributed to Cardinal MAZARIN, *Epilogo de' dogmi politici* (printed several times in the 17th century and later, but of doubtful authenticity). These, especially the latter, discuss the art of simulation and dissimulation, which is to be applied, according to one of the editors (ed. Colonia, 1695, p. 20), "not to deceive others, but to forestall their deceits, and to be used as an antidote against the poison of fraud."

Although the prevalent teaching of the 16th and 17th centuries admitted the use of dissimulation and lying to some extent, there were opinions to the contrary, sometimes expressed in the form of paradox. Thus, M. ROSEO in *Instituzione del principe Cristiano* (1543; based on A. DE GUEVARA, *Relox de los principes*, 1529), in a fantastic account of the life of the Garamantes, attributes to them the law "that every person shall speak the truth, and one caught in a lie, even if innocent of any other fault, shall be beheaded, because one liar is enough to ruin a whole people." Cf. C. CURCIO, *Utopisti italiani del cinquecento*, Roma, 1944, pp. 35-56.

21. The love of truth needs courage and vigor, if truth is to be spread among men. "It is an injury to truth when one hides it, in order to avoid trouble and conflict, when one who should speak remains silent and so favors the triumph of iniquity and injustice." A. ODDONE, *La verità nella carità*, in "Civiltà cattolica," A. 93, Vol. I, 1942, pp. 131-140.

22. On the obligation to keep secrets in general, see D. SOTO, *De ratione tegendi et detegendi secretum*, ed. Brixiae, 1582, where the theme is treated not only in its theological aspect but with psychological and practical considerations, e.g. (p. 329): "Fide secretorum de medio sublata, cessarent commoditates plurimae amicitiae: ut puta, consilia, et solatia, quae amici ab amicis secreto petunt." Cf. also A. VERMEERSCH, *Theologiae moralis principia* (3 ed., Romae, 1937), T. II, p. 629 *et seq.*

23. Professional secrecy is legally protected even in judicial proceedings (see *infra*, § V). The secrecy of letters and all other communications is, subject to limitations, declared inviolable by the Italian Constitution, art. 15. Disclosure of secrets in certain cases can constitute a criminal offense: Ital. Penal Code, arts. 616-623. Cf. A. CRESPI, *La tutela penale del segreto* (Palermo, 1952) and A. DE CUPIS, *I diritti della personalità* (Milano, 1950), p. 122 *et seq.*

24. Doctors do not hold themselves bound to impart an unfavorable prognosis to their patient, especially when the knowledge might weaken his power of resistance. See N. FIESSINGER, *Guida al ragionamento in Medicina* (Milano, 1947), who refers particularly to "anxious, obsessional or suggestionable persons." L. SCREMIN, *Appunti di morale professionale per i medici* (2 ed., Roma, 1934), p. 27, makes similar distinctions. Some would permit the use of the "method of suggestion," e.g. the administration of a *placebo* to raise the patient's morale.

On charity as "the nucleus or the substance of medical ethics," see G. CORONEDI, *Qualche spunto di Morale medica professionale* (in the vol. *La moralità e le professioni*, Firenze, 1934, pp.

101-114). Cf. D. R. PERETTI GRIVA, *Errores medicorum terra tegit* (in "Difesa sociale," A. XXXIII, 1954, III, pp. 41-48); H. THIELICKE, *Der Arzt und die Wahrheit* (in "Universitas," XII, 1957, Heft 5).

The code of medical ethics (*Codice di Deontologia medica*) approved in 1956 by the Italian national federation of medical associations provides (art. 52) that "a grave prognosis may be withheld from the patient, but not from his family, which, if there is danger of death, must be given timely warning, in case religious assistance be desired."

25. MATT., 7, 6; ST. THOMAS, *Summa Theol.*, 2a 2ae, q. XL, art. 3.

26. ST. AUGUSTINE, *De mendacio*, C. X, 17.

27. *Summa Theol.*, 2a 2ae, q. CX, arts. 3 and 4.

28. M. MASSIMI, *La nostra legge* (Roma, 1937), p. 229.

29. MASSIMI, *loc. cit.* Cf. ST. ALFONSO DE'LIGUORI, *Theologia moralis, Tract. de VIII Decalogi Praecepto*, C. I, art. 2 (in 4 ed. by Ninzatti, Torino, 1887, T. I, pp. 373-376), who seems to go too far in allowing the use of such an expedient; C. PESCH, *De virtutibus moralibus* (*Praelectiones dogmaticae*, T. IX, 2 ed., Frib. Bris., 1902), p. 132 *et seq.*; V. CATHREIN, *Filosofia morale* (2 Ital. ed., Firenze, 1913-20), Vol. II, pp. 105-108; A. VERMEERSCH, *Theologiae moralis principia, ed. cit.*, II, p. 634 *et seq.*; T. RAYNAUD, *De virtute morali, cum mendacio et locutionibus aequivocis ac mente restrictis comparata*, in Appendix to L. LESSIUS, *De justitia aliisque virtutibus morum*, ed. Lugduni, 1630, pp. 667-800.

30. MASSIMI, *loc. cit. supra.* Cf. BACON, *Essays or Counsels Civil and Moral*, § VI, in *Philos. Works*, London, 1905, p. 741 *et seq.*: "No man can be secret except he give himself a little scope for dissimulation"; cf. *ibid.* § 1, p. 736.

31. "Omnes restrictiones sunt pro viribus vitandae." D. M. PRÜMMER, *Vademecum Theologiae moralis*, 4 ed., Frib. Bris., 1934, n. 293. GROTIUS, *De jure belli ac pacis*, III, C. I, § 17, 3, declared himself against mental restrictions.

32. ARISTOTLE, *Eth. Nic.*, IV, 7, 6-8. Cf. various maxims *apud* STOBAEUM, *Sentent.*, XII. Fundamental on this topic are ST. AUGUSTINE, *De mendacio* and ST. THOMAS, *S. Theol.*, 2a 2ae, q. CIX-CXIII, *cit. supra.* See also: F. SUAREZ, *De legibus ac Deo legislatore*, II, C. XVI, § 9; L. LESSIUS *De justitia* (*cit.*), II, C. 47, Dub. 6; C. BILLUART, *Tractatus de religione et vitiis oppositis*, in *Summa Summae S. Thomae*, Diss. VII, Art. I-III, etc. Among moderns, see: F. PAULSEN, *System der Ethik* (7

Aufl., Stuttgart, 1906), II, pp. 201-250; V. CATHREIN, *Filosofia morale* (*ed. cit.*) I, pp. 391-392, II, pp. 92-108); and esp. A. VERMEERSCH, *De mendacio et necessitatibus commercii humani* (in "Gregorianum," A. I, 1920, pp. 11-40 and 425-474); O. LIPMANN, P. PLAUT and others in *Die Lüge in psychologischer* (etc.) *Betrachtung* (Leipzig, 1927); J. CREUSEN, *Le mensonge et les mensonges* (in "Nouv. Rev. Théologique"), T. 55, 1928, pp. 50-65); A. KERN, *Die Lüge* (Graz, 1930); J. VERNHES, *Le mensonge* (in "Rev. Apologétique," T. LXIII, 1936, pp. 403-415); M. LEDRUS, *De mendacio* (Roma 1943); W. BECKER, Der Tatbestand der Lüge (Tübingen, 1948); K. HÖRMANN, *Wahrheit und Lüge* (Wien, 1953). Under the psychological aspect, see also: G.-L. DUPRAT, *Le mensonge-Étude de Psychosociologie pathologique et normale* (Paris, 1903); L. BATTISTELLI, *La bugia nei normali, nei criminali, nei folli* (Bari, 1922; 2 ed., 1923); *id.*, *La bugia in Tribunale* (Milano, 1954); V. JANKÉLÉVITCH, *Le mensonge* (in "Rev. de Métaphysique et de Morale," A. 47, N. 1, Jan. 1940, pp. 37-61); M. FAVILLI, *La menzogna* (Firenze, 1945); A. NICEFORO, *L'io profondo e le sue maschere*, *cit.*, p. 39 *et seq.*

33. So PLUTARCH ("On the Education of Children," C. XIV, *ad fin.*, in *Moralia*, ed. Didot, Vol. I, p. 13) rightly said that "it is a holy thing to accustom children to speak the truth, for lying is a slavish, hateful and unpardonable thing." According to C. P. DUCLOS (*Considérations sur les moeurs de ce siècle*, 1751, ch. III, in the coll. *Moralistes français*, Paris, 1838, p. 682 *et seq.*), certain false "politesses" are a kind of "dissimulation permise," as also are exaggerated praises which no one really believes. Yet even these, although of little moment, are not to be approved. VERMEERSCH (*Theol. mor. princ.*, *cit.*, II, p. 636) well says: "Deploranda facilitate multiplicantur hodie mendacia officiosa . . . His artibus puerilis institutio corrumpitur et propriae dignitatis sensus minuitur." See also M. TIÈCHE, *Vivere* (Firenze, 1951), p. 60 *et seq.*

34. SCHOPENHAUER (*Ueber die Grundlage der Moral*, § 17) deduces, from the concept of legitimate defense, "das Recht zur Lüge," in all cases where it would be lawful to use force instead of falsehood. But he goes further, and asserts the lawfulness of lying to defend oneself not from serious threat but from mere unjustifiable curiosity ("Nothwehr gegen unbefugte Neugier"). This seems ethically untenable.

35. Cf. the question whether it is permissible, especially for the police, to use tricks to uncover crimes and find their authors.

Within limits, when such means are employed solely for the discovery of the truth and are not accompanied by physical or mental violence, they may be held legitimate, on the basis of the analogy above. No one claims that a police detective must reveal himself as such. Other common deceptions are less justifiable, e.g., falsely inducing a suspect to believe that a confederate has confessed or has accused him; yet such deceptions are not altogether to be excluded in particular cases, provided always that they do not develop into improper coercion. Absolutely unallowable are all forms of pressure and torture, including mental, directed to extorting confessions, especially since confessions thus obtained are often not true. Cf. E. ALTAVILLA, *Psicologia giudiziaria* (4 ed., Torino, 1955), Vol. I, p. 361 *et seq.*

36. We may recall the lines of ARIOSTO, *Orlando furioso*, Canto IV, 1-8.

37. We must thus definitely reject the saying of VOLTAIRE, that "Le mensonge n'est un vice que quand il fait du mal; c'est une très grande vertu, quand il fait du bien" (*Lettre à M. Thiriot*, 21 Oct. 1736; in *Oeuvres*, éd. Beuchot, T. LII, Paris, 1830, p. 326). The same letter (p. 327) contains the notorious "Mentez, mes amis, mentez," which, however, seems to refer to a particular case in which V. recommended the use even of lying in order to preserve a secret.

Similar, and equally unacceptable, is BENTHAM's doctrine that truth has value only in so far as it is useful: "Les vérités nuisibles, celles qui créent des peines et détruisent les plaisirs, doivent être supprimées" (*Déontologie ou Science de la Morale*, Paris, 1834, Vol. II, p. 83). The suppression of truth is in itself a greater evil than any other, because without truth there is neither morality nor justice. Properly regarded, the above-noted exceptions are only apparent; they are opposed not to truth but to its disregard and abuse. J. S. MILL, although starting from the same principles as Bentham, arrived at an explicit condemnation of lying, with comments practically identical with those of the writers who attribute to truth an absolute value (*Utilitarianism*, ch. II). H. SIDGWICK (*The Methods of Ethics*, 6 ed., London, 1901, Bk. III, ch. VII) acutely discusses various questions concerning the duty of truthfulness and its limits, but, by his own admission, reaches no very definite conclusions.

38. KANT firmly declared against the admissibility of lying, even for humanitarian ends (*Ueber ein vermeintes Recht, aus Menschenliebe zu lügen*, 1797; in *Kleinere Schriften*, ed. Kirchmann, I. pp. 207-215). K.'s extreme strictness led him to maintain that we

ought to tell the truth even to a murderer who asks us if our friend, whom he is seeking to kill, has taken refuge with us. But K.'s proof, although coherent with his system, is unconvincing for the reasons indicated in our text. Even in K.'s own time, his teaching on this point was criticized, see e.g., J. C. MEISTER, *Lehrbuch des Natur-Rechtes* (Frankfurt, 1809), §§ 206-207. ROSMINI (*Filosofia del diritto*, 2 ed., Intra, 1865, Vol. I, p. 237 *et seq.*) inclines to a different and more acceptable opinion, although he does not express it very exactly. Definitely opposed to the Kantian doctrine are, *inter alios*, J. H. v. KIRCHMANN (*Erläuterungen zur Nik. Eth. des Aristoteles*, Leipzig, 1876, p. 121) and J. KOHLER (*Shakespeare vor dem Forum der Jurisprudenz*, 2 Aufl., Berlin, 1919, p. 314 *et seq.*).

On the possibility of permissible deceit, see especially: JHERING, *Der Zweck im Recht*, *cit.* II Bd., p. 457 *et seq.*, 483 *et seq.*; G. MARCHESINI, *I limiti della sincerità* (in "Rivista d'Italia," A. XXVII, Fasc. VIII, 1924, pp. 454-467); B. CROCE, *Dire la verità* (in *Etica e Politica*, Bari, 1931, p. 37 *et seq.*); J. VERNHES, *Le mensonge. Sa nature et sa malice intrinsèque*, *cit.* This last author, although starting from strict theological principles, maintains (p. 409) that "il est possible de tromper positivement le prochain sans le faire injustement"; if he asks us about things which he has no right to know, and, even when he has such a right, if it is in conflict with a higher right. But the first instance would seem to justify silence, not lying; and the second is inaccurately formulated, in that in such cases the conflict is between duties, not between rights. A similar thesis, open to the same objections, has been maintained by W. YUNG (*La vérité et le mensonge dans le droit privé*, in *Droit et Vérité*, Publications de la Faculté de Droit de l'Univ. de Génève, 1946, p. 21). It should be noted that in these discussions the distinction is often not clearly drawn between legal and moral considerations. Thus, e.g., the assertion of a "right to lie" in certain circumstances is taken to imply the moral rightfulness of such a lie and not merely the absence of a legal sanction; and the phrase "right to the truth" is sometimes used where there is a purely moral duty, not legally enforceable.

39. F. PAULSEN, *System der Ethik*, *cit.*, II Bd., p. 213.

40. *Summa theol.*, 2a 2ae, q. XL, art. 3.

41. ST. AUGUSTINE, *Quaest. in Heptateuchum*, L. VI, q. 10.

42. ST. AMBROSE, *De officiis*, I, 29.

43. F. DE VITORIA, *De justitia*, q. 111, art. 1 (ed. Madrid, 1934-35, T. III, p. 243).

44. MACHIAVELLI, *Il Principe*, C. XVIII.

45. *Discorsi sopra la prima Deca. di T. Livio*, L. III, C. 40.

46. A. GENTILI, *De jure belli*, L. II, C. 3.

47. *Ibid.*, C. 3-9. Gentili's discussion was not without influence on GROTIUS, *De jure belli ac pacis*, L. III, C. I; VATTEL, *Le droit des gens*, L. III, C. X; and others.

48. See, e.g., *Hague Convention concerning the Laws and Customs of War on Land* (1907), Regs. Art. 23 and 24 (approved by Italian Royal Decree, 8. 7. 1938).

49. Cf., e.g., P. FAUCHILLE, *Traité de droit international public* (8 éd., Paris, 1921-26), T. II, p. 125 *et seq.*; G. BALLADORE PALLIERI, *La guerra* (Padova, 1935), p. 198 *et seq.*; *id. Diritto bellico* (ed. 1954), p. 175 *et seq.*.

50. Dramatic and artistic fictions, harmless imitations and false statements made merely in jest, where there is no real intent to deceive, are not ethically condemnable, and therefore do not concern us. ST. AUGUSTINE (*De mendacio*, II, 2) makes an exception for games; but elsewhere (*In Psalmum V*, 7) he extends his disapproval even to falsehoods spoken in play or with the aim of helping others. ST. THOMAS (*S. theol.*, 2a 2ae, q. CX, art. 2 and 3), referring to the distinction of *mendacium* into *jocosum*, *officiosum* and *perniciosum* (according to whether it is *causa ludi*, *causa utilitatis* or *causa nocumenti*), notes various degrees of fault according to the various ends; the former two, whose end is not to cause harm, are not mortal sin. Cf. ST. THOMAS, *In tertium librum Sentent. M. Petri Lombardi*, Dist. XXXVIII, q. 1, art. 2. On *mendacium jocosum*, see also M. LEDRUS, *De mendacio*, *cit.*, p. 144 *et seq.*

51. According to VOLTAIRE (*Dictionnaire philos.* s. v. *Lois*, Sect. III), "les lois du jeu sont les seules qui soient partout justes, claires, inviolables, et exécutées." We may admit that the "laws" (better, the "rules") of games are less often violated than other laws; but this is not because they are more just (as V. thought), but because they are valid only for those persons who voluntarily accept them (no one is obliged to play games), whereas civil and criminal laws (and also moral laws) claim the obedience of those whose interest is otherwise and who may therefore be tempted to break them. On the binding nature of the rules of games, cf. J. HUIZINGA, *Homo ludens*, Haarlem, 1938; Eng. tran., London, 1949, but he greatly extends the notion of "games" (cf. his Preface). A similar exaggeration may be noted in G. RENSI, *L'irrazionale, il lavoro, l'amore* (Milano, 1923), pp. 167-172, where all disinterested activities are treated as "games." [The reader may care to speculate on the ethical problems of "gamesmanship" or

"the art of winning games without actually cheating," expounded in *The Theory and Practice of Gamesmanship* (1947) and other diverting writings by STEPHEN POTTER.]

52. ULPIAN in *Dig.* 50, 17, 145.

53. Even in ordinary argument and verbal controversy, the exercise of ability and cleverness must be limited by good faith. He who employs sophisms and other such artifices to confuse the ideas of others shows that he is not aiming at the truth, and he offends both logic and morality. A list of ways, including dishonest ways, to win victory in dispute was compiled by SCHOPENHAUER in one of his lesser and less well-known works (*Eristische Dialektik*), where he expressly declared that he was not concerned whether the victory thus obtained was just or unjust; like the fencing-master who does not care to know which of the parties to a quarrel that precipitated a duel is in the right. The comparison is not particularly exact or convincing, because even in fencing there are "forbidden thrusts," which the combatants must know and avoid. Moreover, while the reason for a duel has nothing to do with the technique of duelling, dialectical tricks enter into the very method of reasoning and disputing. We should therefore conclude that knowledge of sophistic artifices may be useful to put us on our guard against them, but not to furnish us with an example or rule for our own conduct.

54. The distinction between simple *falsiloquium* and *falsiloquium dolosum*, with reference to the distinction between morality and law, is clearly enough drawn by KANT (*Metaphysische Anfangsgründe der Rechtslehre*, Einleitung, Allg. Einteilung der Rechte [ed. Vorländer, Leipzig, 1907], p. 44).

55. On the various types of cases, see L. JOSSERAND, *Le mensonge, la simulation et la dissimulation en tant que facteurs de droit* (in *Evolution et actualités-Conférences de droit civil*, Paris, 1936, pp. 112-134): "Il y a simulation et simulation; les unes sont coupables, d'autres indifférentes, tandis que certaines sont louables et procèdent d'un raffinement de délicatesse" (p. 122). Examples of the last are: donations "disguised" under the form of sale, which are generally allowed by French jurisprudence, save where expressly forbidden by statute; partitions of property "disguised" as compromises of claims; acts of liberality in favor of incestuous or adulterine children, which French jurisprudence allows even beyond the statutory limits, provided the relationship is not expressly stated in the deed of gift.

56. For Italian works discussing the Italian law on this point see n. 58 to the Italian ed. of the present essay (DEL VECCHIO, *Studi sul diritto*, II, p. 207).

57. On this maxim see C. CARDAHI, *L'exécution des conventions immorales et illicites,* (in "Rev. int. de droit comparé," A. III, 1951, pp. 385-411).

58 Cf. n. 50 *supra.*

59. Thus, under the Italian Civil code, art. 9, pseudonyms have legal protection almost on a par with real names.

60. Cf., even for the simile, JHERING, *Geist des röm. Rechts,* III Tr. (4 Aufl., Leipzig, 1888), p. 305 *et. seq.*

61. See, e.g., G. CORNIL, *Réflexions sur le rôle de la fiction dans le droit* (in "Arch. de Phil. du droit et de Sociol. juridique," A. V, 1935, N. 3-4).

62. Among many writings on the concepts mentioned above, see: O.v.BÜLOW, *Civilprozessualische Fiktionen und Wahrheiten* (in "Arch. f. die civilist. Praxis," Bd. 62, 1879, pp. 1-96); R. DEMOGUE, *Les notions fondamentales du droit privé* (Paris, 1911), pp. 238-251; A. LEVI, *La société et l'ordre juridique* (Paris, 1911), pp. 201-244; A. STURM, *Fiktion und Vergleich in der Rechtswissenschaft* (Hannover, 1915); H. A. FISCHER, *Fiktionen und Bilder in der Rechtswissenschaft* (in "Arch. f. die civ. Praxis," Bd. 117, 1919, pp. 143-192); P. KRÜCKMANN, *Wahrheit und Unwahrheit im Recht* (in "Annalen der Philosophie," Bd. I, 1919, pp. 113-190); H. KELSEN, *Zur Theorie der juristischen Fiktionen* (*ibid.,* pp. 630-658); F. GÉNY, *Science et Technique en droit privé positif,* Vol. III (Paris, 1921), pp. 258-447; R. MALLACHOW, *Rechtserkenntnistheorie und Fiktionslehre-Das "Als ob" im Jus* (München, 1922); L. FULLER, *What motives give rise to the historical legal fiction?* (in "Receuil d'études sur les sources du droit en l'honneur de F. Gény," Paris, 1934, T. II, pp. 157-176); R. DEKKERS, *La fiction juridique-Etude de droit romain et de droit comparé* (Paris, 1935); J. DABIN, *La technique de l'élaboration du droit positif* (Bruxelles, 1935), pp. 231-345; J. ESSER, *Wert und Bedeutung der Rechtsfiktion* (Frankfurt a.M., 1940). H. VAIHINGER, in *Die Philosophie des Als ob* (Berlin, 1911), p. 46 *et seq.,* also refers to legal fictions, but improperly extends the notion of fiction to every kind of scientific concept. Thus, all law would be a "fiction," as is indeed asserted, following Vaihinger, by W. STRAUCH, *Die Philosophie des "Als ob" u. die hauptsächlichsten Probleme der Rechtswissenschaft* (*München,* 1923) p. 13 *et. seq.* For criticism, see T. A. CASTIGLIA, *La filosofia dell' "Als ob" nel diritto* (in "Riv. int. di Fil. del dir.", A. VI, 1926, pp. 98-122); E. PROTO, *Finzione e realtà nel diritto* (in "Circolo giurid.," Palermo, A. XXI, 1950, pp. 197-224).

63. On the methods and limitations of ascertaining truth in

court in various legal systems, especially that of Switzerland, see J. GRAVEN, *L'obligation de parler en justice* (in the vol. *Droit et Vérité*, Genève, 1946, pp. 106-157). Cf. in particular on the duties of the parties: G. WURZER, *Die Lüge im Prozesse* (in "Zschr. f. deutschen Zivilprozess," Bd. 48, 1920, pp. 463-508); H. FRITZSCHE, *Wahrheit und Lüge im Zivilprozess* (Zürich, 1921); F. von HIPPEL, *Wahrheitspflicht und Aufklärungspflicht der Parteien im Zivilprozess* (Frankfurt a.M., 1939).

64. There has been much discussion, especially by theologians, and more from the moral than from the legal aspect, of the question whether a person accused of crime has a duty to tell the truth to his judges, when by so doing he will bring about his own condemnation, and whether the transgression of such a duty is a mortal rather than a venial sin. ST. THOMAS (*S. theol.*, 2a 2ae, q. LXIX, art. 1) maintained the affirmative, and has been followed by many writers. Others, however, while accepting in principle the doctrine of St. Thomas, have held that, at least in certain cases, such strictness is "nimis durum," when set against the natural impulse of every one to preserve his own life. Cf. LESSIUS, *De justitia aliisque virtutibus morum*, L. II, C. 31, Dub. 3). St. Thomas himself, when he asserts the existence of the duty, assumes that the trial is a lawful trial, and expressly says that the accused is not bound to reply if the judge questions him on things which he cannot ask him "secundum ordinem juris"; thus he opens the ways to distinctions and reservations (see the full discussion by J. DE LUGO, *De justitia et jure*, Disp. XL, Sect. 1). Some writers have not hesitated here to appeal to the expedient of mental restriction: e.g. LESSIUS, *loc. cit.*, and cf. J. P. GURY, *Compendium Theologiae moralis*, with notes by A. BALLERINI, 6 ed., Roma, 1880, T.I, p. 426.

If we admit that St. Thomas' words, "secundum ordinem juris," may, in a broad sense, refer to natural law when it is confronted by penal laws and procedures that are *absolutely unjust*, we should also allow, as implicit in the right of defense, a dispensation from the duty of veracity even "in foro conscientiae." The question is, moreover, a very serious one, in that it is connected with the much discussed problem of the right of resistance. To arrive at correct solutions, it is necessary to take into account not only general circumstances but the particular circumstances of individual cases. It would seem quite unreasonable to blame (not that any one, so far as we know, has ever done so) the attempt of the hero-patriot Nazario Sauro to escape the gallows by denying his true name before the Austrian military court. [In English (and Scots) law, a person suspected or accused of crime is under no obligation to answer questions or, if he is brought to trial, to give evidence in court. If he chooses to give evidence on oath and knowingly gives false evidence, he is, technically, guilty of perjury; prosecutions for such perjury are, however, rarely brought.]

65. According to ST. THOMAS (*S. Theol.*, 2a 2ae, Q. LXXI, art. 3), the advocate who "scienter injustam causam defendit" commits a grave sin and is bound to make reparation for the harm he has unjustly inflicted on the other party. "Si autem ignoranter injustam causam defendit, putans esse justam, excusatur secundum modum quo ignorantia excusari potest." St. Thomas also considers the case of the advocate who has taken on a case believing it to be just and in the course of the trial discovers it to be unjust; according to St. Thomas, the advocate should abandon the case (but without betraying it to the advantage of the other side) and induce his client to withdraw or to accept a just compromise. These are lofty precepts, but the difficulty of applying them in their entirety is obvious. The theologians themselves admit that the advocate cannot refuse his aid "si causa sit dubia," provided that he advises his client of the uncertainty. This last situation is the most common in practice. Cf. G. PASQUARIELLO, *Questioni morali nell'avvocatura* (Roma, 1934). But we cannot approve the view of A. MAJORANA (*L'arte di parlare in pubblico*, Milano, 1914, p. 388) and others, that advocates, being representatives of the parties, are under a duty to set forth not "the whole absolute truth" but only that "part of the truth" which is in their client's favor. No one requires of advocates (or of judges) "the absolute truth," but one can require that they should not knowingly alter the truth, even by deceitful reticence.

66. Cf. *The Crisis of the Science of Law, infra.* p. 171. On the complex origins of the old reproaches directed against lawyers as a class, see R. v. STINTZING, *Das Sprichwort "Juristen böse Christen"* (etc.) (Bonn, 1875); R. DE MATTEI, *L'esaltazione della Politica* (etc.) (in "Arch. giurid," Vol. CXXXIII, 1946, Fasc. I), esp. p. 21 *et seq.*

67. Thus J. DOMAT (*Les Loix civiles dans leur ordre naturel*, Paris, 1777, T.I, p. xi): "Dans les engagemens volontaires et mutuels, ceux qui traitent ensemble se doivent la sincérité . . . Ainsi le vendeur doit déclarer sincèrement les qualités de la chose qu'il vend."

68. *Dig.*4.4.16.4. But Pomponius here refers only to the price in a sale. On the very limited applicability of the maxim, see GROTIUS. *De jure belli ac pacis*, L.II, C.XII, 26 and PUFEN-

DORF, *De jure naturae et gentium,* L. V,C.III,10. The word "circumvenire" probably does not have the offensive meaning commonly given to it; it can denote (as BARBEYRAC observed in his notes on PUFENDORF) "un artifice innocent, par lequel chacun des contractans tâche de faire son marché aussi avantageusement qu'il lui est possible."

69. On the Roman concept of *bona fides*, see, in addition to the standard works on Roman Law, P. BONFANTE, *Essenza della "bona fides" e suo rapporto colla teorica dell' errore* (in *Scritti giurid. varii*, vol. II, Torino, 1918, pp. 708-747); F. PRINGSHEIM, *Aequitas und bona fides* (in *Conferenze per il XIV centenario delle Pandette*, Milano, 1931, pp. 183-214).

70. CICERO, *De Off.*, III, c. 14-17 (9-12). "Tollendum est igitur ex rebus contrahendis omne mendacium." *Ibid.*, c. 15.

71. There are special rules for contracts of assurance.

72. Cf. N. COVIELLO, *Diritto civile italiano, Parte generale* (2 ed., Milano, 1915), p. 394; G. RIPERT, *La règle morale dans les obligations civiles* (4 éd., Paris, 1949), p. 89.

73. Even for ST. THOMAS (*S. Theol.*, 2a 2ae, q. LXXVII, art. 3 ad 2) "non oportet quod aliquis per praeconem vitium rei vendendae praenuntiet, quia si praediceret vitium, exterrerentur emptores ab emendo." It would be ridiculous to have a crier proclaim "Domum pestilentem vendo": CICERO, *De Off.*, L.III, c. 13 (8). But (cf. Cicero) it would not be permissible to conceal essential defects of the thing which is sold.

74. The monograph of R. TROPLONG, *De l'influence du Christianisme sur le droit civil des Romains* (3 éd., Paris, 1868), although much criticized, is still valuable for its general expositon of the question. Cf. S. RICCOBONO, *L'influenza del Cristianesimo nella codificazione di Giustiniano* (in "Scientia," vol. V, A. III, 1909, N. IX); *id.*, *L'influsso del Cristianesimo sul diritto romano* (in "Atti del congresso int. di diritto romano—Roma, 1933," vol. II, Pavia, 1935). On *bona fides* in canon law, see K. HILDENBRAND, *Geschichte der Bestimmungen des canonischen Rechts über die b.f. bei der Ersitzung u. Klagverjährung* (in "Arch. f. die civil. Praxis," Bd. 36, 1853, pp. 27-49); F. RUFFINI, *La buona fede nel diritto canonico* (Roma, 1944); P. FEDELE, *Il concetto* (Torino, 1892); L. SCAVO LOMBARDO, *Il concetto di buona fede nel diritto canonico* (Roma, 1944); P. FEDELE, *Il concetto di buona fede nel diritto canonico* (in "Ephemerides iuris canonici," A. III, N. 1, 1947, pp. 140-149).

75. G. RIPERT, *La règle morale dans les obligations civiles, cit.*, p. 90.

76. We may recall the considerations advanced by G. FILANGIERI (*La scienza della legislazione*, L. II, C. 23-25) against the "bad faith of traders," and especially against the great number of fraudulent bankruptcies.

77. H. SPENCER, *The Morals of Trade* (in *Essays Scientific, Political and Speculative*, vol. II, London, 1868).

78. J. CARTER, *Commercial Morality* (in "The Economic Review," London, vol. III, 1893, pp. 318-347).

79. A. SRAFFA, *La lotta commerciale* (Pisa, 1894), p. 8.

80. B. BRUGI, *Istituzioni di diritto civile* (4 ed., Milano, 1923), p. 238.

81. On the importance of good faith in law, cf. A. LEVI, *Sul concetto di buona fede* (Perugia, 1912); B. DONATI, *Il primo precetto del diritto*: "*Vivere con onestà* (in "Arch. giur.," vol. XCV, 1926, pp. 157-189); A. VOLANSKY, *Essai d'une définition expressive du droit basée sur l'idée de bonne foi* (Paris, 1930).

82. Italian Civil Code, arts. 2598-2601; Penal Code, arts. 473, 474, 514-517; and the Law on Copyright of 22. 4. 1941, arts. 171-174. To give only one example of judicial decision, the Milan Court of Appeal (5. 5. 1942; reported in "Diritto e pratica commerc.," A. XXI, 1942, II, p. 185) held that the false naming of merchandise gives an action not only to the purchaser but also to any one who has suffered damage through such "unlawful competition," and this in addition to the criminal penalties for fraud.

83. DANTE, *Inf.*, XVII, 3. Among other poetic representations of fraud, we may recall ARIOSTO, *Orlando furioso*, C. XIV, str. 87.

84. Cf. DEL VECCHIO, *Sul fondamento della giustizia penale e sulla riparazione del torto* (in *Studi sul diritto*, I); *id.*, *Justice*, Edinburgh, 1952, Append. I and II.

85. As shown, e.g., by A. BOSCO and G. TARDE, in their studies of comparative criminality.

86. The question "utrum sit licitum defraudare tributa" was discussed by C. BILLUART, *Tractatus de jure et justitia*, Diss. VII, Art. III (ed. Venetiis, 1788, T. II, p. 168 *et seq.*). Among modern writers, P. DE TOURTOULON (*Les trois justices*, Paris, 1933) remarks (p. 230): "Trouver un moyen pour ne pas donner à l'Etat ce qu'il réclame, se soustraire à l'Impôt dans le sens le plus large du mot, est-ce un acte aussi répréhensible que s'approprier la chose d'autrui? On ne le pense pas; personne ne refusera de serrer la main à un fumeur qui aura passé sa provision de cigares en fraude des droits de douane, surtout s'il ne s'est pas fait prendre. Les contrebandiers mêmes jouissent d'une certaine sympathie," and

(p. 233): "La fraude à l'Impôt reste un délit mixte, tenant à la fois du vol et de la désobéissance, ce qui explique le doute qui subsiste dans les consciences et dans l'opinion." Cf. G. LEROUGE, *Théorie de la fraude en droit fiscal* (Paris, 1944), at p. 247: "La fraude fiscale est un phénomène psychologique général que l'on retrouve dans tous les pays et . . . dans toutes les classes sociales," and (p. 248): "Il n'y a sur ce point, tout au moins en France, aucune réprobation collective, aucune coercition sociale sur l'individu." G. RIPERT, in his Preface to Lerouge's work, points out (p. xv) that tax laws at least *seem* to have an arbitrary character ("la règle fiscale est imposée par l'Etat, qui se trouve à la fois être l'auteur et le bénéficiaire de la règle"); cf. RIPERT, *Le déclin du droit* (Paris, 1949), p. 106: "Chaque contribuable se déclare en état de légitime défense contre le fisc. Les gens les plus honnêtes n'hésitent pas à signer des déclarations inexactes." It is a widely-held opinion that the legislator often fixes the rate of a tax excessively high in anticipation of (and thereby almost justifying) false returns by the taxpayer; this shows the serious abnormality of the relations between tax systems and the public conscience. Cf. M. MARSILI LIBELLI, *La moralità nelle azioni economiche* (in the vol. "La moralità e le professioni," Firenze, 1934, p. 119 *et seq.*); G. MATTERN, *Steuer moral* (in "Steuer und Wirtschaft," XXXI Jahrg., N. 9, München, 1954). For refutation of the arguments justifying fraud in tax matters, see especially C. SCAILTEUR, *Le devoir fiscal* (Bruges, 1950).

87. "Si praedonibus pactum pro capite pretium non attuleris, nulla fraus est, ne si juratus quidem id non feceris. Nam pirata non est perduellium numero definitus, sed communis hostis omnium. Cum hoc nec fides debet, nec jusjurandum esse commune." CICERO, *De Off.*, III, 29. The question is, however, disputed, cf. GROTIUS, *De jure belli ac pacis*, L. III, C. I, §§ 17-19 and C. XIX, §§ 2-5; PUFENDORF, *De jure naturae et gentium*, L. III, C. VI, § 11 and L. IV, C. II, § 8; WOLFF, *Jus gentium methodo scientifica pertractatum*, C. VII, §§ 799-800. Different questions are often confused. One can admit as a rule that the obligation to keep agreements is valid even in relation to faithless or hostile persons, but the obligation disappears when the consent has been vitiated by fraud or force, as is usually the case with promises made to robbers; the contradiction is thus only apparent. Another question is that of the dissolution of the bond by "implied resolutive condition" (*inadimplenti non est adimplendum*), see *infra* n. 100.

88. "*Fumisti* (practical jokers) are ruled by the love of deceit for its own sake, a sort of vanity in putting others off the truth."

F. DEL GRECO, *La psiche del simulatore* (Nocera Inf., 1904), p. 24. See also P. PENTA, *La simulazione della pazzia* (3 ed., Napoli, 1905) and I. INGEGNIEROS, therein cited; these authors consider the character of simulators mainly from the psychiatric aspect. Cf. also the works of DUPRAT and BATTISTELLI, *cit. supra*, n. 32.

89. Cf. A. FAVINO, *Note sulla personalità del frodatore* (in "Giustizia penale," A. 49, 1943, P. I, pp. 14-20).

90. Cf. A. ARTHABER, *Dizionario comparato di proverbi e modi proverbiali* (Milano, 1929), p. 284.

91. A. MANZONI, *In morte di Carlo Imbonati.*

92. According to Pythagoras, men approach the divine in two ways: by speaking truth and by doing good to others. (See AELIAN, *Varia hist.*, XII, 59; PORPHYRY, *Vita Pythag.*, 41; IAMBLICHUS, *Protrept.*, 20; STOBAEUS, *Sentent.*, XI; and cf. GROTIUS, *op. cit.*, L. III, C. I, 20.) These thoughts anticipate doctrines which received their highest development in Christianity. On the duty to respect truth in the purely theological sense, see BOSSUET, *Second Sermon pour le Dimanche de la Passion* and *Troisième Sermon* (in *Oeuvres*, ed. Lachat, vol. IX, Paris, 1862, pp. 398-437). See also, on the problem of truth according to Christian dogma, the writings of CH. BOYER and others in "Doctor Communis," A. 1952, III (pp. 169-317).

93. See, e.g., L. TAPARELLI, *Saggio teoretico di Diritto naturale appoggiato sul fatto*, *cit.*, Vol. I, § 372; cf. A. GENOVESI, *Della Diceosina o sia della Filosofia del giusto e dell'onesto* (Napoli, 1766; 2 ed. 1777), L. I, C. IX, § XXXIV.

94. ST. AUGUSTINE, *De vera religione*, C. 39. On the virtue of silence in general, see STOBAEUS, *Sentent.*, XXXIII (*De taciturnitate*). On silence as a means of maintaining the peace of the soul and assisting the development of conscience, see G. TAURO, *Il silenzio e l'educazione dello spirito* (Milano, 1922).

95. ST. AUGUSTINE, *De mendacio*, 3.

96. "Sit omnis homo velox ad audiendum, tardus autem ad loquendum." ST. JAMES, *Epist.*, 1, 19, Cf. PASCAL, *cit.* n. 17, *supra.*

97. We may recall PASCAL (*Pensées.* Art. II [V], 8) on confession: "La religion catholique n'oblige pas à découvrir ses péchés indifféremment à tout le monde: elle souffre qu'on demeure caché à tous les autres hommes; mais elle en excepte un seul, à qui elle commande de découvrir le fond de son coeur, et de se faire voir tel qu'on est. Il n'y a que ce seul homme au monde qu'elle nous ordonne de désabuser, et elle l'oblige à un secret inviolable, qui

fait que cette connaissance est dans lui comme si elle n'y était pas. Peut-on s'imaginer rien de plus charitable et de plus doux? Et néanmoins la corruption de l'homme est telle, qu'il trouve encore de la dureté dans cette loi."

98. See A. BARBOSA, *Axiomatum juris usufrequentiorum expositio* (in *Tractatus varii*, ed. Lugduni, 1660), Ax. 98, n. 7. Cf. *Liber sextus Decretalium Bonifacii VIII, De regulis juris*, 75: "Frustra sibi fidem quis postulat ab eo servari, cum fidem a se praestitum servare recusat." The Gloss on *Codex Just.* 2.3.21 declares "non esse servandam fidem non servanti," but only in certain cases, while in other cases "servatur fides non servanti" (*loc. cit.*, s.v. *uti*). On the value of this maxim, cf. ROMAGNOSI, *Instituzioni di civile Filosofia* (*ed. cit.*), § 2974, p. 1747.

99. More just, in general, is the contrary teaching of GROTIUS (*De jure belli ac pacis*, L. III, C. XIX, 13), inspired by ST. AMBROSE, *De officiis*, I, 29: "Servandam fidem etiam perfidis." But note the necessary limitations on this rule (*ibid.*, 14, and L. II, C. XIII, 16); and cf. n. 87 *supra*.

100. Neither this maxim nor the corresponding *exceptio non adimpleti contractus* belongs to classical Roman law; but the idea appears in certain particular rules. (For modern Italian law, see arts. 1453 and 1460 of the Civil Code; cf. arts. 1165 and 1469 of the previous Code.) Cf. GLÜCK, *Ausführliche Erlaüterung der Pandekten*, L. II, Tit. XIV, § 313; WINDSCHEID, *Lehrbuch des Pandektenrechts*, 9 Aufl., 1963, L. IV, § 321; G. GIORGI, *Teoria delle obbligazioni* (7 ed., Firenze, 1924-1929), Vol. IV, §§ 199-222; R. CASSIN, *De l'exception tirée de l'inexécution dans les rapports synallagmatiques* (Paris, 1914); G. SCADUTO, *L'exceptio non adimpleti contractus* (in "Annali del Semin. giurid. dell'Univ. di Palermo," Vol. VIII, 1921).

101. KANT, *Prolegomena zu einer jeden künftigen Metaphysik*, § 58.

102. It is strange that an apparently similar idea found expression in PLATO, in a much discussed passage, which does not seem to agree with his fundamental doctrines (*Rep.*, III, 389b). But Plato's main thesis (as is shown by the context) is not a justification but a condemnation of falsehoods, which only in a relative sense (that is, in comparison with other falsehoods) would be proper for rulers when they employ them for the safety of the State. It may also be supposed that Plato's partial admission was intended not so much to maintain a doctrine of his own as to refer to ideas already expressed by others (e.g., SOPHOCLES, *Philoctetes*, 109) or current in his time. See R. DE MATTEI, *Politica e Morale prima di Machiavelli* (in "Giornale crit. della Filos. ital-

iana," A. XXIX, 1950, Fasc. I, p. 64 *et seq.*). Noteworthy for the interpretation of Plato is the comment of F. ALBERGATI (*La Repubblica regia*, Bologna, 1627, L. II, C. 6 *alias* 17, p. 52): "The saying of Plato about lies being lawful for the Prince, must be interpreted thus: that, if any one is to be excused for officious lying, so that it seems as it were lawful, it must be the doctor for the health of his patient, and the Prince for the public good. Thus it does not follow that Plato says either that justice is not honorable in its nature or that lying is lawful" (trans.).

103. See, e.g., B. CROCE, *Elementi di Politica* (3 ed., Bari, 1949), p. 25 *et seq.*

104. See A. ARTHABER, *Dizionario comparato*, *cit.*, p. 266.

105. See A. BARBOSA, *Axiomata* (*cit. supra*, n. 98), Ax. 98, n. 4, and (*ibid.*, n. 5), the similar: "Gravius peccat Princeps frangendo fidem quam inferior et privatus." GROTIUS, *De jure belli ac pacis*, L. III, C. I., 20, cites other similar maxims. ROMAGNOSI, *Inst. di civile filos.*, *loc cit. supra*, similarly maintains that "the great ones," that is, the rulers, should "set an example" of truthfulness and loyalty. M. D'AZEGLIO also stressed this idea, especially in his speech to the sub-Alpine Parliament (12 Feb. 1851), on which cf. M. BARONCI, *Il primato dell'onestà* ("Osservatore Romano," 11/21/1943).

106. "It is necessary, it is urgent to set to work again to base politics on morals": MAZZINI, in "L'Italia del popolo," 1848 (in *Scritti editi ed ined.*, ed. Daelli, Vol. VI, p. 232). This idea inspired Mazzini's mission throughout. He contended for "political honesty" as "the cult of truth" and attacked "diplomacy founded on lies" (*ibid.*, pp. 234, 237). "Great thoughts make great peoples" (*Fede e avvenire*, *ed. cit.*, Vol. V, p. 187). "Nations are not regenerated by falsehood. Worship the truth and have the boldness of apostles" (*Ai giovani delle Università d'Italia*, *ed. cit.*, Vol. IX, p. 162). He rejected doctrines according to which "Virtue is an empty name, morality and politics are not sisters, truth and error are equally good according to the case," and "the theories of *useful wrongdoing* and *opportune lying* and such like" (*Ai giovani d'Italia, ed cit.*, Vol. XI, p. 74). His teaching is summed up in the words: "Put away from you the preachers of Machiavellianism, of tactics, of opportunism. That is not how a Nation is created; it is created with truth, boldness in faith, and sacrifice" (*Lettera ad E. Viola Ferretti*, 30. 9. 1861; cf. *Doveri dell'uomo*, *ed cit.*, Vol. XVIII, p. 66).

107. SPINOZA, *Tractatus theologico-politicus*, C. XX. The words are taken from TACITUS, *Hist.*, I, 1.

108. ST. PAUL, *Philipp.*, 1, 9: "Oro ut caritas vestra magis ac

magis abundet in scientia, et in omni sensu, ut probetis potiora." ST. JOHN CHRYSOSTOM's comment (*In Epist. ad Phil. Comment., Homilia II*, C. I, 1) runs: "Non universe quamvis caritatem admiratur, sed eam quae ex scientia proficiscitur; id est, ut non erga omnes eamdem caritatem adhibeatis: id enim minime caritatis est, sed insulsitatis. Quid est, *in scientia?* Adhibito judicio, cogitata ratione, delectu quodam ac sensu." Cf. ST. THOMAS, *Super Epist. S. Pauli ad Phil.*, Lectio II.

109. KANT, *Grundlegung zur Metaphysik der Sitten*, I Abschn.: "Es ist überall nichts in der Welt, ja überhaupt auch ausser derselben zu denken möglich, was ohne Einschränking für gut Könnte gehalten werden, als allein ein guter Wille."

110. VAUVENARGUES, *Réflexions et maximes*, CXXVII.

111. "Isolée de l'éducation morale et religieuse, l'instruction ne fait que donner une forme nouvelle à la criminalité." L. PROAL, *Le crime et la peine* (Paris, 1892), p. 197.

112. *Discours de la méthode*, Première Partie.

113. This has in fact been shown by recent observations in the educational field. See, e.g., the findings of A. E. WIGGAM (in "School and Society," reported in "Selections from the Reader's Digest," Ital. ed., March 1951, pp. 5-7), which conclude by reaffirming the link between intelligence, culture and morality.

A UNITARY PROGRAM OF EDUCATION

CERTAINLY, IN CONSIDERING THE EDUCATION OF CHILDREN AND young people, we cannot ignore the particular elements which are peculiar to different times and places. Not only the physical conditions, but also the language and historical traditions of each State must be subjects of study in order that the individual may become a conscious part of the society into which he is born and where he is to live.

But it is equally certain that education must also consider the universal elements which are innate in human nature; it must clarify and develop the dictates of reason and the principles of morality which are to be found in the soul of every man, independently of the circumstances and details of his existence.

A wise system of instruction must include both the particular and the universal elements. These, if rightly understood, are not in opposition to one another.[1] The consciousness of belonging to a nation can and must be accompanied by the consciousness of belonging to mankind. The work of educators should promote the harmonious development of young minds, avoiding deviation in either direction.

Absolute identity of matter and method in the schools of different countries is impossible, yet some general principles can be indicated, even for that part of the study program which concerns the particular conditions within individual nations. For example, it can be recommended that historical facts should be treated objectively, avoiding fatuous chauvinism and doing justice even to the achievement of foreigners; above all, we must avoid that partisan spirit which would foster the memory of old civil wars. In internal and international relations alike we must aim at harmony and not at dissension. In teaching the history of our nation we must place in bold relief the elements which make for its unity, rather than accidental differences. We in Italy, for instance, far from abolishing the study of Latin (as has been ill-advisedly proposed) should promote its study, using better methods than are presently employed, not only because Latin is an important factor in civilization but also because it is a fundamental element in the Italian language. We should not, moreover, neglect the study of foreign languages, inasmuch as knowledge of these is clearly useful for spreading of ideas and for communication between peoples.

These and other obvious considerations show that lawful and dutiful veneration of one's own national traditions need not lead to isolation, still less to antagonism towards others. But closer international co-ordination and even a uniform scheme of education is possible in subjects which concern the common needs of human nature. Even in the school there can and should be manifest that tendency towards the achievement of a *societas humani generis* which is not merely a postulate of the ethical conscience but a reality of experience, in the sense that, although unfinished, it is yet a real and visible process. Many obstacles remain in its way, but efforts to overcome these are continuing and multiplying in ever wider spheres, and it is becoming clearer and clearer that only thus can the world be preserved from new catastrophes.

In the educational field the achievement of unity in matters of common interest to all mankind should be much easier than where passions and particular interests are in conflict even within the frontiers of a single state. Not only are the theorems of logic and mathematics accepted equally by all human minds, but the fundamental rules of ethics, fully displayed in Christianity, are also at least partially recognized even by followers of other religions. And, leaving theological premises aside, the leading schools of philosophy proclaim these same rules. Even if these schools differ in method, they generally agree as to practical conclusions.

Why then should it not be possible to compile a single text to be used in the educational program of all States? This could include the elements of the various sciences (omitting notions which are controversial or too difficult), as well as a brief description of the physical universe, with geographical data for the different countries. But more important, and indeed essential, would be a clear exposition of the duties and rights which by nature belong to each person. The principles of charity and justice should be explained in full, even in their individual, practical applications to the problems of modern life. Hatred, revenge and those smoldering grudges which poison the mind should be condemned and in their place the sacred obligations of benevolence, mercy and brotherhood to all men enshrined; even cruelty to animals should receive the condemnation it deserves. From the idea of justice, universally understood, will be deduced the duty of respect for the dignity and value of the human person. The natural rights of man and citizen should be clearly affirmed as maxims of reason: freedom of thought, of speech, of work, of meeting, and of association, and the opportunity to share in the legislative power and activity of the State according to one's capabilities. Thus will be defined the concept of the "Justice-State," the State governed by justice, based on the recognition of the natural rights of its citizens.

All human virtues should be briefly set forth in order that their function with reference to the welfare both of the individual and of society may be displayed. Take, for instance, the virtue of prudence; rules of hygiene and health could be given, as well as rules for highway safety.

Perhaps the time for codifying a law for all mankind has not yet arrived, but at least a moral codification should be tried. It might then be adopted as a compulsory educational program by the more advanced nations and by all others who desired to join them in a common organization to confirm and give practical value to the natural unity of mankind.

(1962)

NOTE

1. MAZZINI, addressing the workers of Italy, wrote: "Your first duty is to Humanity . . . You have duties as citizens, sons, husbands, fathers, and these duties are sacred and inviolable . . . but what makes them sacred and inviolable is the mission, the Duty, which is laid upon you by being MEN" (*Doveri dell'uomo*, C.IV).

ON THE STATE-CHARACTER OF LAW

I. THE PROBLEM OF THE RELATIONS BETWEEN LAW AND THE STATE

THE DISPUTES ABOUT NATURAL LAW AND ITS RELATIONSHIP TO positive law having subsided for the moment, no problem attracts modern legal theorists more than that of the relationship between law and the State.[1] It is a problem that touches directly on fundamental questions in several juridical fields and if we are to arrive at their sure systematization, a solution must be found. Moreover, it possesses speculative importance in that it touches on the very idea of "law," which has been, and must always be the basis of jurisprudence and an essential part of every philosophy.

The doctrine that it is for the State, and the State alone, to determine law corresponds to the attitude of practical lawyers who conceive their first duty to be to interpret the law as an expression of the sovereignty of the State. All law would thus be, by definition, State law. This opinion coincides (though with a further restriction) with that which declares all law to be "positive"; Bergbohm, for instance, maintained that this adjective, added to the law, represents a mere redundancy ("law" being, in his opinion, positive law),[2] and more recently, writers like Kelsen have not only maintained the equation between law and State law, but actually between law and State.[3]

Nonetheless, even among the adherents of positive law and, in general, of the inductive method in the study of social life, there can be found expressions contrary to this view. The proposal to inquire into the so-called "historical formation of law and of the State" foreshadowed a distinction which has been confirmed by the results; the data collected seem sufficient for the conclusion that, while law is contemporary with man (since human life does not exist and is not possible except in society, and society is not possible without juridical connections and limitations among those who compose it), the State, on the contrary, arises only by means of a long process, wherein separate clans are synthesized into a new and ampler "super-clan" unity. Law would thus seem to exist, even as an historical and positive phenomenon, before the State.[4]

Considering merely the facts of life today, we cannot overlook the existence of at least two great systems—the law of the Church and international law—to which no State corresponds. The nature of these different systems has been frequently discussed; some contend that they do not truly possess a juridical nature, or else possess it only partially, because certain characteristics which are found fully developed in State law are lacking in them. Such argumentation, however, is apt to fall into a vicious circle, presupposing what has to be proved.

Finally, we must take note of another order of phenomena which seem equally strong as proofs of the possibility of a law which is not State law, to wit, a whole series of minor juridical orders established in the ambit of the State, but independent of it and even, in some cases, in opposition to it. The ancient corporations or *Genossenschaften* (discussed by Gierke in particular) offer typical examples, but similar phenomena may be met with in all stages of juridical evolution, including our own. Every time a society spontaneously forms itself, it tends to form within itself a law (that is, a complex of obligatory rules among its members); to refer such a law to the State, which may even be ignorant of its existence, seems a vain artifice. More than merely an artifice, it would, rather, be a logical impossibility in cases where such societies and their orders are directly turned against the State, so that they formally constitute a violation of its norms. It is easy then to qualify such organizations as "anti-juridical"; and so without doubt they are, if the law of the State is accepted as the starting point. But if we consider those organizations in themselves, it is difficult to deny that the complex of rules in force among them has, either in whole or in part, a juridical character.

From these observations alone, apart from all consideration of ideal or non-positive law, we shall probably be forced to conclude that State law is to be distinguished from non-State law; and that the former represents only a species or a phase, although the most important one, of the genus or logical category of law.

II. THE LOGICAL ESSENCE OF LAW

The problem requires further study, however. First of all it is necessary to determine what really constitutes law. We recognize the essence of this concept in the intersubjective or bilateral relationship, that is, in the coordination of the behavior of several subjects, through which one can claim something (an action or omission) which is obligatory on the other. Whatever the content of such a claim may be, every time a correspondence exists between a demand on one hand and an obligation on the other, we are in the realm of law. From this we perceive, among other things, that a juridical proposition always implies *ex hypothesi* the determination of a duty, that is to say, an imperative.

From the purely logical point of view there are any number of possible juridical propositions. We may suppose any correlation between subject and subject in the aforesaid form and, at the same time, a possible will which affirms it, even if no such will is manifested in fact; and we may multiply such suppositions indefinitely without stepping out of the logical sphere of law. For instance, if in place of the rule actually in force among us—"any act which brings damage to others, requires him, through whose fault it has occurred, to make compensation for the damage"—we were to imagine another by which the obligation of compensation were declared to amount to only the half of the damage or to double or triple of it, the juridical form would still remain unchanged. The series of conceptual constructions of this type may be endlessly extended even when there is no positive law behind them and when the person who conceives them does not really will that they should become effective.

In such matters, however, the human mind cannot be fed on hypotheses alone. By means of an inner call, every human subject is compelled to cooperate with others in the form of law: that is, man derives from himself, even before he does so from extraneous factors, at least an embryonic system of rules for the interrelations between himself and his fellows.

In short, he possesses—and continues to develop—a complex of sentiments and convictions as to what is just and unjust and what is lawful and unlawful for each, whence he asserts claims on others and in his turn recognizes himself to be subject to limitations and obligations towards them. These juridical valuations, upheld by the conscience and will of the subject (which in some measure makes them effective), constitute the first source of the positive juridical order. Thus, this order results from the confluence of individual consciences, and in return strongly influences them.

The connections of these reciprocal actions and reactions in the origin of positive law cannot be easily or briefly described. We shall endeavor here only to establish some fundamental notions.

III. THE PROCESS OF ITS HISTORICAL POSITING

Although separate juridical propositions may be considered in abstraction, they tend naturally to constitute a system. The necessity for logical coherence leads to assembling those which are compatible or respectively complementary and the elimination of those which are contradictory or incompatible. As living logic, will cannot develop, even in the field of law, unless it so links its assertions as to reduce them to a harmonious whole. Hence the perpetual labor (as Vico says), both of individual minds and of nations, to conciliate and develop the various juridical propositions—in their origin so often discordant—into a single organic whole.

The moment in which a juridical idea becomes "positive" is not so readily definable as non-jurists might think. For that matter, even dogmatic jurists who keep their eyes trained on enacted law alone, as if this permitted no access to other sources and did not require tacitly or expressly their concurrence for its actuation, conceive the task to be easier than it really is.

Clearly the will of a single individual asserting a particular juridical rule cannot suffice to render it positive. The positivity of the rule consists in the fact that its effective vigor is rendered independent of the wish of the individual, especially of one who might have an interest in violating it.

Thus, it is necessary for the existence of positive law that a common or super-individual will should be established. The scattered, or merely potential, volitions manifested in juridical ideas asserted by any person whomsoever must give place to a constant and homogeneous will capable of sustaining and imposing effectively a regulative system of social life.

This will, though in a certain sense a new and higher one, is nevertheless not radically different from the will possessed by single subjects. Each one of them may—and indeed, by his nature must—rise above the empirical ego in his consciousness, recognize the subjectivity of others and regard himself *sub specie alteritatis*; thus he can and must conceive and will law as a transubjective, "meta-egoistic" order. The difference between this appearance of law *in interiore homine*, as in a microcosm, and that in which it presents itself to us fully developed in historical and social reality is a difference of manner or degree rather than of substance. A confirmation of this can be found in the fact that the juridical determinations of the individual consciousness ordinarily coincide, at least in great part, with those positively in force; and still further by the fact that the same individual who recognizes this autonomous juridical sentiment within himself may equally feel himself to be both an organ of the law objectively imposed and an organ of the common will which presides over it. This is a psychological attitude which is developed especially in magistrates and public officials but which belongs in a general way to the citizens also: it may be called the "legal sentiment" or the "State sentiment."

IV. THE CONTINUITY OF THE PROCESS AND THE REQUIREMENT OF THE UNITY OF THE SYSTEM

The super-individual or common will, which supports the juridical order and renders it positive, has for its primary function the maintenance of the rules of law which constitute that order. These rules can have various origins, and may in fact precede the constitution of this unitary will to which (through logical attraction, or, one might say, centripetal force) they lead in the end—except when, as is also possible, they fail to merge in this will and are thereby eliminated. In the complicated process of history juridical propositions, or rather the forces which support them, are subject to shocks and conflicts;

and the conclusion of the process (a relative conclusion, be it understood, since the process is infinite) can only be either their insertion in a positive structure or their elimination. It is, of course, true that intermediate degrees, consisting of compromises and adaptations among heterogeneous juridical wills, also exist; this, however, simply denotes the persistence of the crisis, and therefore the continuity of the process.

The maintenance of the juridical order is necessarily accompanied by its reintegration. This arises not only from the inevitable struggle between law and wrongdoing, which requires that the rules in force undergo continual renovation and reaffirmation, but also from the fact that these rules themselves little by little reveal their need of correction and supplementation. Therefore the will, in which the positive juridical order is centered, must simultaneously preserve and innovate; and this second function is distinguished in reality from the first only by a series of almost inappreciable transitions.

As organization proceeds, however, that center or pivot of the common will, which at first had appeared to be oscillating and ill-defined and little more than a potential reference point or a common denominator of volitions still partially in opposition, is gradually consolidated and becomes effective. The compulsory nature of the rules in force, whatever its remote origin may be, henceforth appears as the effect of that unitary will which through its own organs asserts itself as a preponderant power, with sufficient authority not only to confirm preexisting rules but also to abolish them and substitute others for them.

Thus there takes shape a true and proper subject (a "person" in the technical juridical sense), possessed of a supremely autonomous will that is not to be confused with that of the individuals or the minor associations which are comprised in it; and such a will is realized in the rules of law which are in force to the extent that they are willed by it. This subject is the State.

V. DEFINITION OF THE STATE. THE STATE WILL AND JURISTIC ACTS

We can therefore define the State as that subject of the will which imposes a juridical order; or, in metaphorical terms, as the center of radiation of the rules which comprise a positive juridical system.

Consequently, it is clear that the State cannot be subjected to another will; if it could be, the title of State would belong to the subject of that will and to it the validity of the entire system of rules would have to be referred. This essential autonomy or independence of the will of the State is commonly expressed by saying that the attribute of sovereignty is inseparable from the State.

The dogmatic construction of law may now be sketched quite simply. The whole juridical order is, by this measure, a creation of the State; only the State can confer positive value, whether on a law (that may have arisen from custom or some other source), or on a single act of will, since both an act's legality and its capacity to produce juridical effects depend exclusively on its conformity to a norm, which is to say, by hypothesis, to the will of the State. The private will thus has no value *per se* but only insofar as it is confirmed and rendered efficacious by that other superior will which determines it. On this basis is developed, for instance, the common doctrine of juristic acts.

But this construction, while having its own logic with respect to its premise, corresponds neither to historical nor to psychological fact.

The truth is that individual wills can, by meeting together, set a limit to the reciprocal claims in which law consists, prior to and independent of the State. Not only as an abstract principle grounded in pure reason but out of the concrete emergencies of life (that is, with a certain degree of incipient positivity), a juridical relationship among several subjects can grow and develop, and from the relationship arises the rule (as the Romans perceived)[5]; the growing State will then attribute this rule to itself, through a sort of exclusiveness which its aim of assuring the unity of the system makes necessary.

That this is the true order of things is clear not only from past historical phases but also from today's circumstances. When, for instance, the State declares that contracts "have the force of law between the parties," it indeed expresses its will, but only in the sense of acknowledging the existence and adding to the efficacy of the will of others. Must we, out of homage to a dogmatic preconception, assert that the private will of the contracting parties *is* the will of the State and that each party, in making the contract, is an "organ" of the State? The forced nature of such a construction is obvious. The juridical structure of the relationship does not flow from the State as a real entity; the State is only an ideal point of convergence to which all juridical determinations pertaining to the system must be referred. Without this reference, the positive framework of the juridical determinations would appear to be discontinuous or severable, and the single determinations could not in their turn possess fully the character of positivity.[6]

VI. THE STATE AND THE RULES OF AUTONOMOUS BODIES

This applies even more strongly when we turn from mere individual determinations, as in the case of juristic acts, to collective organizations which existed before the State or which have arisen within the ambit of the State but have developed in an autonomous manner (*juxta propria principia*).

Little by little, as the concentration of the social will is gradually accomplished and the State takes shape, the rules of such organizations are referred, so far as is materially possible, to the State will and regarded as its emanations. Thus, for instance, at a certain point in history even time-honored customs seem to be valid because willed by the legislator (a phenomenon well-known to the historian of law); first of all, this is a merely fictitious supposition and becomes partly true only in that later stage of development in which legislative organs truly have the power of abolishing customary rules if they so desire; as a generalized power, however, this is merely a hypothesis or limit-concept.

The evolution of penal law offers striking illustrations. In primitive social groups (families and clans) a certain punitive justice is observed, especially through the authority of the *pater familias*, and this justice would seem to possess not merely a private but in a certain sense a public character.[7] The penal function is later arrogated to itself by the State, which with special rigor asserts and consolidates its exclusive power in this field. Nevertheless it is a significant fact that even in the most advanced stages a certain penal justice continues to be exercised under the name of "disciplinary power"—in the family and in other social organizations (schools, industrial undertakings, various associations and corporations).

This contradicts the notions on which our teaching is commonly based. To solve the difficulty it is not enough to declare that disciplinary penal law (and especially that which in a more restricted sense is sometimes called "autonomous penal law") is not really penal law;[8] this assertion is founded simply on a presupposition which would require proof—viz. that the State alone is entitled to the right of punishment.[9]

This entire subject, which even among penologists is clouded with uncertainty, should be reviewed and explained according to a critical and nondogmatic concept of what is meant by the State-character of law. We should examine, with regard to different types of cases, whether even in the so-called disciplinary field the exercise of the penal function depends, expressly or tacitly, on rules formulated by organs of the State; and how and to what degree the process of referring the disciplinary rules to the State as the center of the whole system is carried out.[10] Even in this field the possibility of divergence and antinomy between autonomous juridical formations and the order of the State should not be excluded *a priori*.[11]

The formation of social aggregations which possess their own specific orders and are totally independent of the State so far as origin is concerned is a phenomenon we are accustomed to observe only in striking cases. Certain corporative organizations of the Middle Ages, the great religious societies and, especially, the Catholic Church are examples. But the phenomenon, except for differences of proportion, truly has a universal character, since every social group tends naturally to generate a law of its own. Perhaps it would be fairer to say that every social group creates within itself—insofar as it is a genuine social group and not a mere chaos—in a certain mode the logical form of law, and it continues to develop its own life in this same form. No common life nor even any collaboration among individuals is possible without a determination, effective even though sometimes unspoken, of the sphere of activity belonging to each, and consequently of their respective obligations and powers. This determination may be imposed by an extraneous and dominant power as something already formed and not to be altered (as when, for instance, a new regiment is created in an army), in which case the new entity is *ipso facto*, almost automatically, inserted into the previous system represented by that power. But the most frequent and normal case is that individuals are not merely passive before the regulations which are to govern their common action but themselves take part in forming them, perhaps by extracting their elements from systems already existing.

The problem of fusing these various organizations into a single will is then the same as that which we have already considered. Here it is most important to note that the alleged dependence of all the social organisms on the juridical order of the State often becomes a mere *fictio juris*; for in reality there are social organisms which live *jure proprio*, attached to the State only by extrinsic bonds or through generic relations which, since they do not affect its structure, leave the autonomy of their intrinsic order intact. That this order has a juridical nature can be deduced with certainty from the presence of the logical characteristics already cited; nor can such a nature be denied on the grounds that a law which is not State-law is impossible. To attempt such a denial would be to fall into the error of a *petitio principii*.

As for the order of the Catholic Church, it is now almost universally admitted, and for sound reasons, that the rules emanating from it (*jus canonicum*) have really the character of law;[12] and incidentally, we may recall that it was because of doubts raised regarding this that some of the most serious investigations into the nature of law in general, like those of Bierling,[13] were started.

A problem which is still discussed, however, is that of the position of the juridical system of the Church in the system of State law, and in particular in the Italian State.[14] The most correct formal solution seems to be that the law of the Church is effective in Italy in virtue of a *renvoi* contained in State law, and thus willed by the Italian legislator.[15] From this point of view we are once again able to defend the principle of the unity of the juridical order; but we acknowledge the existence of an independent juridical order, which only under a certain form (extrinsic as regards its root) enters into, or is reflected in, that of the State. So true is this that a similar difficulty and a similar solution can be found when starting from the opposite point of view, that is, by considering what is the value of Italian State law in canon law.[16] What makes this two-sided consideration particularly important, even in theory, is the fact that it is not a question of two juridical orders each having its own separate sphere of action, as in the case of two different States, but of juridical orders interfering with each other, in force (at least partially) in the same territory and over the same subjects; hence they cannot both at the same time have full State character.

VII. INTERNATIONAL LAW

The problem of the relationship of international law to internal law is the same. Here, too, the fundamental principle is taken to be that the validity of the rules in force in the so-called international society of States is subordinated, so far as any particular State is concerned, to the will of the State itself. The object of this is to maintain the principle of the sovereignty of the State juridical system. On the other hand, it has to be admitted that in the relations between various States a system of rules (partly customary) has established itself which has its own objective existence, distinct from that of the separate State systems, even though in a sense it can be considered as their product.

At least some of these rules, such as the one which declares the inviolability of agreements, have never been adopted either in treaty form (which would obviously result in a circle) or by any formal action of individual States. Nevertheless, they exist and possess a certain positivity (although imperfect) insofar as they are supported by an almost universal will, the presence of which can be assumed in any State which seeks to enter into permanent relations with others. If this common will were to achieve a more precise unity, that is, a perfect organization, the complex of such rules would become a positive juridical order in the full sense of the term, or a State. The consequence would then be that this new order would comprise, or centralize in itself, the others (the single States) to which its rules refer; these would thus cease to exist as States, their quality of being autonomous subjects or centers of radiation of positive juridical rules having, *ex hypothesi*, been lost.

At the same time and for the same reason, international (or rather inter-State) law, which would no longer be formally distinguishable from an internal or State system of law, would cease to exist as such. This is a singular example of a law which can exist only so long as it has an imperfect degree of positivity, since its full perfection would necessarily mark its end as a separate type.

VIII. CORPORATIVE LAW

Corporations of professions, arts and trades tend to elaborate a law of their own, if at the time of their origin they do not receive a ready-made juridical system from an external source. Is this law, elaborated by the organization itself, State-law?

According to the criteria already indicated, we must consider how the relationship between the will which makes this law and that which serves as the foundation of the State's juridical order works in practice. If (as has sometimes happened in both ancient and recent times) there is an antinomy between the two wills, the reference of the corporative law to the State is excluded, even though the possibility still exists of a sort of co-existence between the two different juridical orders, each of which in a way impinges on the other, and tends, potentially, to replace it. This antinomy may take the form of tacit tolerance or of open conflict; in either case the phenomenon may be protracted for centuries, so difficult and wearisome is the process of forming a positive unitary law or, in other words, a solid State structure. In history, the status of unstable equilibrium between social forces is the rule rather than the exception.

The extreme example of conflict is seen in those forms of association which the State deems either illicit or downright criminal. Even associations of this sort can have elaborate statutes and organizational structures with precise definitions of their hierarchy and the powers of their leaders and of the obligations and rights of individual members. Such determinations have formal juridical character and, as far as they are in fact observed and made effective, even positive juridical character; but positivity in this case can only be partial or imperfect, because of the simultaneous presence of another opposing juridical order.

Even aside from this case, which we might term pathological, the co-existence of discordant juridical orders in the same historical setting implies at least a potential crisis which mere silent toleration cannot remedy. A recent instance of such a crisis, the gravity of which manifested itself almost simultaneously in various states, has been the development of syndicalist organizations with anti-State tendencies; these are associations of workers which, by substituting themselves for the State, seek a gradual take over of its functions.[17] The attitudes adopted by different States towards such assaults have taken different forms and would provide material for an extensive table of comparison. Here we are concerned only with the theoretical side of the problem and the possible solutions arising therefrom.

IX. SCHEMES OF POSSIBLE RELATIONS BETWEEN STATE LAW AND CORPORATIVE LAW

As we have learned from studying other cases, the fact that a center of juridical determinations arises and develops independently of the State does not prevent its being attracted, at a certain point, into the orbit of the State itself. There is, indeed, a necessary tendency in this direction, even as there is also a tendency in the opposite direction. Strictly speaking, both bodies have the same nature and differ only in the amplitude and degree of positivity of the norms emanating from them. We give the name of State to the one which has reached the highest degree of positivity, that is, the most ample and solid unitary organization; but we must also recognize that the other body, or center of juridical determinations, is similarly a State in embryonic form. Supposing both to aim at regulating the same relationships, that is, that their spheres of application coincide either wholly or in part, the lines of conflict are marked out *re ipsa*, and it is clear that the two systems cannot avoid testing their capacities and attractive forces with regard to each other.

Hence the possibility of various kinds of solution. The State order may assert its supremacy over the corporative order in such a way as to destroy or dissolve its elements (the French Revolution would be an example of this type). On the other hand, the corporative order may superimpose itself on the State, so paralyzing or transforming its structure that it becomes itself the State (such, in substance, is the meaning of the more recent Russian revolution). Finally, a third type of solution may be adopted or attempted, which consists in the State's reception of the corporative organizations, so that they are brought into the orbit of the State and made subject to its real power. Thus the normative activity, first developed by those organizations in a spontaneous or "autarchic" form, becomes harmonized with direct expressions of State sovereignty. Such a transformation, which touches the inmost fibre and vital centers of the whole regulative system, cannot happen *ex abrupto* but only through a gradual, usually slow process. Nor is it necessary that the change take place through formal or explicit declarations; it may be to a great extent almost invisible, since it is not a superficial variation that is occurring but the displacement (if one may use the term) of the center of gravity of a whole system of rules. Very simply, it is a question of wills which must tend to coalesce; since the foundation of the phenomenon is psychological, the change must take place in the minds of the people. In the consciousness of the particular organizations themselves the State-sentiment must gain ascendancy over the sentiment for class or corporation.

Because of the complicated psychological nature of this process it is possible to have externally, as an intermediate stage, a state of suspense, in which it appears uncertain whether the norms of the corporative organizations have a State character or not. While the process of inserting one system in another continues, this State character itself is a *quid* in process of becoming. No wonder that the functions of the State then seem to be exercised only partially by real and true State organs and partially by various corporative bodies or voluntary associations. And no wonder if, to explain these and other phenomena that typify the crisis, legal theory sometimes has recourse (as it did with custom) to ambiguous or fictitious formulae, such as that of tacit tolerance, or presumed ratification, or delegated authority. Such formulae do not truly correspond to reality; but they permit a provisional interpretation of it and, as it were, serve as scaffolding to support the system while it is being constructed.

Even here, however, it behooves us to be on our guard against illusions which might arise from the metaphorical character of the language used. The process of centralization and of subordination of divergent energies is not accomplished—as might seem from these terms—mechanically, but with mental effort and tension. And these are necessarily tinged with sacrifice.

When this process, in fact and in consciousness, is sufficiently advanced and mature, it becomes easy to formally establish the new arrangements by which the State organizes its sovereignty over the various organizations, which now receive its imprint and become instruments in the development of the normative powers recognized in them or granted to them.

X. RECAPITULATION AND CONCLUSIONS

The conclusions of this summary study may be recapitulated very briefly.

Every juridical proposition which is truly willed—even by individual subjects—and not simply conceived as a theorem or hypothesis, implies an initial degree of positivity, that is, a tendency towards the actualization of the obligations which it signifies.

But effective implementation, that is, positivity in its full sense, comes about only when a connection or synthesis of different wills is accomplished, resulting in a preponderant social will. To this new subject is then formally attributed the emanation of all the juridical propositions which compose a regulative system of social life. This attribution to a single focus or center of radiation determines the unity of the system, which in practice, however, is obtained only by perpetual labor in maintaining the coherence of the different parts of the system during its development. The work of jurists aims chiefly at this; and it is through this that law displays an organic character.

The common center of radiation of the preponderant social will, in a word, constitutes the State. The State in its most general meaning has thus both a moment of absoluteness and a moment of relativity, since it designates that one among several possible juridical systems which corresponds to the predominant will and which has therefore reached, as compared to the others, the highest degree of positivity.

But actually other centers of juridical determinations exist within or alongside of the State, and these, impinging in various ways on the latter, tend to constitute so many other systems and hence, potentially, so many other States. Nevertheless, the "State character" of these can at best only be partial or imperfect (hence latent and not clearly visible, like the microorganisms that dwell in the human body), inasmuch as, *ex hypothesi*, they lack the support of the socially preponderant will.

The relations between the State and these bodies, in the reciprocal effort of each to overcome the other and to attain autonomy, are the source of widely varied phenomena. The complications that thus arise lend a pattern to the web of political history. We have endeavored to indicate summarily the typical forms of such phenomena.

The life of the State necessarily consists of a continual reassertion and reintegration of its authority. It must impose its authority not only on individuals but also, and chiefly, on those other social organizations which operate within its sphere. The latter either refer back to the same center, that is, the State itself, or represent (at least potentially) a disturbing element and a danger to the State's existence.

It is true that in a sense the State cannot perish. The very relativity innate in its concept guarantees its continuity.[18] A revolution of the social energies can transform but not suppress the State, since a new equilibrium must follow on the old and among the various directions the common will can take—no matter what their absolute value—one must emerge as preponderant. This one will then constitute the fulcrum of the new system.

Yet, although this is true as a general proposition, we must not forget that the formation and transformations of the State are the result of laborious historical gestations and not of sudden miraculous creations. Law is coeval with man, and the sentiment for, and idea of, law are constituent and unfailing elements of the human consciousness. The life of a subject is not possible without intersubjective relations, in which the light of that idea cannot help but be reflected (thus one may say briefly, syllogizing: *Ubi homo, ibi societas*; *ubi societas, ibi jus*; *ergo, ubi homo, ibi jus*). Historically speaking the establishment of *positive* law, which we may define as the dictates of individual consciousnesses synthesized in a coherent and organic system, with its own well-defined center in a unitary will, is not, however, so immediate. Indeed, it is possible only by means of a long and complicated process. It is thus no accident that historians distinguish the genesis of law from that of the State and attribute the latter to a much later period.

Similarly, when the structure of the State is altered or destroyed, it must necessarily reconstitute itself through the spiritual forces which constantly draw towards it; but its reconstitution takes place only through a crisis that involves, even to the point of agony, all human virtues and passions.

It would thus be inconsistent to deduce from the relative permanence of the State the legitimacy of a passive or quietist attitude towards it; its life implies the need of continual effort and demands the active and harmonious collaboration of all those who participate in it. A citizen does not belong to the State as a fixture belongs to a building; the relationship between citizen and State is not merely extrinsic or material; it is an interpenetration of spirit which exists to the degree that it is reaffirmed with ever renewed will.

The problem of political organization consists in the establishing of concrete modes and forms for this intimate interpenetration, so that it may be achieved as completely as possible. This is to be accomplished not by suppressing but by coordinating both individual and social elements, that is, the specific organizations which must be brought into harmony with the supreme organization. An erroneous evaluation, and consequently a bad government, of these various elements—whether in the direction of excessive laxity or of undue repression—results in harm to the structure of the State. Thus, for instance, the experience of centuries shows that the attempts of positive legal systems to ignore the natural prerogatives of the human being lead to resistance or uprisings, and that attempts to eliminate or break up all corporative associations, as intermediate forms of life between the individual and the State, fail utterly to prevent the resurgence, open or covert, of similar associations.

Classical doctrines of legal philosophy have always had in view the ideal of a perfect harmony between the authority of the State and the rights of individuals; nor do the errors that have been committed in practice weaken the fundamental legitimacy of the ideal. The theory of the social contract, which in its empirical meaning is so easy to disprove as to be an exercise in futility, in its rational meaning seeks to affirm the categorical necessity of bringing together individual wills and rights—without exception or reserve—in a single authoritative center, the "personality" of the State, so that its structure may be unbreakable and its sovereignty, unassailable.

A State can exist even when it falls far short of this ideal of perfect harmony and compact unity. It can exist in some fashion so long as its centralizing energies outweigh its disintegrative forces, though these latter may be powerful enough to render its life wretched and uncertain and to paralyze its activities. A State fully lives and prospers only when, besides the formal nexus which unites participants in the same juridical order, there is also an ethical bond, a profound identity of wills, a real communion of spirits, and an equal ardor of faith in the civil religion of the fatherland.

(1928)

NOTES

1. Cf. ORLANDO, *Recenti indirizzi circa i rapporti fra diritto e Stato* (in "Riv. di Dir. pubblico," 1926, P. I), p. 273. Orlando, considering the problem with regard to public law, examines *inter alios* ROMANO, *L'ordinamento giuridico* (Pisa, 1918); on which cf. BONUCCI, *Ordinamento giuridico e Stato* (in "Riv. di Dir. pubb," 1920, P. I) and note by DEL VECCHIO: *Moderne con-*

cezioni del diritto (in "Riv. int. di Fil. del dir.," A. I, 1921, Fasc. III). See also EHRLICH, *Grundlegung der Soziologie des Rechts* (München, 1913), p. 110 *et seq.; Die juristische Logik* (Tübingen, 1918), p. 81 *et seq.*; RADBRUCH, *Grundzüge der Rechtsphilosophie* (Leipzig, 1914), p. 83 *et seq.;* HAURIOU, *La théorie de l'institution et de la fondation* (in "La cité moderne et les transformations du droit," Paris, (1925); CAMMÀRATA, *Contributi ad una critica gnoseologica della Giurisprudenza,* I, Roma, 1925); *Il Concetto del diritto e la pluralità degli ordinamenti giuridici* (Catania, 1926); TATARIN-TARNHEYDEN, *Staat und Recht in ihrem begrifflichen Verhältnis* (in "Festgabe für Stammler," Berlin, 1926); PERTICONE, *Il diritto e lo Stato* (in "Riv. int. di Fil. del dir.," A.8, 1929, Fasc. III); CESARINI SFORZA, *Il diritto dei privati* (in "Riv. Ital. per le scienze giuridiche," N.S., A. IV, 1929, Fasc. I-II); G. TEDESCHI, *Volontà privata autonoma* (in "Riv. int. di Fil. del dir.," A. IX, 1929, Fasc. VI); ROVELLI, *Su la statualità del diritto e la distinzione fra diritto e morale* (in "Studi di dir. pubb. in onore di Ranelletti," vol. II, Padova, 1931); PANUNZIO, *La pluralità degli ordinamenti giuridici e l'unità dello Stato* (in "Studi filosofico-giuridici," vol. II, Modena, 1931); RECASENS SICHES, *Estado y derecho; el problema acerca de si son conceptos idénticos o diversos* (*ibid.*); BURCKHARDT, *L'État et le droit* (in "Verhandlungen des Schweizerischen Juristenvereins," II Heft, Basel, 1931); SCHINDLER, *Recht und Staat* (ibid.); CURCIO, *Stato e diritto nella recentissima letteratura italiana* (in "Lo Stato," A. II, 1931, Fasc. XI); C. PETRONE, *Stato e diritto* (Roma, 1932); R. RAVÀ, *La teoria della pluralità degli ordinamenti giuridici e le associazioni sindacali riconosciute* (Firenze, 1933).

2. BERGBOHM, *Jurisprudenz und Rechtsphilosophie* (Leipzig, 1892), p. 49.

3. KELSEN, *Hauptprobleme der Staatsrechtslehre* (Tübingen, 1911), p. 405 *et seq.; Das Verhältnis von Staat und Recht im Lichte der Erkenntniskritik* (Wien, 1921); *Der soziologische und der juristische Staatsbegriff* (Tübingen, 1922); and other writings of K. and his followers, many of them published in "Zeitschrift für öffentliches Recht," directed by K. himself. Cf. CONDORELLI, *Il rapporto fra Stato e diritto secondo il Kelsen*, in "Riv. int. di Fil. del dir.," A. III, 1923, Fasc. III.

4. MAINE, *Ancient Law* (London, 1861); *Early History of Institutions* (London, 1875), p. 386; *Early Law and Custom* (London, 1883; new imp. 1901), Ch. VII, etc.; JHERING, *Geist des römischen Rechts auf den verschiedenen Stufen seiner*

Entwicklung, I. Th. (5 Aufl., Leipzig, 1891), p. 176 *et seq.*, 183 *et seq.*; FUSTEL DE COULANGES, *La Cité antique* (20 éd., Paris, 1908), L. II, Chs. VIII, X; L. III, Ch. III; POST, *Die Anfänge des Staats- und Rechtslebens* (Oldenburg, 1878), esp. p. 103 *et seq.* (where the history of the constitutional law of all peoples is sharply divided into the "friedensgenossenschaftliche"—which comprises the "geschlechtsgenossenschaftliche"—and the "staatliche Periode"); cf. *Grundriss der ethnologischen Jurisprudenz*, I Bd.; L. H. MORGAN, *Ancient Society* (New York, 1878) (this author's divergences from Maine are in this respect not important); GUMPLOWICZ, *Der Rassenkampf* (Innsbruck, 1883), pp. 181, 195; *Die sociologische Staatsidee* (2 Aufl., Innsbruck, 1902), p. 116 *et seq.;* POSADA, *Théories modernes sur les origines de la famille, de la société, et de l'état* (Paris, 1896); WILUTZKY, *Vorgeschichte des Rechts*, esp. III T. (Berlin, 1903); *MacLEOD, The origin and history of Politics* (New York, 1931), esp. Ch. II, "How peoples can live without the State." VANNI, indeed, considers the formation of law to be "parallel with the formation of the State" (*Gli studi di H.S. Maine e le dottrine della Filosofia del diritto* (Verona, 1892, p. 5; cf. p. 63-66), but he rejects the theory that "law could not have existed before the State." "Even before any religious or political authority was constituted, there was an obligatory standard of conduct in the form of vague custom, and *before there was a State* as a special organ of law there was a Justice, also vague and undifferentiated." Cf. his *Lezioni di Filosofia del diritto* (4 ed., Bologna, 1920), pp. 163, 168. More explicit in this sense is KOHLER: "Das Recht besteht vor jeder staatlichen Organisation: es besteht im Herzen des Volkes als das Gefühl des Seinsollenden und Nichtseinsollenden" (*Ueber das Recht der Australneger*, in "Zschr. f. vergleichende Rechtswiss.," VII Bd., 1887, p. 323 *et seq.*). STAMMLER, by another road, reaches similar conclusions, conceiving the State as a sub-species of the legal order (*Das Recht im Staatlosen Gebiete*, Leipzig, 1911, p. 339 *et seq.*; cf. *Theorie der Rechtswissenschaft*, 2 Aufl., Halle, 1923, p. 239 *et seq.*). Cf. also the doctrine of DUGUIT that every society has its own law, even if it lacks that political differentiation which constitutes the State (*L'État, le droit objectif et la loi positive*, Paris, 1901; *Traité de droit constitutionnel*, 2 éd., T.I, Paris, 1921, p. 393 *et seq.*).

According to GIERKE, on the other hand, State and law arise at the same time and presuppose one another as two functions of social life (*Die Grundbegriffe des Staatsrechts und die neuesten Staatsrechtstheorien*, Tübingen, 1874, p. 27); but law can be generated also by associations other than the State (*ibid.*, p. 28; *Das Wesen der menschlichen Verbände*, Leipzig, 1902, p. 32; etc.). So too JELLINEK (*Allgemeine Staatslehre*, 3 Aufl., Neudr., Berlin, 1921), p. 364 *et seq.* Those who assert the political character of primitive family and clan organization approach this conception. Thus, for JHERING, the archaic family represents a "Surrogat des Staats," and the *gens* "die Identität der Familie und des Staats" (*op. cit.*, I T., pp. 179, 184). BONFANTE expresses himself even more decidedly in this sense (*La "gens"e la "familia,"* in "Scritti giur. varii," I, Torino, 1916), and considers primitive social groups as "political organisms," while reserving the title of "State" for the unitary political organization. One writer has gone so far as to assert that "The very first State which ever existed was a human family, consisting of a mother and her offspring . . . The family is a State and the earliest form of State" (W. DONISTHORPE, *Individualism—a System of Politics*, London, 1889, p. 2; cf. MACKECHNIE, *The State and the Individual*, (Glasgow, 1896, p. 55).

For other points in this connection, see: SPENCER, *Principles of Sociology* (1876-1882), Pt. II, § 257 *et seq.*, Pt. V, § 441 *et seq.*; SIDGWICK, *The Development of European Polity* (London, 1903), p. 44 *et seq.*; WUNDT, *Logik der Geisteswissenschaften* (*Logik*, III Bd., 4 Aufl., Stuttgart, 1921), p. 579 *et seq.*; GÉNY, *Science et technique en droit privé positif*, I (2 éd., Paris, 1922), p. 58 *et seq.*; VINOGRADOFF, *Outlines of Historical Jurisprudence* (Oxford, 1920-1922), esp. vol. I, p. 84 *et seq.*; LOWIE, *The Origin of the State* (New York, 1927), esp. p. 74 *et seq.*

5. We refer to the logical procedure actually followed by the Roman jurisconsults, rather than to their theoretical general pronouncements, like that of PAULUS (in *Dig.* 50. 17. 1); "Regula est, quae rem, quae est, breviter enarrat. Non (ut) ex regula jus sumatur, sed (ut) ex jure, quod est, regula fiat." Cf. SAVIGNY, *System des heutigen römischen Rechts*, I Bd., 1840, § 14, p. 47, and JHERING, *Geist des röm. Rechts*, I Th., 5 Aufl., *cit.*, p. 33 *et seq.*

6. A further proof may be found in the fact that in social life even juristic acts between persons lacking capacity, e.g. the contracts of minors, have a real, though imperfect, efficacy, and their imperfection is manifest only in judicial proceedings, that is, vis-à-vis the State.

7. On authority within the primitive family, see the classical account of FUSTEL DE COULANGES, *La Cité antique*, Bk. II, C. VIII; cf. on the phenomenology of criminal law in its earliest

phases E. GARÇON, *Le droit pénal: origines, évolution, état actuel* (Paris, 1922), p. 23 *et. seq.*

8. Thus, e.g., FLORIAN, *Parte generale del diritto penale* (4 ed., Milano, 1934), pp. 12-15, and others there mentioned.

9. FLORIAN, *loc. cit.*; cf. JELLINEK, *System der subjektiven öffentlichen Rechte* (p. 235 *et seq.* of the Ital ed., Milano, 1912); ESPOSITO, *Lineamenti di una dottrina del diritto* (Padova, 1932), p. 177 *et seq.*, and writings there cited.

10. A. LEGAL et J. BRÈTHE DE LA GRESSAYE, *Le pouvoir disciplinaire dans les institutions privées* (Paris, 1938), which appeared after the first edition of the present essay, in substance confirms our thesis (see esp. p. 110).

11. On the antinomy created by, e.g., the duel, cf. CALAMANDREI, *Regole cavalleresche e processo* (in "Riv. di dir. process. civile," A. VI, 1929, N. 2).

12. Against the negative opinions of some (SOHM, WUNDT, JHERING), cf. GÉNY, *Science et technique*, *cit.*, I, p. 60 *et seq.*

13. BIERLING, *Zur Kritik der juristischen Grundbegriffe* (Gotha, 1877-1883), esp. I Th., p. 1 *et seq.*; *id.*, *Juristische Prinzipienlehre* (1894-1917). We do not, however, adhere to B.'s doctrine of "Anerkennung," which has been refuted by PETRONE, *La fase recentissima della Filosofia del diritto in Germania* (Pisa, 1895), p. 120 *et seq.* The *recognition* of law is, in our view, only a mark of *positivity*, which can apply also to morality, insofar as morality is positive, that is to say, actually observed. The really distinctive element of law lies in its bilateral character.

14. See especially the discussion between JEMOLO and SCADUTO in "Archivio Giuridico," vols. 90-93 (1923-1925).

15. As held notably by JEMOLO, *loc. cit.*; see also, with reference to the subsequent Lateran Agreements, his *Lezioni di diritto ecclesiastico* (Città di Castello, 1933), p. 64 *et seq.* On the various possible species of *renvoi* and reception in relations between different legal systems, see TRIEPEL, *Diritto internazionale e diritto interno* (Ital. ed., Torino, 1913), p. 155 *et seq.*; ROMANO, *L'ordinamento giuridico, cit.*, p. 112 *et seq.*

16. See V. DEL GUIDICE in "Archiv. Giurid," vol. 91 (1924) and writings there referred to. According to DEL G., the *canonicatio*, or assumption of State rules into canon law, is not a true "reception" or even a material *renovi*, as such rules are not recognized as having legal existence before the *canonicatio;* the process is thus one of reproduction or, at most, of *"de facto* reception." This subtle distinction does not seem to reveal any substantial

difference from the position reached when one takes State law as the starting point; the State, too, sees the legal validity of the canon law as beginning, strictly speaking, from its reference to the State.

17. On this phenomenon, especially with reference to the public administration, see RANELLETTI, *I sindacati e lo Stato* (in "Politica," vol. V, 1920); ROCCO, *Crisi dello Stato* (*ibid.*, vol. VII, 1921).

18. SANDERS, *Das Faktum der Revolution und die Kontinuität der Rechtsordnung* (in "Zschr. f. öffentl. Recht," 8 Bd., 1919); *Die transzendentale Methode der Rechtsphilosophie und der Begriff des Rechtsverfahrens* (*ibid.*); *Staat und Recht* (Leipzig, 1922).

EQUALITY AND INEQUALITY IN RELATION TO JUSTICE

I.

WHEN WE BEGIN TO REFLECT ON THE IDEA OF JUSTICE, SEEKing its essential principle, we at once think of equality. Pythagoras, the first to consider the problem, defined justice as equality which should manifest itself in exchange. The obvious inadequacy of this definition was soon noted. Aristotle, starting from the Pythagorean theory, introduced an important distinction: namely, that while there is a form of justice—especially applicable to contract—which requires equivalence on each side, there is also *distributive* justice, which considers the dignity or merit of persons and requires that they shall be variously treated in accordance therewith (κατ' ἀξίαν). This doctrine became the classical one and is still held as fundamental. Yet it, too, is open to objection. In contractual relationships, that is, in *commutative* justice, law in fact does not and cannot require objective equivalence of value in what is exchanged but merely (except in the special case of *laesio enormis*) subjective freedom of consent. As for distributive justice, Aristotle did not determine the criterion for valuing dignity or merit; he lacked a concept of the essential value of human personality (as is demonstrated by his justification of slavery), the recognition of which should constitute the first postulate of justice.

II.

A great advance in the conception of justice was made when this ideal postulate, glimpsed by the Stoics, was affirmed by

Christianity. According to the Gospel, all men, as children of God, are brothers; the same spirit abides in all, and the law of charity and love is universally valid for all; hence comes the categorical duty of respecting that which is sacred in every human person; and hence the natural right to claim such respect. Positive legal systems should adhere to these principles, but for all that they sometimes have solemnly proclaimed them, in fact they have adopted them only imperfectly, or even altogether ignored them.

The law which is implanted in human nature itself has been proved by rational analysis (independently of theological premises—thus the dictates of reason and faith coincide); and, notwithstanding the opposition of certain philosophical schools, this law, often and sometimes imperiously invoked by the common consciousness of men, has found expression in the constitutions of the more civilized peoples and in recent international declarations. The various specific requirements of this fundamental law have been set forth in different ways. But if we compare these declarations of principle with the rules of actual legal systems (even systems expressly prefaced by such a declaration), we observe that they have suffered serious deviations and restrictions, in part inevitable but in part unjustified.

III.

The recognition of the juridical personality of each and every human being, such that a fundamental equality is established, is a principle which we must hold as absolutely valid. Rationally understood and applied, this principle should be the basis of a *societas humani generis*, so that humanity might form a single State. And there are reasons to believe that despite the prevailing conflicts this is the goal toward which the history of the human race is in fact advancing.

So long, however, as a diversity of States exists, the distinction between citizens and aliens cannot be abolished. The rule of equality can be established (and in the more advanced States has been established) only with respect to civil and not to political rights.

There should be no exclusion, either from civil or from political rights, on grounds of race or religious belief. This is clearly set forth, for instance, in art. 3 of the Italian Constitution. But some States have not yet achieved perfect legal equality between citizens of different races or faiths, and in some instances a total repudiation of this fundamental principle has led to infamous and shocking persecutions.

IV.

As a general rule, the legal equality of the sexes should also be recognized, as by arts. 3 and 51 of the Italian Constitution. But, for obvious reasons, no legal system confers on the two sexes absolutely identical rights and duties. Military service, for instance, is commonly required only of men. In various States women are also excluded from other posts for which they are considered less suitable. Even in some highly civilized States, like Switzerland, women are excluded from the electorate, although this conflicts not only with the principle of the legal equality of the sexes but also with the principle of universal suffrage. The prevailing modern tendency, however, is towards a progressive rectification of the old systems, in which women were held in a sort of subjection, towards an effective equality. The only exceptions are based, not on a notion of inferiority, but on the natural differences between the sexes.

In modern labor law, for instance, and even in prison regulations, we find special provisions for women who are mothers; on the other hand, admission of women to public responsibilities is always understood to hinge on their possession of the necessary aptitude.

V.

The abstract principle of equality of the sexes gives rise to special problems in family law. Rigid application of the principle would imply the equal authority of the two spouses and deprive the husband of his functions and powers as head of the family (recognized by art. 144 of the Italian Civil Code); thus it would be difficult to maintain that unity which is an essential element in the institution of the family. However, this does not exclude the possibility of broadening the wife's rights (not, however, to the point of complete equality), and certain proposals to that end have been advanced, some of which seem reasonable, while on others judgment should be reserved. It has been proposed, for instance, to apply to both sexes the same penal sanctions for the act of adultery, although the possible consequences of such an act are naturally not the same. The most just solution (to my mind) would be that adultery should no longer be considered a penal offense, but that it should be left to the magistrate, on complaint by the injured party, to determine whether the circumstances demonstrate that a case of *ingiuria* (affront to personal honor or susceptibilities) exists. The present somewhat narrow definition of this offense (art. 594 of the Penal Code) should be appropriately amended by legislation. But this is not the place for full discussion of the problem.

VI.

The dignity of the human being is substantially equal in all stages of his life, but his actual capacity varies greatly, and it would be most unreasonable if, in falsely applying the concept of equality, we failed to take this into account. All legal systems fix—though not always at the same age—the commencement of majority and, consequently, of full civil capacity. But this does not suffice, and there are, therefore, other rules in both private and public law which establish different age requirements for different purposes. In Italian law, for instance (which resembles that of many other States) majority begins at twenty-one, but a young person of eighteen can make a will and enter into contracts of service (arts. 2, 3, 591, etc. of the Civil Code). In view of such exceptions and of present-day social conditions, it would be right (in my opinion) that majority should commence at twenty, if not even eighteen or nineteen.

In criminal law, a child who was under fourteen at the time he committed the criminal act cannot be charged with an offense, and there is a reduction in penalty for one between fourteen and eighteen (arts. 97, 98 of the Penal Code and cf. arts. 223-227).

There are also various distinctions of age in matters of franchise and of eligibility for membership of our two houses of Parliament. These (to which other illustrations could be added) demonstrate the difficulty of achieving organic regulation of this complex branch of law, and certainly the detached and unsystematic rules that now exist provide no satisfactory solution. (A possible electoral reform will be mentioned shortly.)

We must admit that legislation, which must take the future into consideration and provide in general terms for innumerable individual cases, can never be perfectly adequate to cope with the continual flux of changing reality. Even when they permit judicial discretion, legislative provisions always tend to be mechanical, and reflect only imperfectly the actuality of the particular case. Individuals subject to one and the same rule obviously differ greatly in natural capacity; but it is equally obvious that it would be as impossible in practice to subject each individual to an examination to determine whether he had attained a certain degree of capacity as it would be to make the legal period of prescription depend upon the particular circumstances.

Roman jurists, and also the modern legislator, wisely granted a certain limited effect to acts and relationships which do not conform to the requirements laid down in general. This is illustrated by the notion of "natural obligations" as compared with civil obligations; and by the distinction between absolute and relative nullity. The juristic acts of those who, though under age, have natural capacity are not absolutely null and void, like those of the insane, but can be made valid by ratification and by the provision of sureties (arts. 1444, 1939 of the Civil Code). The natural relationship of parent and illegitimate child creates legal rights, subordinate to those of the legitimate. These are merely examples.

All of the foregoing simply shows that even if positive law cannot completely realize the ideal of justice, it can approximate it if the ideal is not enclosed in too rigid terms and if it retains contact with living reality. It is also worth noting that on some points legislation refrains from enacting a precise rule and leaves the matter for the judge to decide according to considerations of equity.

VII.

In modern civilized States—thanks to the past labors of Philosophy, and also to historical revolutions—it has come to be accepted that, while citizens are duty-bound to obey the laws, it is also their responsibility, through voting, through their chosen representatives, and in some cases even more directly, to take part in the making of the laws. It has also been determined that the Government and functionaries of the public administration are subject to the laws and that, in case of misbehavior, the way must always be open to citizens to seek redress through judicial organs, whose independence must be assured.

These notions correspond to the fundamental principle of the dignity and freedom of the human being and are therefore to be held as unquestionable. But their application gives rise to more than a few problems. Even indirect participation in the power to make laws requires, by its nature, a capacity greater than that required for the exercise of private civil rights. Civil capacity, therefore, should logically be distinguished from political capacity. Positive law makes this distinction with clarity by according civil capacity to both citizens and aliens while reserving political capacity for citizens alone. But legal systems commonly impose further, more or less rigorous requirements before granting political capacity even to citizens. For instance, Italian law, until a few decades ago, excluded women from the franchise (an exclusion now justly discontinued) and also required the ability to read and write as a condition of political capacity. Today the law allows even illiterates to vote and—with one exception—at the same age, twenty-one, as is required for civil capacity.

The consequences of this are notorious, since, despite efforts to combat illiteracy and spread education, the number of illiterates, especially in certain regions, is not inconsiderable, and the number of semi-literates is still greater. No one could seriously maintain that either of these groups is really fit to direct the policy of the State.

Another factor to be considered is the formation, in Italy and in other countries, of political parties—some of them strongly organized and rigidly disciplined—whose pressure on the organs of government has often disturbed their proper functioning. One such party, inspired by materialist doctrine and directed from abroad, seeks to replace the existing social and legal order with the rule of the working class, no matter what hardship may be involved for other classes and for individual rights. In some states this party has been made illegal; not so in Italy, where it has spread widely, particularly among the less educated, whose "herd" sense prevails over the sense of individuality. This dangerous state of affairs has naturally provoked discussion. Various proposals have been made, and some have even questioned the principle of universal suffrage, in the belief that it should be held accountable for our present political difficulties.

In my opinion, however, this principle should be maintained, but in its application it should be rendered more rational and compelled to weigh the variance in capacity due to differences of age and education. Instead of a mechanical equality, for justice's sake a criterion should be established which has regard for real values. To put it in Aristotelian terms, equal treatment for unequal merit contradicts the idea of equality and violates the rule of distributive justice.

A system which, in my view, would achieve this would be: A certain percentage (say 40%) of the total would be elected by voters of a certain degree of education (for instance, holding a high school certificate); the majority of the remainder would be elected by voters above a certain age (say, 30 or 35), and the minority by voters under that age—this because judgment ripens with advancing age. (The suggested figures are, of course, merely indicative and could be altered according to relevant statistics so long as the first class were always more heavily weighted than the second, and the second than the third.) Those elected, however, would all have equal dignity, so that the representative Assembly might be homogeneous.

VIII.

In its aims the United Nations organization is among the noblest of human institutions, and it has achieved much towards the progress of civilization and the peace of the world. Yet in its structure and procedure certain defects are manifest. While its Charter declares it to be based on the sovereign equality of all members, five States (the Permanent Members of the Security Council) are placed in a privileged position, thus reducing the other members to permanent inferiority.

The preamble to the Charter voices the determination of the peoples of the U.N. "to reaffirm the faith in fundamental human rights" (and the same idea is embodied in the Universal Declaration of Human Rights of 1948), yet States have been admitted to membership (even to membership in the privileged group) which neither respect these rights in their internal law nor in international relations. Moreover, the possible consequences of this defect have been aggravated in recent years by the admission to the U.N. of many States which are on a low level culturally and whose systems of governance contain no guarantee of the fundamental rights; once such States have been placed on a footing of legal equality with constitutional and highly civilized States, the possibility arises that the votes of the former may paralyze the activity of the latter and of the U.N. itself. Here we see an example of that "equality" which disregards essential values and is thus contrary to justice.

A radical reform, aimed at admitting to membership only States which were "legitimate" or "law-States" (*Stati di diritto*)—that is, where the rule of law prevailed—would seem impracticable at present (especially since it would have to be retroactively applied); all we can hope for is that future admissions will be strictly controlled by such a requirement. Another reform which would eliminate some of the present inconveniences and dangers and ensure a correct and rational functioning of the organization would be to distinguish between these "law-States" (or "justice-States") and those which are not "law-States," although they may become such in the future. In such a case only the former would have the right to vote, at least on important matters. However, we must not delude ourselves that even such a limited reform would be easy under present circumstances. There are, however, other international organizations, with a less extensive membership than the United Nations, that possess a more solid foundation in the sense that they are based on a genuine community of ideas and aims; from these we may expect a greater contribution to the defense of liberty and of peace.

A problem to which little attention has been devoted to date is: whether in international associations it is proper to give equal value to the votes of all States great and small, or whether the size of their populations should be taken into account. The first alternative fits the notion of the juridical equality of States, inasmuch as all are equally sovereign. But Bentham's rule, "Each to count for one," applies also to individuals, and it does not seem reasonable that a vote which represents a population of a few thousands should receive the same weight as a vote representing many millions. These requirements might be reconciled by a system which demanded a majority on both counts for decision. Other solutions are possible, however, and the best solution for one association may not be the same for another.[1]

IX.

Even if the principle of the dignity of the human being is generally recognized and—however imperfectly—applied in the legal systems of more advanced peoples, there is one branch of the law in which the principle seems to be entirely disregarded, namely, in criminal law. Even modern systems still labor under the influence of the ancient prejudice that it is "just" to repay evil with evil, and that suffering inflicted on the author of a crime should be considered "reparation" for his wrongdoing.

In truth, evil is "repaired" only by good. The rule of "an eye for an eye and a tooth for a tooth" has been rejected by the conscience of civilized peoples, who no longer cut off the hand of the thief or cut out the tongue of the slanderer; yet these peoples still retain the false notion that to the evil of crime must be attached the evil of punishment.

Do we show respect for a man's personality by intentionally inflicting pain on him, even if he be guilty? Is not this a duplication of the wrong, ethically unjustifiable, as was observed as far back as Plato? Is it just that a human being should be deprived, for years and even for life, of the opportunity to develop his own spirit and to communicate with other men? Is it just that pain and heavy loss should be inflicted not only on the guilty man but also on those innocents whose only fault is their relationship to him?

Legal sanctions against offenders are necessary, but the problem is to discover what sanctions are admissible according to the ideal of justice. So far as I can see, it is impossible to argue that capital punishment and imprisonment correspond to that ideal.

Both the universally admitted rule of "legitimate defense," the rational basis and limits of which are to be found in the purpose of the defense, and what are called "security measures," whose aim is not to punish but to prevent wrongdoing, may be considered beyond discussion. Similar measures are applied, where necessary, to the insane, and obviously here the intention is not to inflict suffering.

According to Seneca's profound observation (echoed by other thinkers) crime has its proper punishment in itself. Doing wrong is normally (at least in most cases) followed by a feeling of remorse and repentance, which is in itself a punishment. It may be added that, quite apart from the possibility of criminal proceedings, evildoing usually excites social reprobation and discredit, with consequences to which the evildoer cannot be indifferent.

The true and proper field of criminal justice remains to be determined. Its foundation should be that the harm caused by the crime should, so far as possible, be repaired by the criminal, bearing in mind that not only the immediate victim but public order in general—indeed, the whole of society—has suffered.

The provisions of our laws are very defective in this respect. While they assert that a duty to make restitution and reparation exists, it extends only to the individuals harmed and not to the public order; moreover, because of the lack of means of the offender, whose very punishment deprives him of the opportunity to work and earn money, restitution usually remains a dead letter. There is no provision for evaluating the harm which has been done to public order, and where the criminal sanction consists in a money fine, it is fixed quite arbitrarily. While admitting that evaluation of the reparation due would not be easy, we feel that at least the principle and certain rules for guidance should be determined by law.

To make the duty of reparation effective, in my plan those convicted of crime would be required to work and the product of their work would be assigned as payment of their debt. Whether they voluntarily and diligently performed such work should be a matter for their own free choice, in accord with their capacity, though under the supervision of a special magistracy. In serious cases and in cases of default, this magistracy would have the power to impose definite tasks, with certain restrictions of liberty, which, however, should always be in humane forms and determined by law. The same court, or some branch of it, might also be responsible for the surveillance of the way of life of those who had not satisfied their debt *ex delicto*, so that at least the worst offenses against good faith and morality could be eliminated. But always, the respect due the fundamental rights of the human person should be preserved.

The problems involved are difficult and complex, and the above suggestions may well encounter questioning and opposition, especially as on many points they run contrary to prevailing opinion and to existing rules of law. Immediate fulfillment cannot be expected; yet a gradual fulfillment is not impossible, especially since recent developments in penal systems, though more conservative than the radical reform which I believe desirable, demonstrate a tendency to correct some of their defects. Such developments include conditional suspension of punishment (art. 163 *et seq.* of the Italian Penal Code), the so-called judicial pardon for those under 18 (art. 169), labor institutions and farm colonies for the re-education of offenders, etc.

X.

In our search for just solutions to the various problems of social life we have seen that the notion of equality has a part to play, especially insofar as it leads to the recognition of the essential dignity of the human person. Yet it does not suffice for a solution, because while admitting this fundamental equality, justice requires that the differences arising from the varying capacity and behavior of individuals must also be taken into account. We may then ask what is the meaning of such oft-repeated maxims as: "The law is equal for all," "All citizens are equal before the law." Literally understood, these (especially the former) could lead to such absurd consequences as that innocent and guilty, adults and children, should be treated alike. Their real meaning is that no one in the State is above the law (*legibus solutus*) and that ancient privileges (like those of the hereditary nobility) have been abolished, so that all citizens are to be judged by the same measure. Even so, they are of no great value, because they refer generally to the law, and laws can be unjust, and even unjust laws are usually enforced. However, under the present Italian system it is possible that, when the constitutionality of a law is questioned, the judge may suspend proceedings and remit the question to the Constitutional Court. Thus may the principle of the legal equality of all citizens be upheld, within the limits set by the wording of the Constitution.

It must also be observed that it is not always easy to enforce even the most just laws, not only because of their potential for violation but also because the necessary means for enforcement are lacking or insufficient. The Italian Constitution declares that "a period of at least eight years of free school education is obligatory," but the number of schools is inadequate and the economic condition of many families makes the obligation impossible to fulfill. Another provision of the Constitution (art. 24) states that all persons, "even those lacking resources, must be assured of the means to bring actions and to defend themselves before any court," but, although a system of legal aid has been established for this purpose (in particular, for the defense of poor persons involved in criminal proceedings), it is notorious that such aid is often a mere formality and is much less effective than the aid which the well-to-do can obtain.

For all that modern legislation reflects a general advance over that of past ages, even in the most civilized States there still remain many injustices which laws have been unable to cure. Hence arise not only proposals for further legislation, but also political programs which threaten to overturn the entire social order. To place all men in a condition of economic equality would demand an unjust disregard of the rights already acquired by individuals according to their capacity and their labor, as well as of the legitimate provisions made by their ancestors. A rational system of taxation, which would progressively fix the sums due from the various taxpayers, should enable the State to fulfill its function of doing justice for the common good. It is the State's task to provide for the protection of the life and the physical and moral integrity of its members, and above all for the protection of those who are not in a position to provide such out of their own means or the means of those closely associated with them. Everyone should receive education to a certain level. Everyone should be entitled to the use of the tools of labor and the means of production, so that no one would be excluded from productive activity and its fruits.

In a spirit of justice and charity, the initiatives of individuals and of associations must become actively engaged with the State in raising the level of the underprivileged. Law is inseparable from morality. Action in these areas must not hinge solely on State initiative.

XI.

Laws must bear the imprint of generality and not refer to individual persons. Thus, we cannot describe as just laws which condemn particular persons (for instance, ex-monarchs and their families) to exile, without providing the legal process by which they might defend themselves. Inasmuch as the penalty of exile is not provided for in existing penal laws, laws condemning persons to exile manifestly offend against the rule in Art. 25 of the Italian Constitution that "no one shall be punished except under a law which was in force before the commission of the act in question." It would be sophistry to argue that a sentence of exile is not a punishment.

Finally, we may observe that, for law to be truly general, it is not sufficient that it should apply to a group of persons, however numerous. It must apply to *all* persons of the category to which a particular group belongs. Amnesties, pardons and reductions of sentences, granted occasionally, for reasons of the moment, to particular groups undergoing punishment, while all others are excluded, admittedly serve to alleviate the excessive cruelty of our penal systems; they may even be almost regarded as a confession of the defects of the system. But without waiting for the radical reform proposed above, or any other legislative reforms, it would be more just to institute periodic revisions of all sentences of punishment restrictive of personal liberty, followed by such remissions as were found to be really justified by the conduct and circumstances of the individuals undergoing punishment. This would rationally systematize the institution of "grace and favor," which certainly, because of its humanitarian character, ought not to be abolished. Rather, we plead that it should be organically inserted in a wider and more just ordering of this whole field.

NOTE

1. [Del Vecchio's views may be compared with those of J. LORIMER, *Institutes of the Law of Nations* (Edinburgh, 1883, 1884), esp. vol. I, Bk. II, chs. V-VIII on the conditions for recognition of States and chs. XV-XVII on the relative value of States. Lorimer, however, suggested that a State should carry weight, not according to its population, but according to its wealth, and thus to its potential military power.]

THE CRISIS OF THE SCIENCE OF LAW

I. PRELIMINARIES

WHEN WE SPEAK, AS WE OFTEN DO, OF A CRISIS IN THE SCIENCE of law, we must not think that it is a problem pertaining only to our time. It could be said that law and its science, like human existence itself, are locked in a perpetual crisis, intent on a continual struggle and on an incessant labor of adaptation, transformation and re-integration. Such is the drama of our existence that every action corresponds to a problem and represents an attempt at a solution—rarely perfect—to a given problem. We shall now leave these general considerations aside, however, and consider in more detail the crisis of the science of law as it appears in our time.

The fundamental elements of the tension which impels the science of law into a continual and intense struggle can be reduced, simply enough, to the following: on the one hand, law appears to us historically as a datum or a phenomenon, while, on the other, it appears in its ideality as something emanating from, and essentially abiding in our spirit.

II. LAW AS A DATUM OR PHENOMENON. IMPOSSIBILITY OF MECHANICAL APPLICATION OF ENACTED LAW. CONTINUOUS RENEWAL AND THE WORK OF THE LAWYER

The first consideration is the most obvious and apparently the surest. As in all conscious processes, the mind gives itself first to empirical observation, assuming whatever falls within the purview of the senses to be objective reality, absolutely certain and independent of any subjectivity. According to popular opinion, law is a written text, a tangible code which comprises everything. Any juridical question or controversy, according to such opinion, must find its explicit solution in the existing law, which is conceived as a body of enacted rules wherein everything is foreseen. The lawyer and the law are thought of as an almost automatic sort of apparatus, which when set in motion by a mechanical impulse, must in an equally mechanical manner produce a precise judgment in every case. This accounts for that oft-encountered expectation of those untrained in law that they can obtain from the lawyer not a mere opinion but a definite prediction of the outcome of any possible trial. It also accounts for the "unpopularity" of lawyers so frequently noted down through the centuries, which has even been translated into proverbs (*"Juristen, böse Christen," et cetera*).[1] Lawyers are accused of artificially complicating, through professional habit, questions entrusted to them, as if it were their fault that such questions were made difficult and uncertain.

It is hardly necessary to stress how infinitely far from the truth is this popular conception. Lawyers do not artificially complicate human relations; these are by their own nature infinitely varied, extremely complex and almost always new and different. The lawyer must understand them and extract from them the essential elements, which are not always the most evident. He must fit them to a rule if a rule exists, and, if not, must himself labor to formulate the rule which is needed. All this represents a difficult mental task, which, with due respect to other professions, is perhaps the most arduous of all technical activities.

The *jus scriptum*—meaning the product of legislation, and also collections of customs and of case law—is insufficient to reflect the forever-renewed reality or to offer a solution to all the new developments of social life. The inability of the human mind, and consequently of the mind of the legislator, to formulate in advance all possible future cases was explicitly noted by Roman jurists and has since been noted countless times in the course of the centuries. This inability has been most acutely felt in modern times, both because conditions of life have changed so rapidly and also new forms of activity have appeared, which present problems for whose solution it is not always possible to find a secure basis in existing laws. Therefore, the lawyer is not only required to exert himself in interpreting the existing laws so that he may adapt their sense to new social relations; he must also increasingly collaborate in making necessary innovations.

After a fashion every legal system provides for its own renovation, that is, its own modification and supplementation. When it is necessary to add to, rather than modify, the law, such work is ordinarily entrusted to the judge, who is authorized, and thus bound, to found his decision upon one of the so-called subsidiary sources if the principal source or sources are deficient. It then becomes necessary to go beyond the law (and also, where this is allowed, beyond custom) by means of analogy, which makes possible a certain extension of existing rules—in reality a creation of new and related rules. But analogy is not always possible, and, when it is, it is not always permissible. It is necessary, therefore, that the judge discover the criterion for his decisions elsewhere, for no controversy can remain unsolved for lack of a rule. It may be provided, as, for instance, in the Swiss Code, that the judge shall decide "as if he were legislator"; or, as in the Italian Code, that he shall decide "according to the general principles of law"; or there may be no express provision on the point, as in the French and German codes. But the conclusion will always be the same: the judge must find a rule which, while not provided by existing laws, he is nevertheless required to find. How else can he do this except by questioning his own conscience, showing all due regard for the nature of the case submitted and for the logic of the system which his decision is called to add to? We are far from the mechanical or automatic application of a given law.

III. OPPOSING TENDENCIES. NEED OF CERTAINTY AND OF FLEXIBILITY IN LAW. ENACTED LAW, FREE LAW, EQUITY

In modern times, study of the sources of law reveals two tendencies, in a way antithetical, which underline the crisis we are studying. The need for certainty, clarity and order in the determination of law has led in many cases to a preference for the statutory form as that which better answers the logical needs of our mind as well as the practical convenience of settling the greater part of the legal system as firmly as possible. Custom and the authority of judicial precedent are a more unstable and less precise source of law than is legislation. Uncertainty in law produces inconvenience, inasmuch as it directly contradicts one of the very bases of law's existence, namely, the production of order and assurance in social relations. It is for this reason, Bacon said, that the certainty of law is so important: if it be not certain, it cannot be just. For the sake of certainty, in order to establish an adequate basis for determining future cases, the formulation of law proceeds by establishing a sort of stock pattern of the common, constant characteristics of acts and facts which are actually very diverse. The abstractness and schematic rigidity of law, which laymen condemn, is a necessary, practical, and beneficial consequence of the function which law exercises in life. When the legislator fixes the age of reason at twenty-one years, he is establishing a mean which may be unjust in many cases; many youths younger than that have already attained their full capacity of judgment, while others who have reached the legal age remain more or less deficient. But there would be great practical difficulty if the judge had to decide the grade of maturity and the consequent legal capacity of each individual, without any guidance from a definite rule couched in general terms.

The statutory form of law is valued highly in modern times for the assurance it affords in constitutional matters and in every thing affecting the rights of the individual. The formula, "law alone is sovereign and no command can be given which is not based on it"—whether explicitly proclaimed or merely implied in the structure of the system—has enormous historical importance; in a summary fashion it represents the suppression of innumerable abuses which characterized old regimes, abuses which were possible because of the law's lack of certainty. To mention only one point, criminal law in all civilized states today differs essentially from ancient criminal law in that it possesses the fundamental maxims: *Nulla poena sine lege; nullum crimen sine lege*. The same might be said of administrative law, where too the supremacy of enacted law has become synonymous with justice.

Hence, we should not be wrong in declaring that the general tendency of law is to pass from custom and the sporadic decisions of case law to legislation. Further proof is evidenced by the fact that those branches of law which are technically less advanced (such as international law) are the very ones which for various reasons have been unable to achieve true and proper legislative form.

But a contrary tendency is also manifest today, namely, to maintain that the rigidity of legislation constitutes an obstacle to the free development of law, and that, especially in matters which are subject to rapid change and require a greater correspondence between fact and norm, it is better to entrust organs other than the legislature with the task of fashioning the rule appropriate to the concrete case.

We need not here recall the famous polemic of the historical school against codification. We merely note that, even though the idea of codification championed by Thibaut and opposed by Savigny ended by triumphing in Germany, the battle took nearly a hundred years and, except for the particular proposal which occasioned the controversy, the doctrines of the historical school regarding law in general and its origin and development survived and now prevail among jurists. We have even come to take a historical view of legislation and codes, and of the possibility of modifying their sense without resorting to legislation, by employing a broad interpretative process in their judicial application. It would be easy to give examples of legislation which, while remaining formally unchanged, has gradually assumed a different and even, at times, an opposite meaning to its original one, thus restoring that very same condition of arbitrariness and uncertainty which the original legislation was intended to remove.

These are not the only symptoms of the modern tendency to depreciate legislation as a source of law. There is, for instance, that complex of doctrines and ideals which is called "the school of free law." This school maintains that the formal reference the judge makes to the text of the law is scarcely more than a fiction, and that in reality he depends for his solution upon a direct examination of the case and a balancing of the conflicting interests involved. This theory makes legislation a useless ornament which in the name of liberty and truth could even be formally dispensed with. Without going into minute criticism of this doctrine, we may note that, while paying due respect to the small amount of truth which it contains, its basic assumption could not be accepted without shaking the very foundations of the legal order. In this order subordination of judicial to legislative functions represents the citizen's basic guarantee.

A more important phenomenon, manifested especially in countries where changing social conditions have speeded the development of new law, is the institution of special courts to decide controversies in specific matters (such as labor contracts), such courts being freed from subjection to existing rules of law. This opens the door wide to those considerations of mere equity which only in rare cases (and almost timidly) had been admitted as exceptions in the codes. The increasing number of these special courts has complicated the order of the traditional systems. And if they have not diminished the authority, they have at least impaired the universal character of legislation as a uniform criterion valid for all citizens without distinction. Many objections have been raised against the rising tide of special jurisdictions and arguments have been advanced for a change in legislative policy which would again give a unified and homogeneous system. Yet the need for a greater adaptability and elasticity of law persists, and many contend that this can only be satisfied by allowing the judge greater powers of original creation.

IV. THE JUDGE AS "LIVING JUSTICE"

In reality, it is differences of degree and not of kind that are in question, since even in ordinary judicial activity a certain amount of spontaneous creation, *secundum legem* and sometimes even *praeter legem* exists. In interpreting the law the judge is almost never simply passive towards it. All those maxims—including the famous one of Montesquieu—which represent the judge as a mechanical instrument, or an inanimate being, at the service of enacted law must be repudiated in the science and philosophy of law. More truth is to be found in the Aristotelian conception of the judge as "living justice" (δίκαιον ἔμψυχον). In this view, the judge is seen as an organ which sums up in itself the spirit of the law and expresses it in ever new forms, coherent with the system but instrumental in its further development. To disregard this characteristic of case law would mean disregarding the data of experience. From Roman times onward the most perfect and progressive legal systems have been developed with the active, and not merely the passive, aid of case law. Paraphrasing a celebrated philosophical formula, we can say that legislation without case law would be empty, just as case law without legislation would be blind.

This becomes even more evident when we consider that legislation often leaves blank spaces, so to speak, in the legal system. These are the result of the limitation of the human mind (mentioned by Bacon), whereby the legislator is unable to foresee all possible future cases, and also follow from the fact that the legislator often deliberately abstains from determining what can be more opportunely and justly determined by the judge. Every system contains ideas which we may call "safety valve concepts," which allow for expansion and communication with the outer world and serve to prevent that build-up of compression in the legislative system which could provoke an explosion. When the legislator speaks of "good morals" or "public order," he deliberately abstains from defining the terms, which can be variously understood and applied according to the predominant mood of society. Most significant of all are those cases wherein the legislator refers to the "equity" of the judge as the sole criterion for his decision. Here, recourse to "equity," as a criterion for application of an existing law, transcends the ordinary sense of the word. In this case it is a question not merely of interpreting, but of fashioning a norm which the legislature expressly declares it does not wish to formulate.

V. LAW AS A CATEGORY OR NECESSARY RHYTHM OF THE SPIRIT. PSYCHOLOGICAL FOUNDATION OF THE HISTORICAL MANIFESTATIONS OF LAW

Thus, little by little, examination of the life of the law through its own organs has led us to recognize, or at least to glimpse, that point of orientation which we mentioned at the start, by which the law presents itself as an idea rather than a datum. Upon this we must dwell for a moment.

We are born not merely to obey laws passively but to create them, finding their principle in our spirit—not in that part of the spirit which is changeable and doubtful, but in that part which is essential and immutable. There is a rhythm of consciousness, an essential and unfailing moment in the life of the spirit which properly constitutes law. This is its root, its profound reason, its "eternal seed," as Vico put it. In comparison with this, historical phenomena are secondary, supervenient, and bound to the empirical, as the flowering of a plant to its seed. . . . Before law appears as a phenomenon of social organization and a hierarchy of positively constituted forces it is a necessary rhythm of spiritual life. Its essential and characteristic elements, which in historical experience appear to us variously refracted, are already implicit in that primary and fundamental definition, so that we may say with truth: *leges innumerae, una justitia.* Alterity or bilaterality, that is, the simultaneous consideration of several subjects; parity between these same subjects; reciprocity, by which each binds himself to the other even as he imposes an obligation on the other, a holder of rights and claims, subject to restrictions and duties; hence interchange and remuneration—all these elements are no more than corollaries of this idea of justice and just as they flower within the individual consciousness so do they flower and take form historically in positive juridical institutions. They culminate in the supreme requirement of respect for the autonomy of the human being, so that man—not as an empirical personality, but as an organ of universal ideas—may harmoniously develop his nature and fully realize his ends.

We can discover the law in our own nature, *ex interiore homine;* and we can discover it by observation of historical data extraneous to us. This duality would be insuperable if it were not for the help of an insight which was first consciously formulated by Giambattista Vico: "The civil world was certainly made by men and its principles must be found in the human mind." The criterion of truth is the doing of it. The historical data which we called extraneous are not really so if we look a little more deeply. They, too, are spiritual products, products of a spirit substantially identical with our own. All positive juridical institutions, all laws, all customs, are but manifestations or reflections of sentiments, thoughts, and beliefs, no matter how differently expressed. Since they emanate from a multitude of subjects and from the succession of generations, they are imperfectly fused. We would not make a dogma of the historical phenomenology of law, as do some philosophical schools that unfortunately are still in vogue; we merely recognize the fundamentally psychological character of all human historical manifestations, including law. The human spirit follows and in a way reflects itself, witnessing in history the products, however defective, of its roots. We discern ourselves in the innumerable collections of juridical institutions that history offers us, and, even where we find deviations and errors, these are in some way deviations and errors of our own spirit. To recognize them as such is of itself to surmount them.

A circle or uninterrupted activity is thus established whereby the ideality of law, which consciousness draws from within itself, is reflected in its historicity (understood critically and not dogmatically); and in turn, this historical authenticity is reflected in consciousness and becomes intelligible by the intimate echo it finds there. Thus it would not be improper to speak of the "circular life" of law, which, born in the spirit, in the course of history returns to the spirit.

VI. ORGANIC UNITY OF EVERY JURIDICAL SYSTEM AND POSSIBILITIES OF ITS COHERENT DEVELOPMENT

If these principles are true, as we believe them to be, the difficulties which we have indicated as pertaining to the science of law in general and to its modern science in particular become soluble. By this means it becomes possible to trace schematically the criteria which the jurist must observe in his many-sided activity.

Even in its historical and positive existence law is not by nature a physical fact but rather a manifestation of states of mind. Overcoming accidental divergences and antinomies, these mental states compose themselves in a coherent unity or system. Thus, it becomes clear that the jurist, when studying or interpreting a particular positive system, must never halt his efforts at the letter of single dispositions, since these almost always fall short of the intrinsic spirit of the system. Beyond all formulations—almost invariably imperfect and thereby fallacious—lies that reason which animates the entire logical organism. To this reason above all the jurist must pay attention if he is to understand and correctly apply the existing law, even in new cases.

This preference for the spirit over the letter which as a methodological requirement was rightly affirmed by the Roman jurists, and as a universal principle by Christianity, is necessary in the consideration of all phases of the evolution of law. The necessity is even more evident in primitive phases, since here legislative formulation is often absent or at best has a rough character. Jhering, who was among the first to carefully examine the concept of "logical organism" as applied to law, was correct in comparing the rules of law among primitive peoples to the plastic arts of these same peoples.[2] Just as we do not think that primitive men and animals looked exactly like those we see depicted in the embryonic artistic figures of those ages, neither should we believe that their legal systems were exactly the same as might appear from the rules then formulated. Law is a connecting factor in life, a co-ordination, a limit and a guarantee of social relations, and its vigor and true significance must be deduced from an examination of life and its conditions, not from formulae which are more or less approximate, sometimes fallacious, and always incomplete.

Even in the more advanced systems the jurist must make an effort to consider them from within, ideally placing himself at the center or root of the system rather than stopping at the perimeter. This is possible for the jurist since he has, within him, the principle, the measure, and the rhythm of the truth of law in general. The jurist must himself enter into and experience the unity of the entire system conceived as a living organism, following the sap, so to speak, upward from the roots as it spreads its life-giving energies into and through all the organs of the system. He will thus test the power of *logical expansion* which belongs to the system because it has organic character. Without effort he will be able to properly apply the existing rules beyond their literal or apparent meaning. The *ratio juris* (again we call upon the revelatory experience of Roman law), that reason which is the foundation of existing norms, permits —nay, almost compels—extension of their limits, so that cases that are different from and more complex than those originally considered can be solved. In past centuries, the organism of law was developed and enriched to meet inventions such as the printing press, for which the law evolved new institutions without, however, destroying the preceding structure and often without feeling the necessity of express formulation of new norms. And so in our own time, the changed conditions of life and altered modes of activity have created new branches of law, leaving the main trunk substantially unchanged where it was physiologically sound, thus amplifying and perfecting the structure without endangering its fundamental unity. We need only think of the new relations between capital and labor, especially between contractor and worker; of the changed legal rules that govern agriculture in consequence of its now predominantly industrial character; of the entirely new forms of activity which our times have superimposed on the old: the automobile, aviation, wireless telegraphy, radio *et cetera*, all presenting new problems to the jurist, the solutions for which are daily being sought and daily being achieved, partly by new legislation and partly by the ordinary methods of case law, that is, by appropriate recourse to analogy or to the general principles of law.

These practical developments must be accompanied by a corresponding renewal of scholarly elaboration. There is no question of altering fundamental juridical concepts, which remain always the same, as the laws of epistemology and logic remain always the same despite the growth of knowledge in any field. We are concerned here with those conceptual notions whose character is at least partially empirical, that is, they include a content of historically determined juridical experience in such a way as to make possible its construction into a systematic order. We are, in short, concerned with legal dogmatics, not to be confused with philosophy but nevertheless representing a legitimate scientific activity that is perfectly valid in its own sphere.

VII. ELABORATION OF A NON-POSITIVE LAW; ITS LEGITIMACY

While the task which we have outlined for the jurist is vast, it is not his only task. To limit juristic activity to the consideration and elaboration of positive law alone, in however broad a sense, would mean the acceptance of philosophical or pseudo-philosophical positivism. Even though this represents an understandable reaction to the opposite errors of dogmatic metaphysics, it nevertheless does not recognize the essential constitution and most profound needs of consciousness. It would also mean the acceptance of that which true criticism has shown to be logically absurd—that a system historically given can be equal to the infinite capacity of the idea and that from any given system it is possible to derive perfect justice in every case. It would mean, finally, falling into the theoretical and ethical error of worshipping, *a priori*, the accomplished fact, and thus through dogmatic prejudice confusing what is with what ought to be, the phenomenon with the idea. Thus consciousness would be deprived of its most sublime mission, that of asserting and fighting for the eternal value of the idea against its empirical negations.

Even the jurist who devotes the utmost intelligence and good will to understanding the rationality of existing law and improving its formulation wherever it is obscure or insufficient, to fit it to new situations in life and human relations, must at times halt, realizing that as interpreter of the law he cannot force the system which he is examining beyond a certain point. He must understand that it is not permissible for him to contradict or break up the law's unitary structure even in the name of aspirations arising from the most profound depths of his conscience, if such aspirations will inevitably lead to direct violation of the very laws that it is his mission to study and apply. At a certain point the juridical dictates of conscience cease to be reconcilable with the *jus conditum* and become designs and programs of *jus condendum*.

Here we leave legal science in the strict sense and enter the realm of legal philosophy. The transition is inevitable and does not occur *ex abrupto*. Over all the distinctions to be made among the various species of intellectual activity (mathematics, science, philosophy) the unity of the human mind prevails. Hence if we define "jurist," as some do, as only the interpreter of existing law, we must hasten to add that a jurist is not only a jurist but is also fundamentally a man. He is a being who, in the integrity of his conscience and the universality of his reason, can and must nourish idealistic juridical aspirations. And in their ideality these aspirations not only surpass but are often in contrast with actual positive law.

In theory, one might even presume to forbid the jurist to exercise these intellectual and human faculties, but such a prohibition would be not only tyrannical but humanly and practically impossible. The exercise of the superior faculties of the spirit is not subject to the power of arbitrary forces; such faculties have to be exercised and the only effect which prohibitions or exclusions can have is to force men to cultivate in private, or in secret, that which otherwise would be exercised with greater propriety and efficacy in the light of day. For these reasons—if we may digress briefly—the idea that the philosophy of law can be suppressed by excluding it from university programs must be dismissed as erroneous. Educational regulations can reduce the number of teachers teaching a subject, or abolish them all, but they cannot abolish the subject itself when, as proved by thousands of years of history, it naturally and inexorably germinates in the human spirit.

Thus, returning to our argument, it is not only simply permissible for the jurist to operate beyond his duties as judge or interpreter and to conceive and carry out projects for new laws, in other words, to prepare more or less radical reforms *de jure condendo* in any branch of law; indeed, this activity must be actively encouraged for the sake of the positive legal system, that it may be protected from the too violent shocks which would occur if its path to normal and rational development were blocked. Therefore, those systems which have provided for the possibility of their own reform are both better and more secure.

VIII. REVOLUTION AS THE *ULTIMA RATIO* IN THE LIFE OF LAW; CONDITIONS WHICH MAY JUSTIFY IT. LAW AS A PRINCIPLE OF ORDER AND HARMONY

In this manner the occasion for what in the life of law is the *ultima ratio* is reduced to a minimum. Deprecable though it may be, this *ultima ratio* is nonetheless necessary as a crucial experiment, when in the great crises of civilization the innovating forces of a legal system prevail over the conservative and find insufficient outlet within the dikes of legality. This *ultima ratio* is, in fine, revolution. It would be foolish to deny the possibility and even, sometimes, the necessity that social upheavals should occur, whereby a new order of things is set up on the ruins of the preceding. In this great and terrible phenomenon, which Locke called the "appeal to heaven," we have the proof, as irrefutable as it is painful, of the ever possible divergence between positive law and ideal law, and it gives further proof of the error of those who on *a priori* grounds identify justice with fact and the aspirations and needs of peoples with their positive laws.

The only theoretical and ethical justification of revolution is that by its means an inferior, less perfect system is replaced by a higher and more perfect one, that is, one more nearly approximate to the eternal ideal of justice. But this improvement must be attainable by no other means than violation of the established order; to seek by revolution what can be attained by reform is unjustifiable. It is also necessary that the "revolutionists" be capable of more than an uprising, a mere disturbance, an agitation of the established order; they must possess the capacity to install a new and more just order in the place of the old.

There are still further considerations which limit and restrict the conditions according to which any political upheaval can possess rational legitimacy. Not every defect of laws, not every aspiration for betterment which finds an obstacle in the positive laws is a valid motive for refusing obedience to these laws. The stability of the legal order has in itself an ethical value which is not diminished, no matter how great the imperfections of that order may be. For this reason the sacrifice of Socrates has always appeared heroic and sublime: he submitted to an iniquitous sentence rather than give his disciples and fellow citizens the dangerous example of scorning the laws of his country. For the same reason Scholastic philosophy, in the words of Saint Thomas Aquinas, taught obedience even to unjust laws "propter vitandum scandalum vel turbationem," the sole exceptions being the extreme cases of absolute injustice or violation of divine law. According to this philosophy, to disobey or oppose is legitimate only for the sake of reaffirming, not of destroying, law—that law which is absolute and eternal and which, *ex hypothesi*, has been already violated by false and perverse enactments.

Besides all this, we must bear in mind the difficulty of disentangling the motives for opposition to an established order. Even in the holiest of revolutions it is seldom possible to separate the purely ethical contribution of apostles and martyrs from the defiling association of troublemakers and agitators who seek only to free themselves from the restraint of the existing laws. This of itself constitutes one of the strongest warnings against the mirage of revolutionary ideologies for generous but ingenuous spirits, especially the young. Revolution can result from the victory of base and disordered passions as well as from pure ideals. Not all revolutions are to be considered, *a priori,* as vehicles of juridical progress; not infrequently, history has demonstrated that retrogressive revolutions are possible, and it may be added that the most profound and fecund revolutions have often been the least violent.

In the final analysis, all of the foregoing confirms that revolution can be legitimate only insofar as it is truly the bearer of a new and higher law; and law, we repeat, is in essence a principle of order, of equilibrium and of social harmony.

For this reason the Roman jurists conceived their mission as something both sacred and philosophical: in the words of Ulpian "Cuius [juris] merito quis nos sacerdotes appellet; justitiam namque colimus . . . veram, nisi fallor, philosophiam, non simulatam affectantes."

Because of the essentially equilibrating and harmonizing function of their ministry, jurists of all countries feel in a way that they are brothers. They are ministers of social peace, not only between individual and individual and between family and family, but between a nation's various collective organizations and between country and country.

(Lecture delivered, by invitation, at the University of Bucharest, May 11, 1933, and at the University of Sofia, May 16, 1933.)

NOTES

1. On the origin of this and similar proverbs, see STINTZING, *Das Sprichwort "Juristen böse Christen" in seinen geschichtlichen Bedeutungen* (Bonn, 1875). Cf. RIEZLER, *Die Abneigung gegen die Juristen* (München, 1925).

2. JHERING, *Geist des römischen Rechts auf den verschiedenen Stufen seiner Entwicklung* (1 Th., 5 Aufl., Leipzig, 1891), § 3, p. 28.

THE POSTHUMOUS FATE OF ALBERICO GENTILI

IT IS CURIOUS TO NOTE THAT MANY AUTHORITIES HAVE REvealed their ignorance of the true site of the grave of Alberico Gentili. They have assumed, doubtless from the fact that he was for many years a professor of Oxford, that he died there[1] and was buried in Christ Church Cathedral.[2] But throughout this period he also lived in London, where he was an advocate of repute, representing the subjects of the Spanish Crown at the Court of Admiralty. It was in London that he died on June 19, 1608,[3] and he was laid to rest in the churchyard of St. Helen's, Bishopsgate in the City of London.[4]

Returning from a conference at Oxford, where tribute had been paid to the memory of Gentili, I thought it worthwhile to visit the place. The little church of St. Helen's, Bishopsgate, is one of London's oldest. Its origins are unknown, but it was certainly in existence in the first years of the 13th century, and clearly shows traces of architectural styles of the 14th and 15th centuries, all harmoniously blended together. It stands in a little courtyard, access to which is by way of a narrow passage off Bishopsgate, down which one escapes from the hustle and bustle of the financial world to this little oasis of spiritual peace.

Although there is no doubt that Gentili was buried in ground belonging to this church, it is impossible to ascertain the exact spot. The register of St. Helen's records that "Alberico Gentili, Doctor of Roman Law, was buried in the cemetery at the foot of the corner of the window where stood the clump of gooseberry bushes, and less than two feet away from the nun's grating, on the 21st June, 1608."[5]

The impossibility of finding Gentili's remains was asserted by the Vicar of the church, Dr. Cox, in a report which he prepared for the British Government and which was transmitted in 1876 to the Minister of the Italian Government, Bonghi, who had asked for information. It is worth while recalling the origin of this request, and of the interest then shown in Alberico Gentili.

Thomas Erskine Holland, one of his successors in the Chair at Oxford, delivered his inaugural lecture, on November 7, 1874, on Gentili. This fact could not help but be observed in Italy, and it especially attracted the attention of P. S. Mancini, at that time a professor in the University of Rome. He drew the attention of the University of Macerata to it. At this university was the eccentric but high-spirited Professor Pietro Sbarbaro, who then promoted the formation of a committee which discussed the erection of a national monument to Alberico Gentili. The then Prince of Piedmont, who later became King Umberto I, was Honorary President, the active President being Mancini and the Secretary Sbarbaro. A high-flown manifesto was published, and there was a demand for the return of Gentili's remains from England to Italy. As indicated above, this was of course quite impossible.

Some months later a similar committee was formed in England. It arranged to set up a memorial tablet to Gentili in St. Helen's, and to republish his major work, the treatise entitled *De Jure Belli*. Both these plans were executed. The tablet was unveiled in the presence of the Italian Ambassador, among others, on July 7, 1877. The modest memorial of alabaster and marble was placed at the far end of the left wall of the church, above the much more conspicuous tomb of Thomas Gresham, founder of the London Stock Exchange. It carries an inscription surrounded by the armorial bearings of the University of Perugia, the University of Oxford, the Gentili family and the town of San Ginesio, near Macerata, in the Marches, where he was born on January 14, 1552.[6] The inscription is that originally intended for Gentili's tombstone (we do not know with certainty if it was ever really engraved on it: *cf.* De Giorgi, *Della vita e delle opere di Alberico Gentili* (Parma, 1876), p. 15), as recorded by G. M. Konigius (Konig) in his

Biblioteca Vetus et Nova (Altdorf, 1678, s.v. "Albericus Gentilis").

In the same year, 1877, the new edition of *De Jure Belli* was published at Oxford under the scholarly care of Professor T. E. Holland.

The work of the Italian committee was much less effective. The monument at San Ginesio was not erected until more than 30 years later, in 1908, under the auspices of a new committee. Commemorative tablets in honor of Gentili, however, had been placed in 1885 in the Technical Institute of Macerata, which at the same time was renamed after him, and in 1890 in the University of Perugia. In 1930 another was placed in the University of Macerata.

The causes of the long delay were various, but perhaps the principal one was the disagreement that arose because of Gentili's religious beliefs. He belonged, as is well known, to a Protestant family. As a result of this, on one side there was a desire to give to notices in his honor an anticlerical significance, and on the other, there was a desire to raise a protest against any honors supposed to bear such a significance.

Curiously enough, plans for erecting a monument to Gentili had meanwhile been started also in Holland, but protests arose there because it appeared to some Dutchmen strange to honor Alberico in the land of Grotius, rather than Grotius himself. As a result of this singular and rather out-of-place controversy, a Dutch committee was formed to promote the erection of a monument to Grotius in Delft, his native city. This was unveiled in 1886, twenty-two years before the monument to Gentili was put up in Italy. Visitors to this historic Dutch city, where Grotius was born and where his tomb is now, probably do not realize as they behold the statue of Grotius in the beautiful square that it owes its origin to that posthumous rivalry, and was set up as it were to contest the claims of the great Italian jurist.

But statues and tombs derive their value only from the fact that they recall our thoughts to the spirit and the work which are immortal. More important than the rediscovery of Alberico Gentili's bones, or their hoped-for return to Italy,[7] more so indeed than the erection of a monument in Rome where, lay-ing aside all petty jealousies, it could be most worthily situated, is study of, and meditation on, Gentili's teachings. These teachings are truly to be marveled at, and all the more when we think of the era in which they were conceived.

It is a mistake to seek to award unqualified supremacy to either Gentili or Grotius, because each had his precursors, such as the Italian Giovanni di Legnano and Pietro Belli and the Spanish De Vitoria and Ayala, so that it is impossible to boast on Gentili's behalf, as Romagnosi attempted, that he was the founder of modern international law. But there does remain the indisputable fact that Gentili contributed perhaps more than anyone to the modern systemization of this science by applying a more rigorous juridical criterion than that followed by his precursors, and, after him, by Grotius. Here let it suffice to recall his definition of war ("*bellum est publicorum armorum justa contentio*"), which reveals so felicitously its public and at the same time juridical character. This definition is therefore much superior to the later one of Grotius, who conceives war simply as a violent conflict, including thus also private struggles. Or again, let us recall Gentili's doctrine of diplomatic immunity, and of respect for the property of non-combatant enemies and for neutral territory, where Grotius shows himself to be a great deal less just and precise.

In general we may say that Gentili, by his method of collecting facts and his acumen in evaluating them, to a considerable extent paved the way for Grotius and all modern learning in the field of international law. The tribute which Grotius paid to Gentili in the *Prolegomena* of his great work (§38), is itself a significant, though very inadequate, recognition. It would be easy to show how powerful a help and inspiration Gentili was to Grotius, not only by reason of his "*diligentia*" but also by his ideas and the general plan of his work. This fact was long ago brought out by Kaltenborn (*Die Vorläufer des Hugo Grotius* [Leipzig, 1848], pp. 228–231), who was one of the first, if not the first, of scholars outside Italy to acquire a proper understanding of Gentili's work in relation to that of Grotius, yet he is not usually listed in bibliographies relating to Gentili.[8]

If, in the last analysis, the merits of these two great men are perhaps for differing reasons equal, how unlike have been their fortunes at the hand of posterity. To Gentili not even death has brought his "fair meed of glory."

(1956) Translated by H. McN. Henderson.

NOTES

1. *E.g.*, A. FIORINI, *Di Alberigo Gentili e del suo Diritto di guerra*, 6 (Leghorn, 1876); but see note 4 below. Even the contributor to the *Enciclopedia Italiana* (1932) makes this mistake, although the true facts have long been readily available in the Encyclopaedia Britannica and in Professor Holland's article in the D.N.B.

2. *E.g.*, WOOD (quoted by Prof. Holland in his inaugural lecture on Gentili). A. DE GIORGI (*Della vita e della opere di Alberico Gentili* (Parma, 1876)), although he knew Gentili died in London, thought he had no known grave.

3. 1609 or 1611 are the years given elsewhere, but they are without doubt erroneous.

4. *Cf.* G. SPERANZA, *Alberico Gentili*, Vol. I, p. 253 (Rome, 1876); A. FIORINI, in the preface to his translation of Gentili's *De Jure Belli*, p. 43 *et seq.* (Leghorn, 1877); M. THAMM, *Albericus Gentilis und seine Bedeutung für das Völkerrecht*, 11 (Strassburg, 1896); H. NÉZARD in *Les Fondateurs du Droit International*, pp. 43-44 (Paris, 1904); E. NYS in his Introduction to the new edition of Gentili's *De Legationibus*, Vol. I, p. 13a (New York, 1924).

5. *Cf.* G. SPERANZA, *op. cit.*, p. 293; A. FIORINI, *op. cit. supra*, p. 44; note to Saffi's translation of Prof. Holland's lecture, p. 51.

6. Often 1551 is given as the year of his birth, but the 1552 is taken from a note by Gentili in his own handwriting, quoted by SAFFI in the Appendix to his translation of Prof. T. E. HOLLAND's lecture, p. 46 (Rome, 1884). The year 1551, however, appears to be confirmed by the text of the memorial inscription "Aetatis LVIII."

7. It was proposed to transport them, had it been possible, to the church of Santa Croce (in Florence, of course, and not in Rome as written by NÉZARD, in *Les fondateurs du Droit International* 44, *cit. n.* 4 *supra*).

8. Among similar verdicts on Gentili, *cf.* COLEMAN PHILLIPSON, in his introduction to the new edition of *De Jure Belli* (Classics of International Law, Oxford, 1933): "Because of the greater affinity between his point of view and that of modern States and jurists, he is, in that respect, as much as, if not more than, Grotius, the progenitor of the existing law of nations." (Vol. II, pp. 11a-12a, *cf.* p. 18a, where the verdicts of OMPTEDA, LAMPREDI, etc., are also reported; *cf.* also the notices gathered by SPERANZA, *op. cit.*, Vol. I, p. 259 *et seq.*)

INDEX OF AUTHORS